Problem Solving Courts

Problem Solving Courts

A Measure of Justice

JoAnn Miller and Donald C. Johnson

ROWMAN & LITTLEFIELD PUBLISHERS, INC.
Lanham • Boulder • New York • Toronto • Plymouth, UK

Published by Rowman & Littlefield Publishers, Inc.
A wholly owned subsidiary of The Rowman & Littlefield Publishing Group, Inc.
4501 Forbes Boulevard, Suite 200, Lanham, Maryland 20706
http://www.rowmanlittlefield.com

Estover Road, Plymouth PL6 7PY, United Kingdom

British Library Cataloguing in Publication Information Available

Library of Congress Cataloging-in-Publication Data

The hardback edition of this book was previously cataloged by the Library of Congress as follows:

Miller, JoAnn L., 1949–
  Problem solving courts : a measure of justice / JoAnn Miller and Donald C. Johnson.
    p. cm.
  Includes bibliographical references and index.
  1. Courts of special jurisdiction—United States. I. Johnson, Donald C., 1944– II. Title.
  KF8759.M555 2009
  347.73'28—dc22   2009018954

ISBN: 978-1-4422-0080-7 (cloth : alk. paper)
ISBN: 978-1-4422-0081-4 (pbk. : alk. paper)
ISBN: 978-1-4422-0082-1 (electronic)

Printed in the United States of America

For Gus, Carly, and Erin—our hopes and our futures

Contents

Part III Performances and Transformations

Acknowledgments

We are grateful to a number of persons who lit the torch, giving us insights into problem solving courts. They carried the flame, providing us with hours of precious time in their busy lives, their words, and their support. We sincerely appreciate the contributions made by Jeralyn Long Faris, a doctoral student in the Department of Communication at Purdue University. She is the lead author of chapter 11 and presented the model we use to show the tensions between support and control that affect court program participants and service providers. Her home-baked bread is deliciously incomparable, as it symbolizes her dedication to nurturing court participants, her students, and her work.

Rodney Stockment, of Indiana Housing and Community Development, is responsible for turning a moderately successful reentry court into a highly successful reentry problem solving court. Stockment is well-known for two characteristics: determination and delivering the goods, as promised. He visited the court programs, saw the pressing need to add a housing component, and battled on our behalf with a large government agency responsible for released prison inmates. He invited us to apply for a tenant-based rental-assistance (TBRA) program to finance housing. Once we had TBRA in place, only one reentry participant who was supported with housing failed the program. Clearly, Rodney Stockment understood and led the program and its participants to a new world of possibilities.

Stockment monitored the TBRA program carefully. When his agency was awarded a federal Shelter Plus Care grant, which provides permanent assisted housing for chronically homeless and disabled persons, he chose our city to be among the three to receive support. The program initiated a determined effort by the city and its housing experts, Aimee Jacobsen and Adam Murphy, to develop a long-term plan to end homelessness in a Midwestern city. Today, due to Stockment's partnership with the city and its leadership, we have housing for women leaving a domestic violence shelter and housing programs for homeless families.

Our mayor, the Honorable Tony Roswarski, puts problem solving courts in the spotlight, showing the community that every resident has a life to celebrate. His leadership is inspiring, a perfect example of how communities, universities, and the legal system can form partnerships that improve the quality of life for a city and every person who chooses to live and thrive within it. Without the participants in the three problem solving courts that we studied, we would have no tale to tell. We are grateful to all of them, especially those whose voices are heard in this book.

Rowman & Littlefield makes writing a book a professionally satisfying experience. Sarah Stanton, associate editor, guided our work from its initial prospectus through the final edits of a manuscript. We are most grateful for her contributions. The production editor, Elaine McGarraugh, smoothly turned pages into an attractive book. Kevin Krause, editorial intern, managed the review process and prepared our work for production. Two anonymous reviewers provided guidance and a superb plan for revisions. One of the reviewers gave us intellectual and editorial comments that are uncharacteristic for a person whose name is not on the title page.

We thank John J. Contreni, the Justin S. Morrill Dean of the College of Liberal Arts. His leadership makes our work possible and far more enjoyable than we imagined. He represents the land grant mission exceptionally well through his connections to all the populations we serve and his commitment to bringing experts from the community and the university together to solve problems.

Our families, as always, supported and encouraged our work. JoAnn's husband Scott, her beloved partner, was as willing to proofread as he was to listen to our cant. He keeps us balanced and grounded, although he is eager and willing to plan the details of an excursion to distract us from the dreariness of day-to-day life by showing us the beauty of art and architecture, the surprise of quaint restaurants, and the joy of unwavering support.

Introduction

Janise, a thirty-five-year-old mother of four children, has lived in state prison and county jails for more than eight years. She has no history of violent or property crime but was found to be a habitual substance offender and therefore faced a mandatory prison term the last time she was convicted. She finds life on the outside challenging at best, with responsibilities for her children and finding a home and a job, as well as constant feelings of need to see her friends and a relentless craving for drugs.

> The people who celebrate life with me, they are my friends. They know how to have fun. And they really care about me. They get me all the crack cocaine I want and all the other stuff I need. I provide the sex. I'm no whore, you know. These are my friends and when one of us is down, the others pitch in until we get back on our feet. I'd do the same for them.

Janise exemplifies the revolving door problem in criminal justice (Kushel et al. 2005). She leaves prison to return to her home community with a $75 check and a plan for successful parole, which requires her to call the local parole officer within seventy-two hours of release and to live in approved housing.[1] Her pattern is to reoffend within weeks and to be arrested for a minor offense, usually disorderly conduct. She returns to jail where she resides until she is returned to state prison. She clearly lacks the resources to stay out of jail, having no life or occupational skills and no connections to potential employers. She has no money, and she is addicted to drugs and alcohol. Janise unabashedly admits that she has no problem "scoring in prison. There's anything you want. Alcohol and meth are the easiest to get. But if you have

1

good connections, you know what I mean, you can get hash, weed, or crack. Plenty of it. You just need to know the right people and be good to them."

Three of her children live with their maternal grandmother, and upon birth, the youngest was placed in foster care when his maternal grandmother told the prison social worker,

> There is no more room at the inn. This woman cannot take more babies to raise.
>
> I love my kid [Janise], you know, but there are only so many of her babies I can handle. I'm getting old. There's no retirement pay for this job I got.

Janise retained visiting rights but has never even held her son since the baby was born. She talked about how the courts did not help her see her child, leaving her to resolve matters herself.

> After fighting for a year and threatening the judges and everything over it, we— the foster parents and me—finally made friends. They called me every week in prison. They brought the boy [her child] to see me in the prison's visiting room once, and I just signed him over to her [the foster mother] in December. She's adopting my boy. That's the best thing for him.

Janise never mentioned her son's name or age. We knew only that he was her youngest and her only son. When asked about her other children, she said,

> My mom does as good as she can with the kids. They're all girls, you know, so they don't give her a lot of trouble. They all write me letters and tell me they want to see me. I don't think it's such a good idea. Who knows? I don't want them to see me in here.

Janise acknowledges that the prison staff treat her very well, but she claims that judges and the courts treated her unfairly. Her most recent court appearance, on her way to her current term of incarceration, was "amazing. You wouldn't believe how bad he treated me." At the sentencing hearing, the judge did not make arrangements for a time cut or for a specific program for Janise during prison. She had completed her GED in jail and thought her prison sentence should be reduced by six months as a result.

> The judge said he wasn't going give me the 6 months [credit] time. It's not like I caught a new case. I got the GED while I was doing time for this case in jail. . . . Like my mom says, I paid to get out and now they're trying to take my time away from me. And the judge—I don't think he's going to give it to me. Especially because of all the things he said to me before. Cruel! He's the type of person, if you go against his wishes, he's going to do whatever he can. And this

is going against his wishes. Once before he told me never to get pregnant again. But see, I got a letter from my mom that said the judge is getting bad comments in the newspaper. The judge is a jerk, you know.

Janise was interviewed as a candidate for a reentry problem solving court (PSC) program. She was denied admission by the PSC team on the premise that she had too little time left to serve. In a few months, she would be released, giving the PSC case manager insufficient time to plan a program that could keep her out of prison and home for good. What can a reasonable person predict for Janise's future other than more drug abuse, more criminal convictions, and more prison time? How could Janise's life be turned around by a PSC program that works to develop personal and interpersonal strengths and resources for participants like Janise to provide care work[2] for her children, find gainful employment, and complete a drug-addiction program with long-term aftercare?

PURPOSES

For three years we observed and analyzed the problem solving court programs associated with a general-jurisdiction court in a typical city—not New York or Los Angeles but a Midwestern U.S. metropolitan area similar to those that dot the American landscape. The city has more than its fair share of social problems: criminality, drug abuse, homelessness, poverty, and untreated mental illness. Typical for this and all cities is the concentration of social problems in a downtown area. Compared to the metropolitan area as a whole, the downtown experiences more illicit drug trading and higher rates of arrests for burglary, battery, illegal firearms, and robbery. The problematic neighborhoods are downtown, as are the homeless shelter, transitional housing programs, and drug-abuse and mental-health treatment centers.[3] It is only fitting that the PSC programs within this particular state are clustered in the jurisdiction we study.[4]

The purposes of our field research and the preparation of this book are to share state-of-the-art knowledge about PSCs with a broad audience representing three distinctive groups of primary stakeholders in the sociolegal movement that has swept the United States, Canada, Great Britain, Australia, and New Zealand. First are the many thousands of judges, prosecuting and defense lawyers, probation and parole officers, correctional professionals, and social service providers who are deeply invested in the PSC approach to delivering punishment and treatment to individuals within their communities. Second are the law students and graduate or upper-division baccalaureate students within the social or behavioral sciences who study the PSC phenomenon in preparation for their work careers. Third are the local, state, and federal or national-level law and policy makers who tend to weigh in on matters related to problem solving courts. How should they be financed? How should a court's workload and outcomes be measured in our culture of accountability? What services should be provided? Is the problem solving court a promising approach for uncrowding our state prisons and local jails while keeping community residents both safe and feeling safe? These and other PSC questions are important for generating community climates that welcome and value persons returning home from prison or for persons in need of social services (Maruna and LeBel 2003). Nonetheless, we do not ignore the reality that policy makers must be vigilant of perceptions and attitudes to make sure that effective practices are embraced by the constituencies they are elected or appointed to serve. Said differently, we recognize that the social space—the policy space—for implementing innovative and accepted programs is defined by the general population (Bauman 2000; Cusick and Kimber 2007; DeLone 2008; Raco 2007; Rosen and Venkatesh 2007; Whitzman 2007).

Because our purpose is focused while our audience is diverse, we chose (1) to use a dramaturgical metaphor to unpack and unfold the social action that takes place in courtrooms, (2) to review and critique the extant scholarship on problem solving courts, and (3) to illustrate the persistence of social problems with imaginative literature and a classic social-historical study of crime and deviance.

A DRAMATURGICAL METAPHOR

Trial court drama is indeed performance. Prosecuting and defense attorneys argue with each other as if preparing for a duel. The adversarial model, a hallmark of criminal justice in the many nations, is genuine; yet it is simultaneously a ritualized performance, designed for disclosing narratives under the rules and regulations—or scripts—of the courtroom. The prosecutor, on behalf of the state, fights to protect public safety and therefore argues for a criminal conviction. The defense attorney engages in the combat to protect the accused person's constitutional rights, the same rights that all of us can count on.[5] The prosecutor and the defense attorney are, however, members of a courtroom work group (Ulmer and Kramer 1998). Once the performance ends, they may share a moment of despair or laughter at a nearby bar or in one another's office.

We find the dramaturgical metaphor helpful for examining problem solving courts within the traditional criminal court setting. The PSC scripts, the roles the actors and the directors play, and the audiences in the gallery and the jury box are all dramatically different from the traditional criminal court-room. Critics of the PSC are justifiably quick to question the legitimacy of such differences (James 2006; Nolan 2001, 2002, 2003). Are the defendant's rights disregarded in a PSC diversion program? Is the PSC process constitutional?

The dramaturgical metaphor suits our purposes because our observational studies of problem solving courts take place front stage, in the courtroom, and backstage, in the jury room. The traditional criminal courtroom is a public stage that provides seats for the general audience in its gallery and box seats for members of the jury. The drama takes place center stage, with a setting that distinguishes the places for the lead actors, the prosecuting and defense attorneys, to perform. The supporting cast members, the witnesses, enter stage left to provide the jury members the information they need to interpret accurately the script spoken in lawyer-talk. Props are sometimes used in the courtroom—a photo that shows bruises, a map that situates the action. Seated above the stage is the judge who directs the courtroom drama. Cloaked in black, so as not to distract from the center stage drama, the judge presides over the action, directing the actors in situ when necessary to maintain the integrity of the script (the law) or to wrap up the performance. The judge uses the director's copy of the script to ensure the play is performed as intended.

Erving Goffman unfolded the dramaturgical metaphor for social scientists in his first book, *The Presentation of Self in Everyday Life*, yet abandoned it after his third book, *Asylums* (Trevino 2003). Nonetheless, contemporary social scientists use Goffman's metaphor to describe, and sometimes to explain, social interaction as it is performed before large or small audiences.[6] We return to Goffman's metaphor for our study of problem solving courts to observe performances of social actors, the participants in court programs. The metaphor is not intended to present an explanation of social life. It is used here to give our readers and audiences a single language for reading the work completed by a legal and a social science scholar (who admittedly do not on occasion understand what each other are saying). We use terms like *social and legal actors* and *role reversal* in ways intended to clarify issues for lawyers and social scientists alike, for law students and criminal justice students alike, and for judges and policy makers alike.

SHAKESPEARE AND SOCIAL HISTORY

The dramaturgical metaphor is particularly helpful for bridging imaginative and social science literatures for the purpose of understanding contemporary problems in criminal law and criminal justice. Prince Hamlet helps us make sense of contemporary and similar problems—a young university student is obsessed; the ghost-devil speaks to him, provoking him to seek revenge for what he perceives are grave injustices. How can problem solving court principles be used to formulate fairness when a sentencing judge struggles to find the balance between protecting society and considering the needs of the convicted offender? Romeo and Juliet may have been young lovers from well-to-do and highly regarded families, but they clearly represent an urgent need to resolve disputes before too much harm is done to families and their communities. Shakespeare, in *Measure for Measure*, dares the reader to tackle the impossible dilemma of delivering justice and mercy, as do contemporary authors who pen social science studies or law-and-literature treatises (Bennett 2004; Frison 2000; Herzog 2004; Nussbaum 1995, 2004, 2006). We use examples from imaginative literature and social histories to illustrate some of the most pressing and persistent problems faced by the problem solving court movement in the United States.

WAYWARD PURITANS AND WAYWARD DRUG ABUSERS

Wayward Puritans (Erikson 1966) remains a classic in the sociolegal study of deviance and crime. Kai Erikson used social-historical records from the seventeenth century to test Émile Durkheim's theory of criminal law: Is crime a characteristic of society and not merely the behavior of a person? Does every society tolerate a level of deviance or crime for the purpose of establishing moral boundaries? Is legal punishment (especially repressive punishment) useful for maintaining social cohesiveness?

Wayward Puritans sociolegally frames our observations of contemporary problem solving courts. We examine how lawmakers have responded to illegal drug use and dealing over the decades. We explore attempts to fix social problems that have resisted change yet resulted in mass incarceration. We also pay attention to how judges willing to preside over PSC programs threaten the judiciary's understanding of what judges are supposed to do and how judges are supposed to behave. We demonstrate the threat to judicial solidarity posed by the PSC judge. The now classic empirical test of functional theory in *Wayward Puritans* precludes any plausible or intuitive understanding of the problem solving court. It shows that it is imperative to transcend the appearance of success and to uncover the unintended consequences of social and legal programs that are supposed to resolve social issues in contemporary society.

OBSERVATIONAL STUDIES AND INSTITUTIONAL ETHNOGRAPHY

Erikson observed Massachusetts Bay Colony Puritans through historical records, and we observe PSC participants in public and contemporary courtroom settings. Most of the observations we analyze are based on our field notes and court transcripts. We turn to an institutional ethnography method of analysis (Diamond 2006; Smith 2001, 2006; Wright 2003) for one chapter that serves two purposes: (1) to present the experience of a problem solving court from the participant's perspective, and (2) to demonstrate how social actors use written documents (texts) to direct participants through a maze of social, therapeutic, and correctional programs.

A LOOK AHEAD

The following chapters summarize our attempt to make sense of a three-year observational study of problem solving courts.[7] Part I sets the stage. In the first chapter, we ask the reader to consider the problem of meting out appropriate punishments in contemporary and complex societies and examine our definition of problem solving courts, which is influenced by the work compiled by the Center for Court Innovation. Chapter 2 elaborates the purposes and promises of criminal law and criminal justice. It ends with a return to the Attica (New York) prison riot, a moment in recent history that sparked dramatic changes in criminal justice systems and the initiation of a willingness to experiment with new solutions for persistent social problems. Chapter 3 presents the components of a PSC jurisprudence that corresponds to an epistemology for an interdisciplinary study of the problem solving court. The limits of extant theory and the ability to replicate programs pose challenges. Yet, we can identify the key components of PSC programs and how they are used to facilitate changes in individuals' life chances and well-being while reducing the risk of criminal behavior (Andrews and Dowden 2007; Ward and Stewart 2003).

In chapter 4 we turn to one genre of imaginative literature, Shakespearian plays, to help us understand why some problems persist and therefore require new attempts to resolve old or resistant problems. In this chapter we also show how the practices that judges use in problem solving courts can be most helpful in the traditional criminal courtroom.

Part II focuses on courts, prisons, and communities. In chapter 5, we walk through two generations of problem solving courts and examine the grand challenge of delivering reassurance of public safety in the twenty-first century to an audience that does not really want to know the story line. We show how criminal-sentencing laws facilitate the imposition of sanctions that allow convicted offenders to return from prison to their home communities years before the actual time mandated by the sentencing order has elapsed. A paradox becomes clear: there is no end in sight to the effects of the surge in incarceration from decades earlier.

Chapter 6 on blended social institutions shows how hospitals and treatment centers can be like prisons, and prisons like hospitals. Prisons treat more persons with serious mental illnesses than do community mental-health organizations. If prison and treatment facilities blend, do they inevitably lead to a blending of courts and corrections? In the problem solving court, the presiding judge sees the participant over and over and over again. His or her relationship with the offender, whether diverted from prison or returned home from prison, only begins at a sentencing hearing. The community is affected by the social institutions and organizations that respond to crime and social deviance. What does the community need and deserve? How do problem solving courts deliver the appropriate responses to the all residents within the community? We address these questions in chapter 7 through an examination of three PSC programs that serve a single Midwestern city in the United States. An elaboration of how the PSC can address community and PSC participant problems simultaneously is the focus of chapter 8, which features the types of support—emotional, informational, and tangible—participants receive as they experience the social-control mechanisms that come from the PSC and extends into the community (Ward and Brown 2004).

Part III turns to the performances, backstage and front stage, and the transformations that can take place as the drama of the PSC unfolds. In chapter 9, we examine the importance of the master and stigmatized statuses to understand how judges, who declare and impose the stigma, can facilitate its removal. The participant, however, is the only social actor who can complete the transformation from "felon" to "citizen." The participant is the social actor who needs to avoid criminal behaviors.

Chapter 10 turns to the backstage action of the PSC team. Seated at a large table, in a closed room, team members examine reports and exchange information to provide the judge with the director's script to take into the courtroom. We conclude the chapter by comparing the PSC work group to the traditional criminal court work group.

Chapter 11 focuses on the participants' standpoints to discern the struggles of working through a PSC program. We select two participants, a man and a woman, who tell their stories, which we analyze with an institutional ethnography. The method of analysis uncovers the means by which well-intentioned workers see and purportedly understand behaviors through a lens that renders their observations opaque at best. Participants are powerless to influence text-mediated interpretations of rule-abiding and rule-breaking behaviors. The standpoint of participants in PSC programs can be parallel to the goals of the PSC. The wise and strong participant, however, knows when to "go along" with the program to protect his or her liberty or ability to be with family members.

Our final chapter returns to the classic statements found in *Wayward Puritans*. What is different now, and what remains the same? Crime and deviance continue to challenge a sense of safety and well-being, and PSC programs struggle to contain crime and reintegrate (or integrate) the social actor into the fabric of a local community. We conclude by taking a look back at the three PSC programs we studied and justify our plea for the sustainability of the PSC movement—or, in the language of PSC programs, a plea for "going to scale."

Some readers will find the materials in appendixes B through D useful. Included are documents from a reentry court—the participation agreement, waiver forms, and the participant's handbook. The documents can be used to plan or design a PSC in any jurisdiction in the United States, Canada, Great Britain, Australia, or New Zealand.[8] They can also be used to figure out what to do—and what not to do.

DEFINITION OF PROBLEM SOLVING COURTS

Before turning attention to the foundations of problem solving courts, we present our definition of the type of social organization that we study:

> Problem solving courts address the individual participant's and the community's problems simultaneously. They are judge-run programs, in general-jurisdiction courts, that facilitate long-term behavioral and attitudinal change among participants and their communities. Each participant's unique circumstances are addressed, and the court's response is comprehensive. The purpose of the problem solving court is to reduce the probability of repeated criminal acts among those who have been arrested or convicted, thereby increasing public safety and the quality of life for all residents within their communities.

We encourage readers to challenge this definition as well as all implications for delivering the forms of criminal "justice" that it implies.

I

SETTING THE STAGE

1

Measured Justice and Problem Solving Court Principles

PUNISHMENT IN A COMPLEX SOCIETY

All the world's a stage, he wrote.

And each social actor is responsible for knowing social norms, or how to perform the scripted words and how to feel and act appropriately according to directions. What does the decision maker do when a law, the normative script, is violated? How does the decision maker resolve conflict when social actors, returning home following a term of incarceration, break workplace or house arrest regulations?

An eye for an eye, when populations were small, homogenous, and isolated and when criminal or deviant acts were aberrations, was an appropriate dictum, a guiding philosophy that all understood for distributing punishments to those social actors who violated rules and norms. Metaphorically (or not) cut off the tongue of a person who slandered. Hang from the gallows a man who killed his neighbor. Confine the suspected traitor whose loyalty to the state is challenged. Who could dispute the justice of the response? The elegance and simplicity of the judicial decision, based on the eye-for-an-eye perspective, should trouble only those who broke the laws, as long as populations did not grow sufficiently in size or complexity to require change within communities. Yet, they did, and the eye-for-an-eye perspective does now trouble those in pursuit of a justice that reaches beyond the power of the state to reflect compassion or mercy as well.

But mercy is above this sceptred sway,
It is enthroned in the hearts of kings,
It is an attribute to God himself;

And earthly power doth then show likest God's
When mercy seasons justice[1]

Nowadays we live in complex societies and cultures with no shortage of laws and plenty of opportunities for large numbers of social actors to violate them, whether legal violations are grievously violent behaviors, theft, forgery, drug dealing, or vandalism. Too many persons strike out in anger when the frustrations of the workday or a failed effort in school or the community overwhelm the rational self and bring human emotions to dominate behaviors. We all want to be loved, to be cared for, to be nurtured and appreciated. Yet, too many social actors, contrary to the normative script, are abused or punished unlawfully (Loue 2005; Miller and Knudsen 2007; Rivera 2008). Too many are ignored, too few find solutions to personal troubles, and too many seek solace, even if temporary, from illegal drugs, from a fast drive, from some other thrilling albeit illegal act that can fool the social actor into thinking the discomfort or the problem might not happen again (Lyng 2004; Morrison 2004; Schen 2005).

Contemporary societies, unlike earlier societies in search of justice, cannot pretend to subscribe to simple rules to solve the social actor's or community's problems. Towns, cities, counties, and states need general-jurisdiction trial court judges to dispense measured justice, requiring an adequate dose of discretion, to make decisions that are unique to each situation and set of circumstances, yet fit within the boundaries defined by the rule of law. Measured justice means that judges, facing unique law violators, facing endless legal conflicts, must come up with ways to solve problems. Judges in general-jurisdiction trial courts need to estimate the harm to a community that a mentally ill person can cause as well as the harm to the mentally ill person that a community can cause.

THE MEANING OF MEASURED JUSTICE

Measured justice means that a criminal sanction or the resolution to a family conflict may, under the rule of law, be unique and characterized by judicial discretion, and the judge's work is to find the solution most appropriate for all the circumstances characterizing a legal case. Whereas prison may be the only appropriate sanction for a convicted offender who threatens the safety of all others in a community, a community-based sanction may be appropriate for another offender, guilty of the same crime, who can restore or repair harm by working, undergoing addiction treatment, and engaging in volunteer work to help build and not hurt a community. Although statutes and legal cases guide decisions, the trial court judge must predict the future, not by gazing into a crystal ball but by understanding what the evidence (i.e., the facts of the legal case and the research evidence) predicts for those who present different risks of recidivism, influenced not only by a criminal past but also by connections to school, church, friendships, family, and other social institutions.

The judge must look at all the members of a fractured family to estimate what teenage children need in social and emotional support. To predict a future requires the trial court judge to step beyond the facts when making a rational decision that reflects "human needs that transcend boundaries of time, place, class, religion, and ethnicity" (Nussbaum 1995). The truly rational decision considers the person and emotions, not just the facts of the case and the rule of the law. Sans emotion, can a judge be compassionate? Without emotion, which statute, which case, which offense can evoke outrage sufficient to warrant incarceration without the possibility of parole? How can a judge decide what is really in the best interest of the child (Crisp 2008; Fierke 2004; Hartford, Carey, and Mendonca 2007; Nussbaum 2008)?

Measured justice does not mean that judges may act outside the rule of law, that is, the law fixed by statutes, constitutions, and legal cases (Dorf 2003; Ohnesorge 2007). But it does mean that complex decisions need to account for multiple issues that affect social actors and the stages on which they perform social roles and abide by or challenge extant norms. Clearly, measured justice takes place on the bench during problem solving court (PSC) sessions. But it also affects judicial decision making in other courtroom arenas. Measured justice, in many instances, makes characteristically adversarial procedures inappropriate or inadequate. It demands an understanding that incorporates the motivations and emotions of the social actors that can affect how they leave the courtroom with a transformed understanding of how they can or will interact in the future. Consider this excerpt from a transcript of a May 4, 2007, trial court hearing. It is an example of how judges use problem solving court techniques to deliver measured justice. Let's call it the "Nine Dollar Case." Or should it be called the "Importance of Care Work"?[2]

> JUDGE: It is my understanding that the parties have resolved a number of issues but there remains one last issue that you want me to decide. Is that correct? Do the parties agree to handle this matter in a summary manner?
>
> WIFE'S ATTORNEY: Yes, the parties have agreed to you hearing the case in a summary fashion. These parties divorced about nine or ten years ago. The mother received primary physical custody of her daughter, age 15; and her son [Billy], age 17 years. The children go to Harrison High School and now, by agreement of the parties, Billy would like to live with his dad. He moved in about three weeks ago. I've done the numbers and I think the difference [in child-support payments] is $96.00 from dad to mom. Where we are apart is fig-

uring the number of overnight credit that we should give dad for visiting with his daughter, Heather.

JUDGE: Is Billy going to want to spend more overnights visiting with mom than Heather will want to spend visiting with dad?

WIFE'S ATTORNEY: Well, we have a nine year history since the divorce to see what time dad has exercised visitation with the kids, and it's been every other weekend. He has not visited for extended times and not during the week. So we gave dad credit for 52 overnights.

JUDGE: What's the difference in dollars, in terms of weekly support?

HUSBAND'S ATTORNEY: It's about eighteen dollars.

WIFE'S ATTORNEY: We are at ninety-six dollars.

HUSBAND'S ATTORNEY: By our calculation we should be paying seventy-seven dollars per week. Mom has been denying the dad visitation; he wants to visit more.

WIFE'S ATTORNEY: Dad is asking for overnight visitation credit that exceeds what he has actually done for nine years.

JUDGE: I'm thinking of splitting the difference and telling dad to pick it up a little bit.

HUSBAND'S ATTORNEY: Dad hasn't exercised more parenting time with this daughter over this nine year track record because anytime that he has attempted to exercise visitation, it was a very difficult thing to do.

JUDGE: I'm watching mom's response and I am seeing a reaction to the statement, to your claim, that she has been blocking visitation.

WIFE'S ATTORNEY: Our testimony would be that dad has never asked for more visitation. Judge, if he was being denied, wouldn't he have brought that fact to your attention over a nine year period? Dad is just trying to get a visitation credit that he's not earned nor has he ever petitioned the court to receive.

JUDGE: Folks, you told me that these two kids are getting *excellent* grades in school. You must be doing something right as parents. It is not easy to raise kids and have them do so well. You two have been getting along fairly well, and your parenting history impresses me. These kids will become good citizens.

WIFE'S ATTORNEY: Judge, they got along well until this minute.

JUDGE: When the parties walk out of here they're going to have to keep dealing with each other. I'm thinking of splitting the difference between what each party is requesting. How do you feel about that? Nine dollars each, there is no easy answer.

WIFE: I've been trying to be agreeable, so yes.

JUDGE: I can see no sense in getting into a fight over nine dollars.

HUSBAND'S ATTORNEY: Judge, dad would be okay with that, provided that in the future, he could exercise more visitation with his daughter.

WIFE'S ATTORNEY: Ordering support of $87.10 per week is splitting the numbers. And that's taking half away from both. The only other issue is that we are requesting that the support be retroactive back to when physical custody actually occurred.

HUSBAND'S ATTORNEY: We would ask that the support increase be retroactive.

JUDGE: How much time are we talking about?

HUSBAND'S ATTORNEY: About three weeks.

JUDGE: I'll make the support increase effective today. Dad, I am giving you the benefit of the doubt, and I have faith in you that you will exercise additional visitation with Heather. Mom, I do not believe that you are impeding visitation. I wish each of you good luck as you keep doing a good job with your children.

The trial court judge, during a child-support hearing, used the principles and practices of the PSC, although he was not deciding this case within a PSC, to deliver measured justice (Farole et al. 2005). By that we mean he engaged in an internal dialogue and self-overhearing to render a decision that can potentially benefit all parties. As his comments suggest, he initiated a process of self-overhearing, or a decision-making process in which he weighed both sides of an argument in consideration of the facts of the case, his experiences with similar situations, the relevant materials that he has read, and the push and pull of ideas presented in the courtroom by attorneys and litigants. During the process of self-overhearing, he needs to think through the issues to size up the problem, the parties, and potential solutions that would benefit the children and not further damage an already fractured family. He needed to know the parties and the problems—not only the legal facts—to construct the best solution.

In this instance, he began by simply observing the parties as they settled into their court roles with their attorneys, thinking that the mother and the father both had done reasonable jobs. He asked the attorneys if he could pose questions to their clients for the purpose of knowing who they were and how they were thinking. The judge, on May 4, 2007, reported,

I like to ask the parties how the children are getting along in school. Are the children in extra-curricular activities? What kind of grades are the children getting? Are the children happy? How is each parent cooperating with the other—to work together as parents—though they are no longer married? Do the children talk about what they want to do when they are young adults?

I try to divide up the questions between the parties so that I can get a feel as to how the parties are engaged in the parenting process. My goal as a judge is to reinforce the positive parenting qualities that appear to be in place and to determine where there is disagreement. Though my job is to make a decision and resolve the conflict and issues, I knew full well, in this case, that the parties will continue working together in the best interests of the children after their court appearance. Instead of referring to the parties as "petitioner" and "respondent" I used the terms "mom" and "dad" and encouraged the attorneys to refer to their clients as parents.

Language is important. I must decide legal issues, yet I strive to maintain the position that encourages the parties to continue their work in being loving and nurturing parents for the benefit of the children.

The nine-dollar decision gave neither party what he or she wanted; yet the judge preserved, enforced, and reinforced important parental relationships. During the hearing, he asked questions and listened to responses for the record, focusing on fact gathering that would become the basis for a decision based on the law. Yet, this type of case invites judicial discretion, eliciting an internal dialogue to weigh and consider what each parent is saying and promising to do in order to provide care work for their teenage children.

For the record, the legal decision is represented by a number, that is, a dollar value assigned to child support. The search for the methods and means to reinforce parenting, for the sake of the children, requires a continuous process of self-evaluation by the trial court judge. A wise decision represents problem solving court skills, not the absolute wisdom of a King Solomon. A good decision establishes an emotional reality. Mom and Dad will walk out of the courtroom satisfied that they are good parents and understanding that being a good parent requires care work and is never easy.

Measured justice accounts for discretion and an understanding of what judicial decisions imply for disputing parties or for convicted felons. In response to a criminal conviction, it refers to the distribution of sanctions designed to protect the community and change the needs of an offender that led to law violations. In the United States, with an ever-increasing prison population, there is a corresponding need to respond effectively to the men and women who return home from prison.

Problem solving courts are the public stages upon which trial court judges mete out measured justice. Evolving from the earlier drug court movement, they are designed to ensure public safety through ongoing judicial monitoring and intervention (Dorf and Fagan 2003; Fulton Hora 2002; Nolan 2001). It is no longer possible to incarcerate all the persons charged with or convicted of felony offenses. The prisons have simply run out of room. One consequence of a period of mass incarceration in the United States is the emergence of problem solving courts, which supervise persons within the community in lieu of handing down prison or jail sanctions. No society can expect to be free of a crime problem[3]; yet no society or social group can afford to punish all those who break the laws (Erikson 1966).

No longer can a criminal-sentencing judge cease thinking about the future of a convicted offender when the social actor is sentenced to prison. Maura Corrigan, chief justice of the Michigan Supreme Court and chair of the Problem Solving Courts Committee, Conference of Chief Justices, reviewed the 2003 book, judging in a therapeutic key, and claimed: "Perhaps no other movement in the past decade has so influenced American trial courts as the emergence of thousands of problem solving courts. To appreciate this movement and its growing impact, judges should learn principles [of this jurisprudence] to enhance their critical mission."

OBSERVING AND UNDERSTANDING PROBLEM SOLVING COURTS

This book takes an inside look at problem solving courts, judge-run programs in general-jurisdiction courts designed to facilitate long-term behavioral and attitudinal change among convicted offenders within their communities. It articulates the principles of a jurisprudence of problem solving justice designed to take place in the special court session, which the trial court judge generalizes in other courtroom experiences to resolve legal conflicts. In response, other members of the courtroom work group—the prosecuting and defense attorneys—subscribe to the practices of a problem solving jurisprudence. We argue that a problem solving jurisprudence represents a merger of three distinctive legal positions: (1) legal pragmatism or legal realism, a position that claims the law is judge-made, albeit within the boundaries of the rule of law; (2) therapeutic and crime-prevention jurisprudence (i.e., a position claiming that court processes can build the strengths of an individual to facilitate the person's commitment to a good life and the avoidance of crime); and (3) the law-and-literature position that claims rational legal decisions[4] must consider the person holistically and within the context of a society's social structure and its needs.

The conceptual framework that guides the analysis is articulated in Émile Durkheim's *The Rules of Sociological Method* (1893) and in Kai Erikson's *Wayward Puritans* (1966). We examine four sociological themes regarding crime, criminal law, and community: (1) Punishments or consequences for rule or law violations have a more proactive than reactive purpose. (2) A symbolic and proactive purpose of punishment is to communicate shared values or the shared identity of a society or social group. (3) Crime or deviance is not a property of the person. It is socially constructed by laws that define certain behaviors as criminal. (4) Punishments for crimes and rule violations are not delivered exclusively for the purpose of preventing harm in a community. They are delivered partly to reinforce a sense of community and public safety.

Unlike the social-historical accounts that Erikson presents, we use observational methods and analyses of court dialogues to present a detailed account, from the perspective of problem solving court participants and the judges who preside over the PSC programs. All told, three years of observations, court transcripts, and field notes make up the data we analyze. The participant-judge dialogues, although informed by social and criminal justice agency representatives, are impromptu. There are no stage directions, analogous to the rules of the court, and there are no scripts for participants. Moments of comedy, followed often by reports of tragedy, are spoken indicators of expectations for personal transformations.

Our study examines how judges and legal actors work to deliver PSC justice. It examines the successes and setbacks experienced by participants and court programs, while reporting on the use of evidence-based practices and principles in contemporary criminal justice settings. We pay attention to what researchers call input, output, and outcome data. Our research findings are largely qualitative, based on analyses of court documents, texts, dialogues, and court transcripts. We focus nonetheless on how the problem solving court works to bring a sense of citizenship to the person, making him or her responsive to programs designed to prevent crime (Andrews and Dowden 2007). Ultimately, we are interested in demonstrating what works in a problem solving court and how the PSC works to prevent crime and increase a sense of well-being among the general population.

2

The Purposes, Promises, and Magic of Contemporary Criminal Law and Criminal Justice in the United States

INTRODUCTION

Criminal law and criminal justice processes continuously change as law and policy makers seek principles and practices to increase public safety and reassure the general population, saints and sinners alike, that social problems can be resolved by using fair procedures. Some problems, such as poverty, alcohol and drug abuse, behavioral and physical illnesses, and intolerance for imagined or real "outsiders," persist, unaffected by criminal law (Erikson 1966). Witch hunts plagued Salem, Massachusetts, centuries ago when twenty-two persons, all within one year, were suspected of or condemned for witchcraft (Erikson 1966). Beginning in the early 1980s, an overzealous prosecuting attorney initiated a witch hunt in Jordan, Minnesota. The "witches" in Jordan, some of whom were outsiders, were identified as satanic child abusers by supposed victims, coaxed into disclosing false reports of molestations and other forms of torture and victimization. With a population of fewer than four thousand persons, twenty-four adults in Jordan were arrested for child sexual abuse, satanic ritual abuse, and child pornography. All were exonerated. The witch hunt ended only when a minister's wife was added to the list of suspects.

Contemporary societies are governed by law; yet the law alone stands impotent in attempts to resolve persistent problems, many associated with poverty and social disorganization. Critics may point to the social structural factors that underlie the visible problems, taking the position that until the fundamental causes are addressed, attempts to resolve problems can only be futile. We disagree strongly and contend that it is a moral imperative to respond to individuals, families, groups, and segments of society *now* in well-informed attempts to alleviate suffering and pain, including that caused by criminal misconduct or the legal response to crime.

The criminal law has use, value, or instrumental, as well as symbolic value, to all societies and local communities. The challenge for contemporary and future law and policy makers is to understand the evolution of criminal justice to avoid repeating mistakes and to strive for improved social conditions.

PURPOSES OF CONTEMPORARY CRIMINAL LAW

It is simply wrong to burn down a church. Keith, a nineteen-year-old high school dropout, pled guilty in January 2007 to burglary and arson in connection with a fire that completely destroyed a Baptist church in a Midwestern community in the United States. As a consequence, the criminal court judge faced the responsibility of determining an appropriate sanction. By law, Keith could be incarcerated for up to eighteen years by the Department of Corrections. At his sentencing hearing, the nineteen-year-old claimed the torching of the church was not really his fault. He felt forced to do it by his friend Jim, a former member of the church. Together the two boys planned to steal money from the safe.

Jim, according to his own statements, had emptied cans of lighter fluid on the church pews and the curtains and commanded Keith to strike the matches to start the fire. Keith claims that Jim also talked him into dropping out of high school in his senior year because school was a waste of time. Both boys agreed to take the GED and pursue business opportunities together. Jim passed the GED, but Keith failed and laments that he should never have listened to Jim. Some would say Keith is a good example of "a follower."

A comprehensive psychosocial evaluation was ordered in preparation for the sentencing hearing. The psychologist stated that Keith is not mentally ill in any way, but he is indeed easily manipulated by others and is willing to do whatever is asked of him, largely because he is starved for friendship and acceptance.

As the judge listened to Keith disclose what he was thinking, as Keith described how he cut the safe out of the church floor and then watched Jim throw lighter fluid around, he began to understand that Keith does not have a well-developed sense of who he is or who he could become. He simply wanted to be a friend and thus went along with Jim's demand to light the fire. Keith told the judge that he understood fully the wrongfulness of a church burning. "It makes God angry," he said. Yet, the emotions and thoughts he expressed aloud communicated clearly an inability to grasp the realization that his criminal actions had destroyed a building where community residents gathered each week. He willfully destroyed not only a sacred place but a community space.

The judge struggled to consider what Keith said and felt, to measure the danger he posed and the fear and dread he brought to his community. He wondered if Keith could comprehend that fire personnel dispatched to the church could have been injured or killed. He tried to understand, according to the way Keith viewed the world, the importance of wanting to be accepted by others, while imagining how church members felt about losing their meeting place. The judge understood fully that the law is written with harsh consequences for persons who intentionally burn down churches; yet he was perplexed by what could be done to deliver law and justice to Keith, a teenager with few prospects for doing well in society. The judge experienced a sense of sadness as he visualized what life would be like in prison for a person like Keith, a follower and not a leader, who only wants to be a friend and to have friends.

The rule and spirit of law bind the judge to balance the rights of the individual with the interests of the community. He is responsible for meting out a fair sentence, knowing full well that he cannot fix Keith's thinking or bring the church back from a pile of ashes. He must retain compassion for Keith, although personally he may be disgusted by his criminal acts and intents. Ironically, he is required to consider what the church is asking for: absolute forgiveness. The victim's statements must be considered a mitigating circumstance, albeit balanced with the aggravating circumstances regarding the harm caused to the entire community. The law, and the law alone, guides the determination of the number of years of prison time warranted for this offender and his offense. The law reiterates to the community its most important values by determining the appropriate range of punishment. Simply put, the law's function may be utilitarian, but it is certainly symbolic. Utilitarian or instrumental purposes may be deterrence or rehabilitation. Simultaneously, the purpose of law pronounces the values and norms of a society and the degree to which criminal behaviors are disvalued or intolerable.

In this case, the judge sentenced Keith to fifteen years in state prison and Jim to twenty-two years. The defendants were ordered, once released from prison, to share the payment of more than the $900,000 in damages to the church. The judge suffered from no illusion that either defendant would ever be able to pay monetary damages, but he did hope to restore a sense of community to those who lost their church.

What is the purpose of criminal law, the law invoked to identify the seriousness of the church-burning event and the appropriate sentence for those who committed the criminal act? Criminal law and the criminal justice process have the purpose of responding effectively and fairly to types of behaviors and types of social actors deemed intolerable by society. The overarching purpose of criminal law is to protect the general population from harm and to punish criminal offenders appropriately. No social group, social institution, or culture can accept arson or murder, theft or rape. How behaviors are defined and classified as crimes—and not the justified taking of another person's life, sexuality, or property—is subject to change over time and across social spaces in nations and societies around the world.

Historical accounts of criminal law in the United States and Western Europe highlight evolutionary and revolutionary thinking and experimentation with the appropriate punishments to hand out to persons found guilty of criminal wrongdoing (Foucault 1975; Friedman 1993, 2002). Capital punishment and corporal punishment, once required for many offenses, were replaced with what most social groups consider to be more humane forms of punishment, ranging from solitary confinement in prison to a term of probation within the community. As social identity changes or threats to a community's identity emerge, the law's responses to deviance change (Erikson 1966). All told, social histories of crime and punishment conclude that social-structural and cultural factors, population changes, and the process of social institutionaliza-tion account for changing definitions of and responses to crime. The rule of law changes as a function of social change. Simply put, the rule of law itself is normative (Bauman 2000; Ducci 2000; King, Massoglia, and MacMillan 2007; Kruttschnitt, Gartner, and Hussemann 2008; Levin 2002; McCall, Parker, and MacDonald 2008; Oh 2005; Rocque 2008; Yates and Fording 2005). Nonetheless, the stated purpose of criminal law was and is the delivery of a socially legitimated form of control and discipline that stops and prevents deviant and criminal behaviors.[1]

REHABILITATION, INCAPACITATION, DETERRENCE, AND JUST DESERTS

Students of criminal law and criminal justice are familiar with the four central purposes of criminal law in the contemporary United States. Rehabilitation is the first and the oldest. It is articulated in state and federal constitutions, statutes, and court decisions (Birgden 2002, 2004; Bonnet 2006). Convicted criminals are not "bad"; they are unprepared or unequipped to live success-fully and independently in society. Rooted in the British Poor Law tradition, incarceration was supposed to provide treatment, education, and the devel-opment of work skills, along with the internalization of social norms and mainstream cultural values (Citti 2004; MacKay 2001; Murdoch 1998). The convicted felon could be transformed into a productive citizen and would leave the poor house or the prison with a new opportunity to succeed in society. If the released prisoner fails to follow the rules of probation or parole that follow the social actor upon reentry into free society, the once-convicted felon returns to prison to receive more rehabilitative attempts.

The second purpose of criminal law, one of the utilitarian-based justifications, is incapacitation. Catch the thief, incarcerate the thief, and end theft in the community. The convicted offender is not free to commit more thefts (or burglaries, drug deals, batteries, and so forth). He or she is incapacitated. No community or state can afford to incapacitate all convicted offenders. Thus, the law is expected to deliver selective and not general incapacitation (Auerhahn 1999). Identify the very worst thieves or the most dangerous drug dealers, and incapacitate them with long terms of incarceration, while acknowledging that a lesser or minimum punishment is sufficient for the offenders less likely to repeat their crimes.

Selective incapacitation (Auerhahn 1999) presents the criminal law as a double-edged sword. Using actuarial-type prediction devices to estimate the likelihood of repeated crime, it is possible to incapacitate the persons who, if they had remained free, would never have committed subsequent crimes. As a consequence, the social and personal costs for incarceration are misallocated and undeniably unfair. Using the same prediction devices, a person not predicted to repeat crime may remain free in society under selective-incapacitation principles, only to commit countless thefts, drug deals, or batteries. Undeniably, the decision to punish insufficiently has grave social costs. All told, the infinite diversity of thought, behavior, and social circumstances characterizing all social actors and social acts renders any actuarial tool for predicting future behavior problematic. Thus, the selective-incapacitation purpose of criminal law is left with an unanswerable question: is it more egregious to incapacitate the individual who does not need the punishment or to fail to incapacitate the individual who continues to commit crime (Auerhahn 1999; Burdon and Gallagher 2002; Kessler and Levitt 1997)?

The third purpose of criminal law is deterrence, also a utilitarian approach for responding to deviance and crime. Deterrence implies that social actors calculate the subjectively perceived costs of crime and weigh them against potential or perceived benefits.[2] If the costs outweigh the benefits, social actors are likely to avoid criminal acts. If the benefits trump, criminal behavior is more likely to occur. Make the criminal punishment severe enough, deliver it soon after the criminal event, and be certain to punish the offender (Ward, Stafford, and Gray 2001). The specific offender, having experienced the pains of punishment, will be deterred from subsequent criminal activity. Others in the general population, although they may not directly observe the punishment, develop perceptions of the costs of punishment as the media portrays life behind bars, as the news reporter dispatches the sentence meted out in court, and as a driver reads the highway sign that says "click it or ticket," reminding her that she is somewhat likely to be fined for failing to buckle her seat belt.

The fourth purpose of criminal law is to punish those who deserve sanctions, including the deprivation of liberty, because they have been convicted of crimes. Known as just deserts, or retaliation, the purpose can be accomplished through various sentencing procedures, such as guidelines that examine only the offender's offense and prior criminal history (Frase 2005), or mandatory-minimum sentencing laws that leave no room for consideration of the circumstances that account for a more discretionary sentencing decision process (Bjerk 2005; Courtwright 2004; Sabet 2005). Although just deserts gained widespread popularity during the 1980s and 1990s, it fell out of favor as more and more prison inmates returned home from long-term incarceration, only to reoffend without the tools needed to remain productive and self-sufficient within their local communities.

The purposes of criminal law change. The reader needs only look back to mid-1970s to see the supposed demise of the rehabilitative purpose. Yet, this first decade of the twenty-first century has witnessed an absolute return to the rehabilitative ideal with an increasing dependence on drug courts, reentry courts, and community court programs. Analysts account for changing criminal law by examining changing social problems and the irresistible impulse to experiment. Across the states and across time, we see social experiments designed to uncover how punishment "works" to affect social actors' behaviors (Miller 2003; Sherman 2000; Terry 2004; Toch 2003; Ziegler and Mitchell 2003). Most recently, social experimentation has turned to the judiciary to resolve problems that once were considered only the prison-probation-parole problem to resolve.

PROMISES OF CONTEMPORARY CRIMINAL LAW

Contemporarily, the ever-changing citizenry depends on criminal law to define and apply law and consequences in ways that meet the government's interests, society's interests, and diverse cultural interests. We can peek into the soul of U.S. society and its core values through the eyes of criminal law. How do we treat persons convicted of criminal misconduct? How do we create, or prevent the creation of, an underclass through criminal law and mass incarceration? How do we respond uniquely to problems in unique cities, counties, states, and towns?

Criminal law promises to protect society by responding mostly to individuals, that is, by taking into account the social act and the mind of the social actor.[3] Courts examine *actus reus*, the criminal act defined by law, and *mens rea*, the intent to commit a criminal offense, to determine appropriate punishments or responses. How harmful or potentially harmful was the act committed? Did the social actor deliberately engage in behaviors, alone or with others, with the intention to set in motion a chain of events that could or would harm persons or society? Although strict liability offenses do not require the state to prove mens rea for certain criminal acts (e.g., possessing a small quantity of narcotics), for most criminal charges the prosecuting attorney must prove the criminal case based on the state of mind as well as the criminal act.

Fairness and justice, equal or equitable criminal sentencing, and punishment appropriate to the offense constitute the three foremost promises of criminal law in the United States. Each remains nearly sacred; yet each is impossible to achieve in all cases, or even in the majority of them. What constitutes fairness or justice tends to remain unstated. It is as if everyone is supposed to know the meaning of the terms and how to mete out fair and just punishments. When formulating arguments, it is not unusual for a legal actor to justify the purpose of a punishment by linking it to the words "fair" or "just," inferring erroneously that the purpose follows the promise. The just deserts sentencing model uncritically accepts the notion that a punishment deserved for an offense is a just punishment. As a result, important issues, such as the use of power and influence in the lawmaking process that identifies the putatively just punishment, remain unexamined (Engen and Steen 2000; Jacobs et al. 2007; Mayrack 2008; Petrucci 2002). Similarly, the fair punishment remains illusory (Corrado et al. 2003; Hadfield 2005; Miceli and Segerson 2007; Persico 2002). Critical analysis is needed to ask if fairness is a quality of the sentence that applies to the individual judgment, the individual offender, or the sentencing law in general. Suppose a five-year term of incarceration is legislatively prescribed for a particular charge of burglary. Is that a fair level of punishment? Does the punishment fit the crime or the criminal act, the criminal mind, and the circumstances surrounding the offense? Perhaps the fair punishment should reflect the harm an individual or the community experiences, or perhaps it should reflect the fear that spreads through a neighborhood following a church fire or some other crime. Fairness and justice are deeply rooted cultural values that social actors, including lawmakers and law breakers, subscribe to. Yet, in practice, it is difficult to specify what the fair and just criminal sanction is.

Equally untenable is the promise to deliver equality in sentencing practices (Arvanites and Asher 1998; Decoursey 2003; Yates 1997). Should all persons convicted of the same category of crime be punished alike? Without equal punishments, some argue, biases result. Worst are the individually biased decisions and the social-institutional biases that result in social-structural-level discrimination. Even shifting to a standard of equity, rather than equality, keeps the promise of criminal law at bay. One limitation to the promise of equal or equitable criminal law is its key value protecting each unique person's rights, of making sure that every individual social actor gets his or her day in court. Because no two social actors and no two social acts are alike, equitable punishments are unlikely. We posit that equality, even that which becomes transformed in the equitable criminal law, represents a symbolically important value across the United States; however, working to achieve equal or equitable punishments or a criminal law that promises equality is futile at best and, in meaningful ways, unfair.

What should the criminal law promise? It must promise fairness and equality in the procedures used to achieve lawful arrests, convictions, and punishments. Regardless of whether the offender stole $5 from the collection box or set the church on fire, the same procedures must be applied to ensure that each person is treated according to the rule of law, which, in a nutshell, tells legal actors to follow the rules specified by statutes, court decisions, and constitutions.

The criminal law should also promise that punishments or sanctions will be appropriate to the offense, offender characteristics, and circumstances surrounding the crime. It is easy to promise appropriate punishments for extreme forms of criminal behavior or for the most and least serious offenses. Life in prison is perhaps appropriate for first-degree murder, and a fine is fine for a first-time loitering offense. Difficult to specify, however, are appropriate punishments for acts that fall between the extreme anchors on a continuum of crime seriousness. Social groups and their lawmakers must come to a shared understanding of the range of crime seriousness (Evans and Tyson 2001; Ip, Kwan, and Chiu 2007; Kwan et al. 2002; Lyons 2008; Piquero, Carmichael, and Piquero 2008; Sellin and Wolfgang 1991; Vogel and Meeker 2001). If, for example, on a crime-seriousness scale, loitering is valued as "10" and first-degree murder is valued as "100," how serious is a home burglary? How serious is marital rape? Once agreement has been achieved as to crime seriousness and the law reflects the appropriate categorizations, how do lawmakers determine the punishment level that fits the degree of crime seriousness? Although a research literature exists to establish a general consensus with respect to determining crime seriousness, identifying appropriate punishments for the diverse array of criminal misconduct identified by criminal law remains akin to the quest for the Holy Grail (Alter, Kernochan, and Darley 2007; Buchanan and Young 2000; Darjee, Crichton, and Thomson 2000; Herzog 2006; Hochstetler and Shover 1997; Miller, Rossi, and Simpson 1986, 1991). The sociolegal community has weighed in on the issue and concluded that variations in perceptions of appropriate punishments across regions and social groups in the United States, the harmfulness of the crime, and the history of law in any given state together prevent widespread agreement on the determination of the punishment or a punishment scheme to provide a good fit for the distribution of crimes along the dimension of seriousness (Alter, Kernochan, and Darley 2007; Darjee, Crichton, and Thomson 2000; Sanderson, Zanna, and Darley 2000).

MAGIC OF CRIMINAL LAW

The magic of criminal law lies in its symbolic value and ability to alter as a function of social change. Criminal law can process, if not resolve, disputes that could become transgenerational and tragic blood feuds, like those Shakespeare described in *Romeo and Juliet* or American folklore proclaims in accounts of the Hatfields and McCoys.

A contemporary example of the magically malleable criminal law is seen in the criminal courts' responses to drug offenses. The War on Drugs era (identified by Richard Nixon in 1971) was characterized by harshly punitive responses to users and dealers, typified in many ways by New York's Rockefeller drug laws (Spunt 2003; Tinto 2001). Across the states, "three-strikes" laws, habitual-substance-abuser laws that required sentencing judges to execute and not suspend sentences, mandatory-minimum sentencing laws, and presumptive terms of incarceration for drug dealers that exceeded the punishments for manslaughter were typical. We call this sociolegal approach "punitive jurisprudence," meaning that legal institutions, organizations, and activities communicate the centrality of identifying and punishing wrongdoers for the primary purpose of controlling and preventing harm. The common-law theme of determining a defendant's guilt is paramount (Miller and Knudsen 2007). Applied to drug offenders, a punitive jurisprudence model promotes the creation of law that defines criminal behaviors and criminal sanctions. It encourages law enforcement and the courts to develop and implement policies and procedures aimed at capturing and punishing wrongdoers. A required or mandatory punishment is preferred over a discretion-based judgment by the court. To sum it up, using police jargon, a punitive response to drug offenders, and an appropriate one, is "Trail them, nail them, and jail them."

Punitive jurisprudence gave way to what was initially called a therapeutic jurisprudence for responding to drug offenders. Since 1989, the courts

have adopted a somewhat remedial or therapeutic approach when responding to drug users and abusers (especially those pronounced to be addicts),
to persons appearing in court with serious behavioral-health problems,
and to those returning home from state or federal prison (Arnold, Stewart,
and McNeece 2001; Berman 2004; Jessup et al. 2003; O'Connell et al.
2007). It is imperative to realize that regardless of the therapeutic termi-
nology, because responses to offenders or ex-offenders are court-based,
persons are held strictly accountable for their behaviors within their communities.

We use the term *problem solving jurisprudence* (not therapeutic jurisprudence) because the problem solving court programs in the twenty-first
century work to resolve community and defendant/convicted offender/indi-
vidual problems simultaneously. A returning prison inmate presents clusters
of personal problems, and clusters of returning prison inmates present community or social problems. Both clusters need attention from the courts, and
the dual approach required by the problem solving court presents enormous
challenges. Arguably, it is far easier for a court—a judge—to order an individual into treatment than it is for the judge to resolve community problems
resulting from an inadequate supply of affordable housing for a number of
drug-addicted offenders (or a large number of persons returning from prison)
living within one or more areas of the city.

No longer does the lawyer or the social scientist conclude that offenders are simply criminal and require punishments, not services within the
community, or that the severity of an addiction is anything but a multidimensional problem, representing some combination of family, work,
residence, medical, psychological or psychiatric, and social-interaction
issues. Problem solving jurisprudence entails focus by legal institutions,
organizations, and activities on practices that can reform or rehabilitate social deviants while helping victims. Intensive programs, including counseling or probation, center on helping the perpetrator to develop work skills,
attain education certification, establish or reestablish family relationships
across the generations, develop improved everyday-living skills, and
manage and minimize criminal thoughts, feelings, and behaviors. When
necessary, courts working with a problem solving jurisprudence model
typically order program participants to enroll in medical, psychological, or
dental programs.[4] A problem solving jurisprudence communicates a strong
crime-prevention, work, and education message. Coupled with health and
mental-health programs, as well as housing programs, problem solving
jurisprudence brings a comprehensive approach to resolving defendant and
community problems.

SOCIAL CONTROL

Punitive and problem solving jurisprudence models communicate and symbolize different social-control purposes, but they do not represent mutually exclusive, or even competing, practices. Social-control methods may vary, but both models aspire to maintain high levels of social control. A punishment theme dominates punitive jurisprudence and appropriate responses to offenders and social problems, whereas a social-problems solution dominates the most contemporary jurisprudence model. In principle, punitive jurisprudence imposes relatively harsh sanctions. In practice, however, problem solving jurisprudence models may impose sanctions that are as harsh, or even harsher, than those imposed under a punitive jurisprudence model.

Consider the following example from a diversion problem solving court program designed for addicted substance abusers: Joe was convicted for driving under the influence, and his criminal history included a prior conviction for a DUI that resulted in serious bodily harm to his victim. Rather than sentencing Joe to the local jail for one year for his second conviction, the sentencing judge placed Joe in the problem solving court. Nearly twelve months into the diversion program, Joe was arrested once again for DUI. As a result, he was convicted as a habitual substance abuser and sentenced to three years in state prison. Joe's placement in the diversion program allowed the judge to stay his one-year sentence, but when Joe was arrested once again, the stayed sentence was executed along with the sentence for the new offense. All told, Joe served at least twice the time he would have served for his second conviction, and he served more than the usual time for a DUI because of the habitual statute. Problem solving court programs attempt to address the individual's and the community's needs by imposing an amount of social control that is no less than a traditional criminal sentence would impose. The perpetrator, in this case Joe, remains in the community, but he is subject to a high level of monitoring and surveillance, as well as drug and alcohol testing, and required to follow all program regulations while in the community.[5]

In sum, the magic of criminal law lies in its ability to process disputes between the state and the accused and to change or transform the methods used by the courts to address social problems. Criminal law helps victims experience revenge without requiring vengeful acts (Frison 2000). Disputes between the state and the individual social actor can be addressed, victims can be compensated, and the general population can experience perceptions of public safety or an increased quality of life within a community (Fisler 2005; Petersilia 2001), in part because recidivism rates can be reduced (Lovell, Gagliardi, and Peterson 2002; Marbley and Ferguson 2005; Yu 2000).

SOCIOLEGAL MOVEMENTS

The law is never static, although its critics charge that it changes and moves much too slowly to keep pace with social change. Nonetheless, over the decades and centuries, continuous but gradual sociolegal change has characterized U.S. law.

Changes in law are sometimes provoked by tragic and newsworthy events, a death resulting from child abuse, for example, but most of the legal changes that researchers can document can be classified as sociolegal movements. Sociolegal movements are somewhat like social movements, but they differ in terms of what provokes or sustains them. A social movement may be initiated and maintained by identity politics, protests, or perceptions of grave injustices within social organizations or social institutions. Groups of social actors, often outsiders to mainstream politics and power centers, challenge the legitimacy of extant practices. Sociolegal movements, on the other hand, are initiated and sustained by insiders. They are social-change movements *from within* legitimated institutions, such as politics and the law.

We look inside the relatively new sociolegal movement of problem solving courts. Basically, they are judge-created court programs that evolved from the drug court movement of the 1990s (Cooper 2002; Fulton Hora 2002; Harrison and Scarpitti 2002; La Prairie et al. 2002; Turner et al. 2002). Problem solving courts are typically community, family, prisoner reentry, or prison diversion courts (Anon 2005a; Berman and Feinblatt 2001; James 2003).

Be it a diversion or reentry program, the problem solving court addresses the consequences of a period of mass incarceration in the United States (Jacobs and Kleban 2003; Roberts 2004; Vogel 2004; Wacquant 2002). Incarcerating large numbers of nonviolent offenders, especially drug dealers whose offenses are defined by the type and quantity of the illegal substance involved, resulted in increased poverty, neglected families, and a host of problems for already disadvantaged neighborhoods (Anon 2008; Comfort 2003; Jacobs and Kleban 2003; Kruttschnitt 2006; Lazare 2007b; Oliver 2008; Pettit and Western 2004; Roberts 2004; Wacquant 2002). The problem solving court movement reflects clearly the realization that "something different" must be done to address the population's concerns for crime, safety, prison overcrowding, and prisoner reentry.

ATTICA: THE SEEDS OF SOCIOLEGAL CHANGE

We can see the seeds of this demand for sociolegal change at a specific and ironic moment in criminal justice history, the Attica prison riot. Attica was selected as the state prison in New York where drastic reform measures would be implemented and their consequences measured. However, shortly before the reforms were implemented, the riot occurred (Light 1995).[6]

The prison held more than twenty-two hundred inmates on September 9, 1991, with the facility operating to confine and punish, not rehabilitate, them. Attica, at the time of the riot, ran no meaningful work, education, or psychotherapeutic program. During the riot, 123 persons were killed or wounded by officers' and inmates' gunfire (Attica 1972). What lessons were learned? What needed to be done? We interviewed a man, John, who was at Attica. This is what he told us:

> On September 9, 1971, a general prison uprising at the Attica Correctional Facility in Attica, New York, galvanized public attention to the condition of prisoners in the United States during the 1960s and early 1970s. The riot, sparked by racial issues, overcrowding, and demands for better living conditions, including educational and vocational opportunities, was the bloodiest prison confrontation in American history. After Governor Nelson Rockefeller ordered the state police and national guard to retake the facility, on September 13, tear gas was dropped into the yard, shots were fired, and, in all, forty-three persons, including ten hostages, were killed on that single day. The overwhelming loss of life and injuries suffered by the inmates generated a flurry of federal civil rights complaints, along with a state civil class-action suit filed against the state of New York.
>
> At the time of the Attica riot, I was a young, second-year Federal Bureau of Investigation agent, among those dispatched by the Albany Field Office to Attica to conduct civil rights investigations, following complaints filed by inmates against guards, the state police, and the national guard.
>
> I was twenty-five or twenty-six, with a law degree in hand. I had no expectation for what I would find at Attica. The individual I was scheduled to interview was a file—a case—not really a person. I knew the name of the man but nothing more. I was merely doing my job, doing a routine investigation.
>
> The imposing, austere, stone facility was designed for twelve hundred inmates but housed one thousand additional persons at the time of the riot. It was a dreary place. Over half the inmates were African Americans, yet all of the guards were white. It was well-known that the guards were openly racist and that they routinely assaulted inmates with their batons.
>
> I entered the facility through the large, imposing front gate. There was a small space for me to put my personal belongings, including my gun. I carried my photo ID with me. The entry door had black bars, and behind it was a guard, staring at me. He asked, "Why are you here?" I told him who I was, he asked to see my FBI identification, and he asked me who I was going to interview. He directed me to a small, locked room with two metal chairs and a table, nothing more. I can still hear the clanking sounds of being locked in the interview room—without my gun. I knew the guard was directly outside the room I was

in. But I knew that he resented me being there. I doubted that he would lift a finger in my defense, if that had become necessary.

All the guards were cold toward the FBI agents, and quietly but obviously hostile toward me, coming into the facility to investigate civil rights violation allegations. It is possible that they felt guilty or worried or angry. It was clear that they hated the FBI for investigating. According to them, *they* should be able to file suit so that the government would look at the situation from *their* point of view.

They told me that they believed that the inmates who were injured or killed during the riot "got what they deserved." A grim bitterness between inmates and guards over the riot and its consequences pervaded the facility.

I interviewed Dossie, a very tall African American with bulging biceps shaped by daily heavy weight lifting. He appeared matter-of-fact as he sat facing me in a small, sterile, windowless interview room. Dossie seemed to be in his late forties; his cropped, black hair was flicked with grey. He was more than willing to speak with me because I had come to the facility responding to his civil rights complaint. He believed that he was the victim of excessive force. Even Dossie had the feeling that nothing would result from the interview, but he seemed to appreciate the opportunity to talk with a visitor who was there only as a matter of routine.

Dossie unashamedly pulled off his prison shirt and pulled down his shorts to display marks showing where he had been assaulted by guards. There were numerous small scars and various bruises of differing colors. I could not tell when or how he received them as many of the scars appeared to be thin, old knife-cut scars. Dossie calmly insisted that each of the marks on his body had come from the guards and the riot.

Toward the end of the twenty-minute interview, Dossie slowly reached into his shirt pocket and pulled out an old-fashioned, thick pair of glasses, saying, "Look, they broke my glasses." Dossie somehow could endure the unfairness of receiving arbitrary physical injuries, but he could not comprehend the despair he felt because he was now unable to read, an activity that empowered his imagination to take him beyond the walls of his cold confinement. Dossie needed his glasses, and he needed to share this moment with another human being who might care about his condition. I left the interview, and Attica, with the feeling that the civil rights complaint would in all likelihood not be substantiated. I was also convinced that I had truly been in a hellhole, filled with guards and inmates who desperately hated one another, though fellow human beings, for which there was no redemption. I didn't think I would ever look back at that day, but later on I understood that Attica was a watershed moment. Everything changed. (October 9, 2007)

Following the interview with John, we retrieved from the New York Court of Claims Dossie Walls's claim (No. 57710) against the state of New York. Dossie was from Brooklyn, the city in which most of the inmates had lived,

yet far away from the Attica facility, located in a primarily white and somewhat rural population. He reported[7] that on September 13 guards did

> shoot, threaten, menace, beat, strike, injure and otherwise harm [him,] causing
> serious injuries, mental and emotional anguish, pain and suffering;
>
> Steal, convert, and appropriate without due process . . . clothing, food, per-
> sonal effects, books and writings, including a manuscript;
>
> Order him to disrobe and to *throw his glasses and watch to the ground* [em-
> phasis added] and to march in formation while disrobed and without shoes for
> approximately one hour upon a surface that contained gravel;
>
> Ordered and forced, while still naked, to run with his hands over his head, in
> between lines of officers while they beat [him] with clubs and bats. [He] was
> struck 25 times or more on each buttock, 25 times or more across the back, ten
> times or more on each arm and elbow, three or four times on each knee, and
> once on the upper left stomach. . . .
>
> Thereafter an officer pressed an automatic pistol against [his] chest and
> threatened to kill him. He was struck on the right side of his forehead with a
> club and knocked to the floor.
>
> [He] did not receive medical attention for three days after he was injured
> thereby aggravating his injuries.

Harry Costas, now retired and living in Connecticut, represented Dossie
Walls. He demanded a judgment against the state for the sum of $500,000.
The claim was dismissed in June 1989 for lack of evidence. We phoned
Costas about this case. He was eager to talk to us, perhaps as eager as Dossie
had been to talk with John back in 1973. Costas told us that he represented
Dossie, having been recommended by the New York Bar Association. He
didn't receive any compensation. He remembers vividly that Dossie was in
solitary confinement when the riot broke out. He could not have contributed
to it in any way; yet he was humiliated, tortured, and injured. Costas thought,
at the time, that people would forget about Attica. He was, of course, wrong.
Although Dossie Walls remained in prison and received no compensation for
what happened to him, the United States will always remember Attica.

Attica represents the beginning of a wave of prison riots, some more brutal
and deadlier than Attica's (Hamm 1998; Huspek 2000; Useem 1985; Useem
and Piehl 2008). It also caused a heightened sense of the need to reform
policy and law. With hindsight, we can see that the Rockefeller drug laws ex-
acerbated the imprisonment problem in New York State, and other strict laws
led the states down an extremely punitive path for twenty years. Although
no current reform can undo yesterday's harms, the problem solving court
movement today—court and judge initiated—is taking a step forward toward
rehabilitative programs that are proven to be effective and cost-efficient. The

problem solving court movement is perhaps the most comprehensive and realistic approach to changing lives and preventing recidivism.

Although we need time to reflect upon the movement, its current status is at least promising and probably highly successful. Today's problem solving courts represent social movements generated "from the inside" (Mirchandani 2005) rather than provoked by an urgent need to respond to a problem using untested methods.

The problem solving jurisprudence that influences the movement represents a merger of highly regarded perspectives, such as legal realism (Farber 2001; Levinson 2000), pragmatism (Posner 2000, 2004; Sullivan and Solove 2003; Wells 2000), law and economics (Krecke 2003; Posner 2006), and law and literature (Crane 1997; Nussbaum 2006).

A PREVIEW

The studies we present in this book are based on three problem solving court programs. Each program has (or had) public court sessions that we systematically observed over a period of three years. Detailed field notes were taken. In addition, we interviewed court team members and analyzed transcripts of public court sessions. All the data collection was approved by a university-based institutional review board to protect human subjects in research studies.

We analyze the dialogues and documents that come from three different problem solving courts. One, a prisoner reentry court, is an unmitigated success. Another, a forensic diversion program, is only moderately successful. The third, a reentry court for sex offenders, is a complete failure.

We contend that failures provide excellent tools for advancing our knowledge of problem solving courts. Like the morbidity and mortality conferences held in hospitals to determine what went wrong, analyses of failed court programs tell us how to better deliver services and programs designed to improve public safety. We cannot learn such lessons by looking only at successes. Further, we contend that successes must be understood within the context of community building. When a court program brings an increased quality of life to a community's residents and neighborhoods, its key components and characteristics must be identified for the purpose of promoting success in other communities.

Comparing the extremely successful program with the moderately successful and the failed programs requires a strong analytical approach. Yet, the stories participants tell provide perhaps the most valuable lessons. No quantitative data can communicate how a parent feels when reunited with a child who was too young to visit him or her in prison. No data can capture the anguish of trying, but failing, in a court program and being reincarcerated. That said, we introduce you to Jack and Donna.

Jack is a forty-one-year-old reentry problem solving court graduate. He was incarcerated for eight years on A-level felony drug-dealing charges and readily admitted a methamphetamine addiction, a problem that he developed after he began using the drug regularly at age seventeen. At the time of his arrest, he was cooking methamphetamine in front of his children.

Soon after his head was shaved on his way into the Department of Correction, he decided to grow his hair for Locks of Love (an organization that collects donated human hair to make wigs for children who suffer hair loss from cancer treatment, alopecia, or some other illness or disease). Jack successfully petitioned the court to modify his sentence by ten years and appeared in the reentry court with a ponytail down to his waist. The judge asked him about his family. Jack told the court that he was living with his girlfriend, the woman who stood by him during his incarceration. She had two children, and Jack intended to care for them. "They are my second family," he claimed. The judge persisted:

> JUDGE: Do you have any children of your own?
>
> JACK: I do, your honor, but I don't know where they are. But I know I owe child support.
>
> JUDGE: Now, how are you going to pay child support? Do you have a court order?
>
> JACK: No sir, my wife, my ex-wife that is, didn't keep up with the paperwork. I just know that I owe a lot of money for the kids. I have a son and a daughter. I never saw them after I went away.
>
> JUDGE: What's your future plan about your kids?
>
> JACK: I want to be part of their life, but, you know, there's a lot of bridges I burnt, and I don't blame their mother at all for how she feels about me. Because . . . we were married for twelve years and she's seen that addiction, so I'm gonna have to prove myself to her and that will take time. (February 19, 2007)

Three months into the reentry problem solving court, Jack reported that he had located his children and his ex-wife living about ninety miles away. No one wanted to see him, but Jack wanted to make amends to his children. His ex-wife appeared in court and was awarded back child support. Jack was ordered to pay $120 per month. Jack continued living with his girlfriend and her children. He eventually obtained a full-time job at a manufacturing plant that uses advanced technologies, voluntarily doubled his monthly child-support payment, and also supported his "second family."

A year after entering the program, Jack graduated and was placed on probation. Once a month he returns to reentry court. During one session that took

place about eighteen months after Jack came into reentry, he was quizzed
again:

> JUDGE: Now[, Jack], how are you doing with all those kids you're supposed to
> be taking care of? How's your ex-wife doing? Is she letting you see the kids?
>   JACK: Well, i don't know quite how to say this. . . . My ex-wife, she likes me
> now. She says i'm the man she knew. I'm the man she fell in love with.
>   JUDGE: Are you thinking about getting back together?
>   JACK: No, no, your honor. I will never leave the love of my life. She was
> always there for me when I was in prison. This is my family, too.
>   JUDGE: What about the kids? How are you going to take care of all four of
> them?
>   JACK: Well, your honor, it's not a big problem. There aren't a lot of things that
> I want. I save my money for the kids. I can't give them much, you know. But I
> see my own kids at least every week, and now my girlfriend can stay home and
> take care of her kids, on account of my job and my pay. (July 14, 2008)

Throughout the time he participated in the problem solving court program,
Jack was sanctioned for only one program violation: missing curfew. He
completed eight hours of work crew and never looked back. He continues to
do well at work and to support both of his families, and he has helped other
reentry court participants get jobs. He volunteers to drive new participants
around town to help them transition back into the community. His story
comes from a dramatically successful reentry problem solving court program.
Of all the persons who came into the program ($N = 58$) during the time we
observed it, three were arrested, and eight additional persons were expelled
from the program and returned to prison for violating program regulations.
Reentry garnered indirect financial support from the state in the form of a
housing program that set a low level of rent for twelve months, enabling
participants to pay down bills, including back child support that accrued
while the participant was incarcerated. It also became the centerpiece for a
five-year federal grant, awarded to the city, focused on improving the quality
of life for all residents and a five-year federal grant, awarded to United Way,
designed to build assets that can be used to purchase higher education credits
or a first home.

Donna was a participant in the less successful forensic diversion problem
solving court program.[8] She was convicted of dealing crack cocaine and suffered from numerous health problems, including diabetes, related peripheral
neuropathy, and hepatitis C. She found it difficult to keep a job or a suitable
apartment. In forensic diversion, she saw a case manager twice a week, who
made sure that she attended counseling sessions for depression, treatment
for cocaine addiction, and family counseling so that she could reunite with
her adult daughter. Donna started out doing well, maintaining a cheerful de-

meanor as she met the judge in weekly court sessions. She had trouble getting a job, however, as the forensic diversion problem solving court included no formal employment program. As a result, Donna had difficulty paying the rent with her disability check, and when she returned to her old ways, meeting up with men to pay her expenses, she quickly slid down the slippery slope into depression and returned to drug use and drug dealing.

Eventually, she missed a court session and tested positive for cocaine. In court, she admitted to selling cocaine to another forensic diversion participant. She was expelled from the program and sentenced on May 30, 2007, to six years in the Department of Corrections. Donna's story comes from her participation in a problem solving court program that is only moderately successful. In its fourth year, approximately one-half of the participants had failed—usually during the time they spent on probation after completing the active phases of the four-phase program—and were sentenced to prison time. What accounts for the rate of failure? First, the participants engaged in behaviors that violated program regulations and sometimes the law. Second, case management was woefully inadequate: social workers were uninformed and as a consequence misinformed their clients. Third, the measurement instruments used to assess needs and risks to reoffend did not include adequate indicators of psychological or psychiatric problems, a major concern for problem solving court programs designed for defendants with mental-health issues (Butler et al. 2006; Senior et al. 2007; Webster et al. 2006; Wolff, Blitz, and Shi 2007). Fourth, the team put up serious resistance to changing the way it usually did business. Finally, although the presiding judge worked diligently to keep up with the research literature on treating co-occurring problems (drug addiction and mental illness) within the community, he encouraged the team to make what are, in reality, judicial decisions. No one factor explains success or failure for an individual participant or for a court program. Nonetheless, we document in subsequent chapters the patterns we observe that account for variation in the outcomes of distinctive problem solving court programs. Before we present the empirical evidence, however, we turn attention in the following chapter to the jurisprudence behind the sociolegal movement: a problem solving jurisprudence.

3

A Problem Solving Court Jurisprudence

Problem solving courts require leaders—judges or judicial officers—willing to exercise an energetic and entrepreneurial spirit with unimpeachable ethical standards and a tolerance for taking risks. Problem solving courts are state court programs that depend almost exclusively on judges, as individuals or as small groups of judicial officers, to design and implement programs and to sustain them in constructive ways that benefit participants and the community simultaneously. PSC work, albeit with exceptions, tends to remain unrewarded or unrecognized by other judges, the state court systems, and the communities they serve (Fulton Hora 2002; Wolf 2008). Ironically, many strategies used in PSC work have found their way into the traditional courtroom setting. Judges take problem solving approaches to respond to a custody or visitation dispute in a civil court hearing or to determine the appropriate sanctions in a criminal court hearing without consciously realizing how the deliberative practice was devised (Farole et al. 2005).

THEORY AND MEASUREMENT
LIMITATIONS AND POSSIBLE SOLUTIONS

Effective and efficient problem solving courts, be they mental-health, family abuse, community, diversion, or reentry court programs, need to be theory driven and continuously evaluated empirically. Yet, there is no prevailing theory or jurisprudence to guide problem solving courts. Earlier-generation drug courts subscribed to key principles (yet no theory), especially if they sought state or federal funds. In operation for years before systematic evaluative studies were published, drug courts could claim success by appealing to the general population with the claim "we are doing something different to solve the drug problem."

Skepticism, at times unspoken, about problem solving courts nonetheless remains. By and large, criticism of what goes wrong in courts, not praise for the benefits that result, rules the day (Berman 2004). Two central explanations are offered for this seemingly naïve or unfair reality. First, the news media tends to report the bad news and not the good news that comes from court activities. The adage "When it bleeds, it leads" applies to court hearing as well as PSC programs. We do not pick up newspapers or watch televised news to measure all the day's good news coming from general-jurisdiction trial courts. However, if a person participating in drug court relapses and causes a drunk-driving accident resulting in serious injury, expect to see a headline story in the local section of the newspaper.

Second, whatever centralized office accounts for judicial workloads tends to treat PSC work as community volunteer work. In those states that use a weighted method to sum up the supposed time it takes the court to handle diverse types of cases, where does the problem solving court fit it? In those reports, distributed by each state with some data compiled nationally by the National Center for State Courts (NCSC), no measurement component accounts for problem solving courts and their caseloads, that is, the participants who appear in the court each week.

There is, however, some progress on this issue. After all, problem solving courts are here to stay, making it important to measure and account for their specialized work. More than twenty years ago, the NCSC disseminated a report on trial court performance standards for the purpose of giving courts effective management tools. In May 2008, the NCSC issued *A Unifying Framework for Court Performance Measurement—Final Report*, which stresses the importance of bringing the effectiveness and efficiency of problem solving courts into the courts' overall performance assessment.

Consider an important outcome measure (i.e., crime committed following court rulings). Called "alternative court customers" by the NCSC (2008, 15), problem solving court participants, as a group, fare better than they would if their cases were adjudicated by traditional court processes.[1] In other words, PSC programs are more effective at reducing the likelihood of recidivism than traditional criminal court procedures. A comment in the NCSC report claims, "Performance measures in specific types of courts [problem solving courts] need to link up to broader measures of court performance."

REPLICATING SUCCESS: IS IT POSSIBLE?

Each problem solving court is unique, taking into account local community circumstances as well as the specific social problem it is designed to address. It is impossible to imagine, as the social scientist would prefer, that a model problem solving court program could be established and replicated and that the various sites could then be studied and compared. It is important to realize that this limitation is not unique to problem solving courts. A more dramatic example is the cluster of mandatory arrest experiments to deter spousal abuse. During the 1980s, the Minneapolis Police Department agreed to participate in a randomized, controlled experiment on the premise that arrest has a specific deterrent effect on what was then called "domestic violence." Police randomly assigned cases to the arrest (i.e., treatment) group, or to the no-arrest (i.e., control) group. As predicted by a simple deterrence principle that specified punishment certainty and severity would prevent recidivism, researchers did indeed show a deterrent effect: "The arrest intervention certainly did not make things worse and may well have made things better" (Sherman and Berk 1984, 236). Eager to find a potential solution to the social problem of domestic violence, researchers replicated the quasi-experimental Minneapolis program in five other locations: Milwaukee, Wisconsin; Omaha, Nebraska; Charlotte, North Carolina; Colorado Springs, Colorado; and Metro Dade County, Florida. These studies, known as the Spouse Abuse Replication Program (SARP), unfortunately did not support the initial study. Cities varied, and offenders varied. Some of the cities had substantial unemployment problems, especially among the African American population; others had substantial Latino populations. A number of arrested offenders were repeat offenders, while other first-time offenders were unemployed. With hindsight, it is difficult to imagine why social scientists expected to see "what worked" in one city would necessarily work well in another. Needless to say, the initial findings did not hold up under replication studies. In Colorado Springs, no deterrent effect was found. Worse yet, reports based on three experiments (Charlotte, Milwaukee, and Omaha) concluded that arrest either had no deterrent effect or caused an escalation of violence within six months following police intervention. A meta-analysis of all the SARP experiments concluded that "a more complete and sobering look at [the arrest experiments] . . . indicates that the initial claim of the deterrent value of mandatory arrest policies may well be the social science equivalent of cold fusion" (Gelles 1993). Ironically, few studies paid attention to what the victims experienced (Miller 2003). Imagine how victims differed: Did they have children? Were they employed? Did they have family members in town?

There is no one-size-fits-all problem solving court because no two communities and no two offenders are alike in all relevant ways. The SARP experiments taught that lesson well.

Imagine, for instance, the drug-abuse problems in three states: Maine, Indiana, and Kansas. The U.S. Drug Enforcement Administration reported in 2008[2] that Maine's marijuana is locally grown or imported from neighboring states. Dominican traffickers are the primary suppliers of high-quality heroin, and PCP is available only in the southern part of the state. Indiana, on the other hand, is "an active drug transportation and distribution area," although heroin is not available in the central and southern regions of the state. Club drugs are not a significant problem in Indiana, although methamphetamine, imported from Mexico, remains a problem. Elkhart, Indiana, is a major distribution center for Mexican methamphetamine. High-quality and highly refined ice (crystal methamphetamine) is "predominant throughout Kansas," and cocaine and crack cocaine are readily available throughout the state. Yet, PCP is available only in Kansas City and Wichita, and OxyContin is the abused pharmaceutical of choice.

No two states face the same set of drug problems, and no two jurisdictions in a particular state or region have the same population characteristics. There is no value in trying to fit a single prepackaged program into a court system that responds to unique problems. There is, however, tremendous value in measuring process, output, and outcome data in all problem solving courts. Moreover, the prospects for any PSC's succeeding at any level are largely a function of how well it is guided by the appropriate theory or perspective for its unique purpose. Said differently, a good problem solving court recognizes the jurisprudence that drives it and measures the successes and setbacks that participants and the program itself experience. Together, theory- or jurisprudence-driven and empirically studied PSC programs generate the archetypical program.

ARCHETYPICAL PROGRAMS, UNIQUE COMMUNITIES

The value of understanding the archetypical PSC is to figure out how to design and implement successful programs for unique communities. We illustrate this point with reentry problem solving courts in Indiana. The state created reentry courts by statute, and the Indiana Judicial Center was charged with responsibility for promulgating rules and regulations that would apply to all the state's reentry court programs.

Indiana has a moderately sized general population relative to the other states, although sociodemographic characteristics vary widely across regions of the state. The state certified four prisoner reentry problem solving courts, which together cover the geographical areas in which the majority of inmates return to live upon release from Indiana Department of Correction[3] facilities. The first reentry court, in Fort Wayne, was established in a large urban area and followed the ten key components of the model drug court:

1. integration of substance-abuse treatment with justice system case processing
2. use of a nonadversarial approach in which prosecution and defense promote public safety while protecting the right of the accused to due process
3. early identification and prompt placement of eligible participants
4. access to a continuum of treatment, rehabilitation, and related services
5. frequent testing for alcohol and drugs
6. a strategy coordinated among the judge, prosecution, defense, and treatment providers to govern offender compliance
7. ongoing judicial interaction with each participant
8. monitoring and evaluation to measure achievement of program goals and gauge effectiveness
9. continuing interdisciplinary education to promote effective planning, implementation, and operation
10. partnerships with public agencies and community-based organizations to generate local support and enhance drug court effectiveness (Fulton Hora 2004; Wolfe et al. 2004)

The Fort Wayne (Allen County) reentry court program was not funded with any federal or state dollars, relying instead on the reallocation of state funds to assist the transition from prison to the community.[4] No particular jurisprudence guided the PSC's design, implementation, or operations. To the contrary, all persons returning from prison to one quadrant of the city were subjects in a black-box, experimentally designed program that randomly assigned persons either to a control group or to the reentry court program as the treatment group. Programs such as the Allen County reentry court, especially during its initial and experimental period, are possibly more influenced by public policy that mandates a response to prison overcrowding and saving taxpayer dollars than by the social science theory and research that can guide the process of transforming "felons" into "citizens" who can contribute to their communities (Jacobson 2006; Kurlychek, Brame, and Bushway 2006).

   In the reentry program (the treatment group), participants had access to adult education classes, cognitive skills training, substance-abuse programs, an "employment academy," mental-health intervention, and assistance with driver's license reinstatement. Once the county evaluated the reentry program, concluding that it reduced recidivism substantially and significantly and was a cost-efficient program relative to prison, it expanded the program to persons returning to all parts of the city. In 2005, four years following implementation, the program showed that among the participants remaining in the county, 18.9 percent reoffended, compared to the typical 45 percent, during the first year following release from prison. The recidivism rates include new offenses and parole or probation violations that result in revocation hearings. Clearly a success at reducing the crime problem among returning prison inmates, the Allen County model was the focus of the spring 2007 Department of Justice and Community Capacity Development online publication titled "INsites." Although Allen County works to deliver comprehensive responses to released prisoners, the jurisprudence- or theory-driven research that determines the contours and elements of the program remain unspecified.

The Allen County reentry court program, in its initial phase, was a black-box experiment to determine if it succeeded in reducing recidivism. Of the three other reentry problem solving court programs in that state, one is designed for a small and homogeneous population and the others for midsize cities with sociodemographically diverse populations. Each is guided by unique circumstances, the key social problems that returning prisoners bring to the county or the city, the rural or urban location within the state, and the characteristics of the community the court serves. On account of the Fort Wayne model, the reentry courts in other parts of the state had empirical evidence and some conceptual or theoretical work inferred from Fort Wayne to build on.

One program is in a small, nearly all-white rural county in a relatively isolated region of the state; one is in Indianapolis, the state's capital; and one (documented and analyzed in this book) is in a county with a population of over 156,000 persons that includes a major university. This particular county is among those throughout the United States with the largest recent growth in their Hispanic and Latino populations. Finally, this particular program, in Lafayette, Indiana, has a large homeless shelter that attracts persons from surrounding counties. It is also in a county committed to ending homelessness within ten years. As a result, it enjoys the benefits of a substantial Shelter Plus Care program that provides permanent supportive housing for the chronically homeless who are disabled by mental illness, drug abuse, or HIV/AIDS.

The reentry PSC established in Lafayette is designed to bring persons who are drug addicted and suffer from behavioral or mood disorders out of prison early, on average, by two years and reintegrate them into the community. The targeted population returns with a higher than typical risk of recidivism. Thus, the challenge is to provide the PSC with efficient, evidence-based programs that effectively reduce crime. The rationale for targeting the high-risk offender is straightforward: if those most likely to commit crimes desist, the community will enjoy a higher level of public safety and quality of life. Thus, in contrast to the Fort Wayne model of accepting all returning prison inmates into the reentry court program, the Lafayette model operates on the small-is-better principle. Identify the small number of persons most likely to commit most of the offenses upon their release from prison and provide the most comprehensive reentry court program possible to address the constellation of needs and problems that account for this particularly high-risk ex-prison population.[5] Moreover, the reentry PSC in Lafayette was designed deliberately to reflect the integration of five contemporary perspectives of law and society in the United States.

Without accounting for the theory and perspective that explain successful reentry or the jurisprudence that guides a problem solving court, programs can only fail. Project Greenlight, funded by the Vera Institute, is the best example of a prisoner reentry program that, though well designed and well studied, was not based on theory that explains recidivism (Ritter 2006). The eight-week, prison-based program provided cognitive skills training, housing services, and employment assistance. Empirical study found that program participants were significantly more likely to recidivate than released prisoners not in the reentry program.

When implemented, Project Greenlight did not focus on high-risk offenders. Evidence-based practice principles would predict failure for the program on the grounds that it delivered too many services to a group of state prison inmates who did not need them. As with giving a small woman a dosage of medication intended for a large man, problems and failures were inevitable. While other programs may fail and go unnoticed, prisoner reentry programs, unlike other PSC or rehabilitation programs, are more critically scrutinized by the media and the general population.

UNSYMPATHETIC AUDIENCES

Reentry problem solving courts everywhere encounter a daunting problem that the earlier generation of drug courts did not face: a lack of resources. There is no large sum of money distributed by the U.S. Office of Justice Programs to implement pilot court programs.[6] Ample national- and state-level professional organizations respond to the reentering population, and there are federally sponsored programs to support dimensions of reentry (such as education and work skills for participants), but there is no reentry court funding program sponsored by the U.S. Department of Justice or by the state governments.

Reentry falls outside the general public's sympathy zone, which must be approached by policy makers who urge the use of taxpayer's dollars to support social programs. The general population has never perceived ex-felons as the "deserving poor" (Chunn and Gavigan 2004; Goren 2003), warranting support in their transition from prison to their home communities. This has an important implication for the jurisprudence of problem solving courts, which judicial officers depend on to design, implement, and evaluate reentry court programs.

The classic and experimental reentry studies in the United States conducted by Peter Rossi, Richard Berk, and Kenneth Lenihan (1980) in the late 1970s could specify the complex path that communities must pursue to reduce recidivism. Researchers clearly specified the financial and emotional benefits of reducing crimes committed by returning prisoners. Nothing that social scientists demonstrate, however, can sway the general population's attitude or perceptions toward ex–prison inmates. Whereas drug courts treat those who are perceived to be addicted and therefore possibly ill, reentry courts are set up to respond to those who have been convicted of criminal offenses and sentenced, in most cases, to lengthy terms of incarceration (Aviram 2006; Chunn and Gavigan 2004; Goren 2003). The mad versus bad distinction (Bell 2001; Moss 2007) implies that it is socially acceptable to treat those who are ill but not to provide a therapeutic process to those deemed criminal, therefore bad, by a jury or criminal court judge. Hospitals are supposed to be for the ill, and prisons are supposed to be for the criminals.[7]

The general population's less-than-sympathetic view of the need to provide services for the reentry population, coupled with widespread fear of crime (Eschholz, Chiricos, and Gertz 2003; Kanan and Pruitt 2002; Roh and Oliver 2005; Schafer, Huebner, and Bynum 2006; Walklate and Mythen 2008; Wilcox, May, and Roberts 2006), makes the implementation of a reentry problem solving court especially challenging. Thus, it is imperative to design a reentry PSC with a clear understanding of the jurisprudence it can put into practice.

JURISPRUDENCE: PRACTICAL OR ASPIRATIONAL?

We posit that all problem solving courts, but especially reentry courts, must be informed by a well-articulated jurisprudence (i.e., an underlying philosophy or theory that guides legal processes, procedures, decisions, and programs that are nested within the PSC).[8] Simultaneously, we recognize that the best-laid plans—those informed by theory—can be destroyed by a number of factors, such as resistant service providers, criminal acts that seize the imagination of the general population, and changes in the socioeconomic circumstances that characterize a community.

A typical problem solving court jurisprudence builds on the quintessential traditions of legal realism and legal pragmatism. The American realist perspective acknowledges that judicial decisions are not merely the result of objective, logical interpretation of statutes and careful study of precedents or prior and similar cases. American realists (e.g., Karl Llewellyn and Jerome Frank) argue that law itself is indeterminate and ought to reflect an interdisciplinary explanation of human behavior. Further, and most importantly for problem solving courts, realists contend that the law can and should be used instrumentally (i.e., to achieve specified purposes such as reduced recidivism) (Dagan 2007; Kennedy 2000; Miles and Sunstein 2008; Norrie 2000).

Many, but not all, legal scholars argue that legal pragmatism is closely related to realism. To illustrate, a student may read Oliver William Holmes Jr. as an American realist or legal pragmatist. Both perspectives focus on judicial decision making as a human behavior and not merely a function of legal facts, logic, and precedent; both also recognize that law can, or should, be instrumental. The legal pragmatist is consciously aware of the social and historical context of decisions and is likely to acknowledge that, while the rule of law is among the tools used to achieve decisions, other factors operate, such as the need to solve problems. The pragmatist argues that "the concepts we use to describe the world—whether in the form of moral rules, legal doctrines, or scientific theories—are not given in nature but are human creations. Truth, then, is neither absolute nor transcendent but, rather, emergent in human action; truth is valid only insofar as it helps us to act authentically and effectively" (Sutton 2001, 137–38). The layperson's version of "what is practical" is not an accurate understanding of pragmatism.

Pragmatist philosophies as well as legal pragmatism have been well critiqued for being descriptive and not explanatory. Most who espouse the pragmatist perspective or jurisprudence insist that the value is in the method, not the explanation: What does the decision maker intend to achieve? How can decisions move toward achieving a particular objective? In these ways, legal pragmatism is as much an aspirational as a practical jurisprudence (Alan 2003; Kellogg 2004; Knudsen, Vorobjovs, and Gordon 2008; Posner 2004).

The focus is on experience and results as well as the decisions made to achieve the intended or unintended results. Pragmatism has a rich, American history; therefore, its key contributors contend that "the law embodies the story of a nation's development through many centuries, and it cannot be dealt with as if it contained only the axioms and corollaries of a book of mathematics. In order to know what it is, we must know what it has been, and what it tends to become" (Holmes 1881, 1). A decision maker, a judge, may look at, and be informed by, prior cases without pretending to be absolutely influenced by the rule of precedents. The contemporary judge looks at previous cases and at the offender before him. What is the offender's criminal history, or how does his educational, familial, and medical or psychiatric history influence where he is today? The pragmatist-judge, perhaps guided by a larger problem solving jurisprudence, estimates the likely results of his or her decisions based on experience and an awareness of the social context in which decisions are made. If I order Rita to an alcohol-abuse program, is she likely to follow the rules and avoid drinking and driving in the future? Does she have family to support her efforts to maintain sobriety? If she fails, is she likely to cause an accident that could seriously injure or kill her or other victims?

A problem solving jurisprudence clearly must incorporate principles of legal realism and legal pragmatism. In addition, a fully developed jurisprudence integrates two additional strands that guide the judge and the processes leading up to court sessions and trial court decisions. One strand, the more recently articulated jurisprudence, is known as therapeutic jurisprudence (TJ). Its founders, David Wexler and Bruce Winick, are responsible for TJ's becoming the foundation for the drug court movement. Basically, TJ posits that either legal procedures, and especially legal actors, can be helpful or therapeutic in their deliberations and how they render decisions or they can be hurtful and revictimize or traumatize court participants. TJ posits that lawyers and police officers, as well as judges, can be therapeutic or not. This is most obvious when a person suffering from a serious mental illness is arrested and the case is adjudicated. Imagine Doug, who is wrestled to the ground and handcuffed by a police officer. He is booked into the jail, found guilty of resisting arrest and disorderly conduct, and sentenced. Nothing helpful or therapeutic occurs to prevent Doug from encountering the same problematic situation over and over again. Next, imagine Richard, who manifests the same symptoms and behaviors. The police officer, trained to deescalate problems encountered with the mentally ill, talks to Richard, concludes he is ill, and calls a psychiatric social worker. Richard appears in court and is ordered to treatment at a residential mental-health program instead of jail. The public defender, although protecting Richard's rights, knows it is in her client's best interest to receive treatment at a facility that can help stabilize him and thus prevent the episode from reoccurring.

Therapeutic jurisprudence, although once the focus of mental-health courts only, has been translated into practices for drug courts, family-abuse courts, and reentry courts. The court participant needs criminal justice intervention, not necessarily criminal sanctions. Defense and prosecuting attorneys are encouraged to work together to do what is best for the participant. The net result is a beneficial outcome for the participant and the community (Casey and Rottman 2000; Maze and Hannah 2008; Tauber 2001; Wexler and Winick 2003; Winick 1999, 2008).

A fully developed problem solving court jurisprudence incorporates a second strand, the tenets of the law-and-literature perspective, an orientation to understanding legal controversies and issues that emerged in the 1950s and had gained widespread popularity in U.S. law schools by the 1980s (Anker 2008; Baron 1999; Hanafin, Geary, and Brooker 2004; Sheehy 2004). Scholars distinguish law "in" literature from law "as" literature from law "and" literature. Law-in-literature proponents use fiction, especially novels, to understand the basic human condition. Law-as-literature scholars apply literary-analysis techniques to legal texts for the purpose of understanding and interpreting the law. Law-and-literature writers bring law and literature together to transcend the limitations of the specific event, the specific case, the specific person in court (Barmash 2004; Cavallaro 2004; Fortier 2004; Freedman 2002; Roberts 2003; Skinner 2003). The purpose of law and literature is to understand human nature and society and how they affect each other in ways that characterize circumstances faced by social actors in this century, how they did so in an earlier century, or perhaps how they could influence social actors in a future society.

One of the most influential, controversial, and prolific writers in the law-and-literature field is Martha Nussbaum, a philosopher and ethicist whose body of work focuses on capabilities and emotions. Apropos of a problem solving court jurisprudence, Nussbaum argues that the law is not an abstract logical entity, and those who make, decide, and are affected by it are persons with emotions who tend to influence social actors and therefore communities. Further, she argues that certain emotions, especially love, compassion, and fear, are important to law. Trial court judges must be compassionate when they sentence a convicted offender, regardless of how the judge feels about him or her. The judge should simultaneously recognize the fear that the convicted offender has caused the community or that he or she feels in the courtroom. The ability to understand the other—what it must be like to be homeless, or drug dependent, or remorseful—requires an understanding of emotions. This aspect of law and literature shows us, for example, that Shakespeare had something to say about love and family disputes in *Romeo and Juliet* that may apply to intended marriages in the twenty-first century. It shows us that Charles Dickens, himself a child of a parent imprisoned for poverty, can shed light on how a convicted criminal feels fear. Thus, problem solving court jurisprudence must incorporate the law-and-literature movement as it addresses the importance of emotions. It directs the judge and the court advisors to acknowledge the importance of compassion and fear. And it warns the problem solving court to reject shame and disgust resolutely, because such emotions undermine community and stigmatize social actors, making them outsiders (Nussbaum 2004).

All told, a reasonable problem solving court jurisprudence takes into account legal realism and pragmatism, therapeutic jurisprudence, and a law-and-literature perspective. It makes transparent the human nature of judges and arrested or convicted offenders. It encourages attorneys to work on behalf of their clients and the community concurrently. A problem solving court jurisprudence represents what guides a decision-making process. It also connects readily to methods for studying the effectiveness and efficiency of PSC programs. Do they work? How do they work? Who benefits? At what cost?

4

Timeless Problems, Innovative Solutions

A NEW APPROACH, OLD PROBLEMS

Problem solving courts, of which there are more than twenty-five hundred nationwide, represent a new approach toward responding, with criminal law and the criminal justice system, to seemingly permanent social problems, especially high rates of drug abuse, mental illness, and family abuse and violence. The problem solving court approach emerged in the 1990s because law and policy makers remain convinced and optimistic: we can and will resolve, or at least minimize, the effects of certain problems on communities throughout the United States.

While problem solving courts are new, the intention is to respond effectively to a number of social problems that persist across time and space. Charles Dickens wrote about experiences of poverty in nineteenth-century London that are no less painful for the poor adult or child living in an urban neighborhood or rural area in the United States today. In *Romeo and Juliet*, Shakespeare referenced the illegal purchase of drugs, which had fatal consequences. He spoke in *Hamlet* about problems that we would call hallucinations and the products of the obsessed mind, as did Dostoevsky in *Crime and Punishment*. Moving from imaginative literature to the classic social science literature, Kai Erikson (1966) demonstrated how social responses to behaviors defined by the social group as deviant or criminal are important attempts, whether successful or not, to maintain a collective identity or a sense of community. Erikson's illustrations and tests of Émile Durkheim's theory (1895) are no less salient today than in 1966, and the social response to "crime" matters as much in the United States of today as it did in the Massachusetts Bay Colony of 1636.

Contemporary cases of drug abuse associated with accidental death or suicide are described in novels and films as well as in the obituaries in daily newspapers. Substance abuse is a timeless problem that has, in the United States, evoked dramatically different social and legal responses across time. We have experimented with prohibition, incarceration or commitment to psychiatric hospitals, residential treatment programs, and outpatient or community treatment. Why are some problems, such as crime, drug or alcohol abuse, and mental illness, timeless? We now accept the clear and convincing claim that schizophrenia, for example, has a genetic or biological basis, offering a partial explanation for why the illness will not disappear as society changes. Biology, however, is anything but a sufficient explanation for schizophrenia (Carrington 2001). Social problems such as drug abuse, crime, and delinquency are correlated with age. Age-specific crime rates do not tend to change over time; yet, age, or the distribution of age groups within the population, remains an insufficient explanation for crime rates (Levitt and Miles 2006). Economic, political, social, and cultural factors, sometimes clustered together and referenced as social-environmental factors (Chandler et al. 2004; Friedmann, Taxman, and Henderson 2007; Madden and Wayne 2003), are associated with the onset of symptoms and the relative success of treatment (Kelly 2005) for mental illness and desistance from crime (Bushway and McDowall 2006; Immarigeon 2003; Kurlychek, Brame, and Bushway 2006).

Plus ça change, plus c'est la même chose directs our inquiry of persistent social problems with social science and through the lenses of imaginative literature. We look at some of the consequences of social problems to understand better what transcends time, place, politics, and social circumstances. We look at the social science literature to contextualize problems that seem to persist across the centuries.

Although scientists and social scientists, historians, and psychologists provide no definitive responses, social actors seeking knowledge of what has been tried and what works to resolve problems can turn to imaginative literature for a humanistic understanding of persistent social ills. We begin here with comments on *Romeo and Juliet* and then compare *Hamlet* to a patricide in a Midwestern city. In subsequent chapters, we turn to imaginative literature to round out the social science and legal understanding of issues.

ROMEO AND JULIET

Romeo and Juliet: Are they young and innocent star-crossed lovers, too naïve about the underlying cause of their families' ongoing blood feud? Are they the ultimate or sole solution to a deep, sustained grudge between two respectable and dignified families. A watchman, guarding the Capulets' tomb where Juliet lies waiting for Romeo, tells us,

> The ground is bloody; search about the churchyard:
> Go, some of you, whoe'er you find attach.
> Pitiful sight! Here lies the county slain,
> And Juliet bleeding, warm, and newly dead,
> Who here hath lain these two days buried.
> Go, tell the prince; run to the Capulets;
> Raise up the Montagues: some others search:
> We see the ground whereon these woes do lie;
> But the true ground of all their piteous woes
> We cannot without circumstances descry.

Only after acknowledging their children's deaths do the fathers decide to declare their feud finished, or terminated, but not resolved.

> CAPULET: O brother Montague, give me thy hand;
> This is my daughter's jointure, for no more
> Can I demand.
> MONTAGUE: But I can give thee more;
> For I will raise her statue in pure gold;
> That while Verona by that name is known,
> There shall no figure as such be set
> As that of true and faithful Juliet.
> CAPULET: As rich shall Romeo's by this lady's lie;
> Poor sacrifices of our enmity!

The *Romeo and Juliet* theme, representing a cultural expression that is reproduced and modified to fit the context of an era, illustrates how some social problems, even those that seem most contemporary, represent ageless and persistent problems. While the younger generations have not seen the play or film *West Side Story*, nearly all are familiar with the basic story. The star-crossed lovers of the late 1950s, Tony and Maria, belong to different social groups, in this case New York gangs that act as substitute families for the gang members. Like Romeo and Juliet (who come from two equally high-status families), the lovers tragically believe that they can transcend, or even conquer, ongoing and entrenched rivalries. Like Shakespeare's play, *West Side Story* ends with the hope or promise that the fights between rival groups will stop. We know, of course, that gangs thrive. Can we therefore assume that some noble or respectable families, similar to the Capulets and Montagues, have resumed their rivalries also? Because a number of social problems persist across centuries, such as family or neighborhood disputes, drug and alcohol abuse, interpersonal violence, and juvenile delinquency, literature in the form of novels, plays, and poetry is an ideal place to ask questions about the offender's motivations, or society's need for exploring issues of stigma, crime, and strong disagreement among groups (Bruegge 2006; Castillo 2008; Korobkin 2007).

HAMLET

Consider another Shakespearian tragedy, *Hamlet*, which conjures up images of revenge, madness, brutal crime, and incest. Surely it is difficult to envision how the play, focused on the troubled and tortured or obsessed mind, can be useful for analyzing a contemporary criminal case. Why would a trial judge read *Hamlet* to make sense out of a murder? Perhaps because the story, although told centuries ago, can help the judge solve the timeless and disquieting question, what is the appropriate punishment for a man who kills his father? Here, the trial court judge works to make sense out of a patricide, committed by Elbert, by returning to *Hamlet*.

It is a few minutes past midnight; the weather is bitter cold as two sentries exchange greetings, preparing for a shift change on the walls of an ancient Danish castle. Although Denmark is not at war, there are active military preparations to protect the royal family and the country from pending or potential danger. The sentries are on full alert, filled with a dark sense of foreboding, for all is not well. After all, the royal family is in disarray. Claudius, the deceased King Hamlet's brother, has taken the throne and (in an unseemly short span of time after the king's funeral) married Gertrude, the king's widow. The natural order of the universe has been disrupted as the world is filled with uncertainty, and secular and spiritual boundaries show signs of stress.

The ghost of the dead king appears to the sentries, leaving them horrified by the apparition, and they are honor bound to report the disturbing sighting to Prince Hamlet. The prince is a young, brave university student, insightful and superbly intelligent. Yet, he is grieving deeply over the loss of his father. The prince himself comes face-to-face with the ghost of his father, dressed in full battle regalia. Obligated by oath, Prince Hamlet vows to avenge his father's murder. The ghost cannot rest in peace, as the king died before taking the opportunity to make amends to God and receive forgiveness for his sins. Yet, he instructs Hamlet not to hurt his mother for her disloyalty, her quick marriage to Claudius. Gertrude is, in principle, being punished sufficiently by her own guilty conscience. Hamlet vows revenge.

Three hundred years later, in the United States, not Denmark, Elbert, a somewhat ordinary university student and by no means of royal blood, struggled with his fast-growing addiction to amphetamines. The addiction became manifest when he began abusing a prescription drug. Elbert's father, although not a king, was a highly regarded high school math teacher, the winner of awards and community praise for his devotion to his work and his students. Elbert had been a popular high school basketball player and at the university was earning excellent grades, working on a baccalaureate in history. Somehow he simply did not feel at home in his world. He acknowledged that the future seemed dark, and he felt fragile. His A and B university grades became impossible to achieve, and a string of failed courses led to his departure from the university.

Elbert began to feel a growing resentment toward his father and namesake. His father was a beloved teacher, and no one seemed to care about Elbert Jr. He loved his mother; yet, he was troubled by her tendency to side with his father when family arguments erupted. Elbert openly resented his father's popularity, despised the fact that father was financially comfortable, and accused him of always trying to control his life.

Father and son continuously argued over drug abuse and how the medications and eventually the illegal drugs made Elbert feel invincible and in command of his life. Amphetamine abuse grew worse as Elbert seemed to slip into madness, showing signs of mental illness that his parents did not ignore.

Was there a similarity to Hamlet, who continues to grieve over the death of his father yet procrastinates in fulfilling his promise to the ghost who has demanded blood revenge? The ghost of the king represents an older generation of warriors who made sense of the world through retribution and killing enemies in the name of God. Prince Hamlet is a privileged beneficiary of the old world order, however harsh and cruel; yet, his intelligence and imagination make him pause. His passions ebb and flow; his emotions eat away at his conscience.

> HAMLET: Why then 'tis none to you; for there is nothing either good or bad but thinking makes it so.
> To me it is a prison.
> ROSENCRANTZ: Why, then your ambition makes it one: 'tis too narrow for your mind.
> HAMLET: O, God, I could be bounded in a nutshell and count myself a king of infinite space—were it not I have bad dreams.
> GUILDENSTERN: Which dreams indeed are ambitious; for the very substance for the ambitious is merely the shadow of a dream.
> HAMLET: A dream itself is but a shadow.

Hamlet is driven by forces beyond his own will. He must take bloody revenge to enable the ghost of the dead king to find peace. Simultaneously, he is hounded by his conscience, and he cannot get away from his horrible dreams.

He tries to rationalize his place in a world that allows no space for individual conscience to prevail. He is trapped by the bad dreams.

Demons and dreams also affected Elbert. He explained at his trial that he could not sleep because the demons kept him awake, trying to control his thoughts. In his dreams and in his awakened states, in drugged-filled days, his father kept hounding him about his substance abuse. Both parents felt compelled to help and therefore had him committed to a psychiatric unit for a seventy-two-hour observation. Elbert was a bright, articulate patient and therefore was able to convince the doctors that he was really okay and would not use methamphetamines or illegally obtained pharmaceuticals in the future. The psychiatrists released him.

While his parents, especially his father, reassured their son that they loved him, Elbert openly admitted that he despised his father for what he had supposedly done. He resented his father because he continually had to ask him for money. Elbert even tried to access his father's bank account because they had the same family name. After all, the money really belonged to Elbert, according to his delusional thinking, although his specific name was not on the account.

He began to obsess about Christianity after finding a West Virginia church called R. A. West Ministries. Elbert would listen to taped sermons by Brother West for two and three days at a time without sleeping, and he described to the court how God "was turning pages in the Bible faster than he could almost read, and God was underlining what he wanted him to read." He attempted to travel to West Virginia on a bus to meet Brother West but returned the same day because "half the people on the bus were evil and they were yelling at me in my mind and God was yelling back at them. The bus driver was in on it, too, so I couldn't take it being in the bus anymore."

We feel Hamlet's emotional turmoil in his inner struggle to make sense out of his life as he engages in what seems to be endless periods of self-talk and reflection. He asks important questions about what it means to be human, to suffer because of circumstances beyond one's control. He debates whether and how to go forward in the face of adversity, and he contemplates his existence and imagines his death as a way of finding peace.

> To be, or not to be, that is the question:
> Whether 'tis nobler in the mind to suffer
> The slings and arrows of outrageous fortune,
> Or to take arms against a sea of troubles
> And by opposing end them. To die—to sleep,
> No more; and by a sleep to say we end
> The heart-ache and the thousand natural shocks—
>   . . .

To grunt and sweat under a weary life,
But that the dread of something after death,
The undiscovered country, from whose bourn
No traveler returns, puzzles the will,
And makes us rather bear those ills we have
Than fly to others that we know not of?
Thus conscience does make cowards of us all—

Hamlet sees how fear paralyzes his will and how persons tend to endure their burdens rather than jump into the unknown, thereby becoming incapable of action. Yet, Hamlet continues to be driven toward those acts that unleash a string of events leading to tragedy and his own death. Perhaps primitive emotions of guilt for not avenging the death of his father and restoring his honor override reason.

Elbert, like Hamlet, was confronted by his parents on account of his bizarre behaviors. He responded to them by saying, "You don't know. That's because you're controlled by demons. There's a purple one sitting on your head right now, mom. I hate them. Why are you lying to me? You say you love me, but you are two-way. There are demons inside there. Your tears do not mean anything."

Elbert was thinking "words, words, words. They mean nothing." He began limping as a consequence of endless walks around town that caused an ankle injury. When his father asked what had happened, he said, "I broke my ankle." When asked if he wanted medical attention, he said, "I know about you and the devil. Why are you keeping me here like a prisoner?"

Elbert decided that something had to be done to free himself from his parents' attempts to dominate his life. He purchased a handgun but then pawned it at a loss so that he could buy ten to fifteen bibles. He distributed the bibles at a local bar and at a tattoo parlor. He felt good about what he had done: he had handed out bibles for Jesus. The demons, however, would not let him rest. He needed to act.

In *Hamlet*, there is no separation between the secular and the religious, and before the advent of the rule of law, there were precious few avenues for following individual conscience except death. Prince Hamlet felt a human desire for vengeance in the form of the blood feud that continued to bubble to the surface of his consciousness. He experienced a deep conflict between a will for retaliation without limits and an aspiration to suffer personal loss and to move on with his own life. Yet, there were no laws giving room for personal grief and providing measured and public justice. The desire for personal justice continues to grow.

As Claudius prays for forgiveness for murdering the king to obtain his crown, for his ambition, and for taking the king's wife, he wants to repent but

cannot because he is trapped in his position with no way out. Hamlet passes
up the chance to put the sword to Claudius, whom he finds on his knees, pray-
ing to heaven for forgiveness. Hamlet cannot act because he knows that killing Claudius during prayer will send him to heaven in a state of forgiveness,
an outcome Prince Hamlet deems too good for Claudius. Hamlet decides to
wait for another opportunity.

> Now might I do it pat, now he is a-praying,
> And now I'll do't. [Draws his sword.]
> And so he goes to heaven;
> And so am I revenged. That would be scanned:
> A villain kills my father, and for that
> I, his sole son, do this same villain send to heaven.
> Why, this is hire and salary, not revenge.
> He took my father grossly, full of bread,
> With all his crimes broad blown, as flush as May.

Elbert attended a birthday party in his honor at his own house, rented for
him by his father. During the celebration he professed that he was Jesus and
talked about the evil world conspiracy. Later in the day, he took his sister
for a drive to a local cemetery and pointed out to her where he wanted to be
buried because he "hadn't been feeling well." He said that he "didn't think he
would be here that much longer."

Hamlet also went to the graveyard and gazed at the skull of Yorick, who
"hath borne me on his back a thousand times," yet now is dead. He contemplates the finality of death for even the most powerful of men:

> Alexander died,
>   Alexander was buried, Alexander returneth to dust, the dust is earth, of earth
> we make loam, and why of that loam whereto he was converted might they not
> stop a beer-barrel?
>   Imperial Caesar, dead and turned to clay,
>   Might stop a hole to keep the wind away.
>   On that earth which kept the world in awe
>   Should patch a wall t'expel the winter's t'aw.

Elbert also thought about the man he considered to be great, R. A. West.
He listened to one of West's recordings, saying, "I just kept going back and
forth. Am I supposed to do this? You know, and I kept hearing, 'You got to
do it.' It's right. Am I supposed to do this? Then I put one of my R. A. West
CDs, and I hit play. You gotta go. And I, I thought, you know . . . I pushed
stop. Alright, well, I gotta go." He took these words to mean that he must kill

his father. There would be no more demons, and he would have control over his life once the deed was done.

When Elbert's parents came to check on him that night at about 11:00 p.m., he met them as they got out of the car. Elbert shot his father six times. He watched him stagger across the yard to a ditch where he fell. Elbert then went back into the house and reloaded his gun with a second clip of bullets; he got a flashlight and followed his father to the ditch where he shot him six more times. Before emptying the second clip of bullets, he told his mother to "step back. I do not want to hurt you."

Elbert's mother called 911; an ambulance took her dead husband to the hospital, and a police officer took Elbert to the jail. While riding in the patrol car shortly after his arrest, Elbert spotted a White Castle and asked the officer if they could stop so that he could buy a hamburger. Nothing seemed out of the ordinary to him.

In *Hamlet* we read that we should not defy superstition or our fates; there is divine meaning even in the death of a common sparrow. Whatever comes will be. No person knows what is left behind through death, so why should one care? Hamlet laments,

> Not a whit. We defy augury. There is a special
> Providence in the fall of a sparrow. If it be now, 'tis not to come; if it be not
> to come, it will be now; if it be not now, yet it will come.
> The readiness is all.
> Since no man of aught he leaves, knows aught, what is't to leave betimes?
> Let be. (Act 5, scene 2)

freeing himself from the tension between his inner will and the expectations imposed on him by his life circumstances. There is a letting go of an innate desire to survive and to live, for he has now fulfilled his destiny.

At the end of the play, when all are dead and the tragedy has come full circle, it is left to the loyal and true Horatio to say, "Now cracks a noble heart, Good night, sweet prince/And flights of angels sing thee to thy rest!"

At the end of Elbert's trial, he was found guilty of first-degree murder, committed under aggravating circumstances. At his sentencing hearing, with a framed picture of Jesus on the defendant's table, he heard the judge pronounce a forty-year prison term. His only concern was that the duration of the sentence would get in the way of his need to become a preacher, to teach the word of Jesus. "I want to be a preacher you know. Forty years is a long time (December 28, 2006)." The sentencing judge reassured him that he could prepare and read the Bible while in state prison.[1]

IMAGINATIVE LITERATURE AND CASE STUDIES

Shakespearian plays (Friedler 2000; Frison 2000; Sokol and Sokol 1999) portray timeless personal, interpersonal, and social structural problems: mental illness, discrimination, unfairness, deceit, feuding, unacceptable illicit sex, murder, and the struggle to achieve justice. Indeed, authors of legal documents and published opinion are more likely to turn to Shakespeare than any other literary source to drive home a point (Alexander 2005; Auberlen 2003; Decoursey 2003; Hart 2005; Murray 2003; Park 2004). Why? Because the problems that persons and communities face today are unique and explained in part by the social and legal circumstances and contexts that surround social interaction; yet, they seem too close to the basic human condition and basic human tragedy that trial court judges and attorneys must address in the course of work.

Although some social problems have persisted across historical eras, social change brings about new social problems, including new forms of crime. This point is no less important than the acknowledgement that some human circumstances are universalistic. The Industrial Revolution in the United States and elsewhere resulted in urban problems, including poverty, crime and delinquency, child labor abuse, and child neglect (Barrett 1999; Lane 1974). The U.S. Civil War may have resulted in the abolition of slavery, but it could not erase the consequences of slavery, which persist today in the form of institutionalized discrimination, family problems, and a social-class structure heavily influenced by race (Cross 2003; Decoursey 2003; Levin 2002; Rocque 2008; Smith 2005; Wacquant 2002).

Sociodemographic changes in the general population, immigration and migration patterns, urban growth, and suburban sprawl are nowadays considered important social forces that explain increases in drug and alcohol abuse, crime, and delinquency in the United States (Carrington 2001; Craddock et al. 1997; Fox and Piquero 2003; Hochstetler and Shover 1997; Levitt 1999; Muir and MacLeod 2003; Myton, Carnwath, and Crome 2004; Pridemore 2007).

Since the 1970s, the United States has experienced dramatic increases in the arrest and incarceration of persons for drug offenses, resulting in mass incarceration across the states (Clear 2005; Comfort 2003; Doob and Sprott 2006; Jacobs and Kleban 2003; Kruttschnitt 2006; Lazare 2007; Manza 2007; Pettit and Western 2004; Roberts 2004; Vogel 2004; Wacquant 2002). Critics argue that urban problems, racial discrimination, an impaired labor market, and other social problems are consequences. Millions of caretakers (mostly women) and children, none of whom have been convicted of crime, are brought into the criminal justice system as offenders (mostly men) are incarcerated.

The United States, historically and contemporarily, is eager to find solutions to social ills, including the drug problem. Looking exclusively at the 1970–2005 period highlights supposed solutions to the drug-abuse policies that focus on punishment. The now infamous Rockefeller drug laws (Sabet 2005; Spunt 2003; Tinto 2001) represent a benchmark in contemporary state drug laws. The laws had two important features: (1) mandatory minimum sentences were supposed to be imposed for most convicted offenders, including first-time offenders, and (2) sentencing judges were not supposed to consider the offender's potential for rehabilitation or individual circumstances. Judges were supposed to consider only the weight or the amount of drugs found at the time of the arrest.

These and other state laws led to increased problems but few solutions for the augmented use and distribution of illicit drugs, especially heroin, in New York State. Mandatory sentences or protracted terms of incarceration for drug-distribution convictions filled prison cells but did not decrease the social problem of drug abuse (Courtwright 2004; Feather and Souter 2002).

The punitive criminal justice landscape shifted, however, toward a rehabilitative model as the drug addict was characterized as sick or mad but not necessarily bad (Heidari et al. 2007; Kelly 2005; Kushel et al. 2005; Prince 2006; Riches et al. 2006; Skeem, Emke-Francis, and Louden 2006; Stevens et al. 2005; Tenorio and Hernandez 2005). Although substance abuse was medicalized to a degree, the states persist in attempting to reduce the level of illicit drug use through arrest, criminal conviction, and incarceration (Bourgois 2003; Fulton Hora 2004; Garrity et al. 2002; Gottfredson, Kearley, and Bushway 2008; Herd 2008; Lovell, Gagliardi, and Peterson 2002; Shapiro 2002; Spunt 2003; Turner et al. 2002; White 2002). As a consequence, a large number of offenders continue to be incarcerated, and returning prison inmates who receive inadequate social intervention are likely to recidivate. Communities suffer, racial and ethnic disparities in sentences persist, and the public health problems associated with mass incarceration, such as the widespread transmission of sexually transmitted diseases and hepatitis C, threaten social well-being (Braude and Alaimo 2007; Jordan-Zachery 2008; Kushel et al. 2005; Needels, Jarnes-Burdurny, and Burghardt 2005; O'Connell et al. 2007; Reisig et al. 2007; Seal 2005; Thomas and Sampson 2005; Zasu 2007).

A number of social problems escalate to a level beyond that which traditional legal and criminal justice responses can control. Family feuds, urban and prison gang fighting, drug problems, family abuse and violence, and neighborhood and community disputes are as inevitable as the sun's rising in the East. Nonetheless, in contemporary societies, including the United States, we seek solutions and different methods to achieve them. Sometimes, the problem faced by a society compels attempts to do things differently. Right now, the large number of persons returning home from incarceration presents such a problem. What should we do? What can we do? U.S. society always seeks potential solutions. Problem solving courts may indeed provide excellent opportunities to reduce the social and personal costs associated with serious mental illness and drug abuse, family abuse and violence, and returning prison inmates who repeat their crimes.

II

COURTS, PRISONS, AND COMMUNITIES

5

Responding to Reality

They All Come Home

THE FIRST-GENERATION PROBLEM SOLVING COURTS

The problem solving court is a dramatically successful sociolegal phenomenon. Judges, beginning in 1989, established drug courts, gained a stamp of approval from many state court systems and financial support from the federal government, demonstrated success, established a professional association, and held national meetings that garnered media attention. What began as a small number of atheoretical experiments in local courts became a large sociolegal movement that supported the creation of programs in every single state (Cooper 2003; Fulton Hora 2002).

Now known as first-generation drug courts or problem solving courts, the early programs were diversion programs. To divert persons charged with drug or alcohol offenses from the formal criminal justice process, they were enrolling in drug court. If they succeeded and graduated, criminal charges were dismissed. Diversion programs are attractive to the states and local communities as long as public safety is assured and the programs deliver the promised results (Grudzinskas et al. 2005; Hartford, Carey, and Mendonca 2006; James 2006). Even the cynic must acknowledge that diversion programs, in criminal justice and in mental health, cost less. Cases are kept out of the systems that find persons guilty or ill, and costs for community surveillance and treatment are a fraction of those incurred by hospitalization or incarceration. The secondary costs of supporting family members while the bread winner is institutionalized can also be avoided (Clark, Ricketts, and McHugo 1999; Wilhite and Allen 2008).

Second-generation problem solving courts approach a different type of clientele or participant. The newer programs, building on the success of the

67

first-generation programs, are driven by sociolegal theory and evidence-based practice principles (Bouffard and Taxman 2004; Burdon et al. 2001; Goldkamp, White, and Robinson 2001; Osher, Steadman, and Barr 2003). Armed with confidence derived from empirical results and solid theoretical rationales, the second-generation problem solving court tends to be a diversion program that approaches either a co-occurring mental-health and criminal justice problem or a prisoner reentry problem. Second-generation programs are more difficult to sell to the community because they are riskier—at least the population thinks they are. If a general-jurisdiction trial court is willing to establish a diversion program for persons with serious mental illnesses, it needs to convince the general population that public safety is the first priority. If a court is willing to establish a reentry program, it needs to address the real or imagined problems, including recidivism, that a reentry population brings to a local community.

PRISONER REENTRY:
A SECOND-GENERATION PROBLEM SOLVING COURT APPROACH

An irony that no proposal for a reentry program or reentry problem solving court should ignore is this: without prisoner reentry programs, a known percentage of those released from incarceration will threaten public safety in every community; yet, no community wants to support a prisoner reentry program to prevent recidivistic criminal behavior. After all, although "they" may move into the neighborhoods where children live and go to school, where families work and play, "they" do not deserve to be supported with law-abiding citizens' tax dollars.

Persons are released from prison and returned to their home communities every day or every week or every month, often with a small amount of money that is insufficient to pay a month's rent or buy a month's worth of food. Without resources and services to live outside of prison, a return to criminal activity, and in many cases prison, is inevitable. Every community in the United States faces the same problem. If nothing is done for persons returning home from prison, crime rates are likely to increase, and public safety is threatened. However, if a court puts together a reentry problem solving court program, it announces to the community a definite reality: they all come home.

SENTENCING LAWS

Most convicted felons sentenced to state prison[1] return to their home communities sooner or later. Exceptions in the United States include the handful of persons executed under capital punishment laws each year, a number of persons killed by fellow inmates, and those who die as a result of suicide or disease while incarcerated (Heflick 2005; Jacobs and Kent 2007; Kariminia et al. 2007; Perez-Carceles et al. 2001). It is reasonable to estimate that 97 percent of inmates eventually come home to local communities.

Each state and the federal government has unique sentencing laws that guide judges in their determination of the appropriate jail or prison sanction for convicted offenders (Caulkins 2001; Feld 2001; Ladipo 2001; Sorensen and Stemen 2002; Tinto 2001). Moreover, each state varies in terms of the percentage of time that an inmate is expected to serve (Bushway and Piehl 2007; Caulkins 2001; Engen and Steen 2000; Feld 2001; Frase 2005; Griset 2002). For example, one state maintains sentencing laws that permit inmates, in jail or in prison, to receive one day of good-time credit for each day served. Other states and the federal government require that 75 to 80 percent of the sanction meted out by the judge be served (Bjerk 2005; Corrado et al. 2003; Diederich 1999; Engen and Steen 2000; Frase 2005; Griset 2002; Roberts 2003; Sabet 2005; Schmertmann, Amankwaa, and Long 1998; Shepherd 2002; Sorensen and Stemen 2002; Stone, Winslade, and Klugman 2000; Ulmer and Kramer 1998). To complicate matters further, most states permit or encourage sentencing judges to impose split sentences (i.e., a sentence with some time executed in prison, followed by a period of probation or community or local corrections). Further, the states maintain laws and regulations that permit judges to modify or reduce the severity or the duration of the sentence or criminal sanction initially imposed. Finally, the states vary in terms of their parole systems. Only a handful of states maintain discretionary parole release (though all states must follow the laws that applied when the person was sentenced; therefore, even in a state without parole in 2008, a person may be released on parole), and some states require a fixed number of years on parole for each person released from prison. Nowadays, the sentencing judge sets the initial sentence, but the prosecutor with the inmate may petition the court for a sentence modification.

This was the sentencing order for Fabian, convicted at a plea hearing and sentenced to fifteen years for a Class B felony. His sentence was modified at the time he was accepted as a participant in the reentry problem solving court.[2]

Sentencing Order

Comes now the State of Indiana by Charles Smith, Deputy Prosecuting Attorney, and comes also the defendant in person, in the custody of the Sheriff of Tippecanoe County and by Ann L. Holmes, his attorney. The Court accepts defendant's plea of guilty and the plea agreement. IT IS ORDERED, ADJUDGED AND DECREED that the defendant is a male person 23 years of age and that he is guilty of Count I, Possession of Cocaine, a Class B felony.

The Court finds no mitigating factors.

The Court finds as aggravating factors the defendant has a history of criminal or delinquent activity, the defendant was on supervised probation at the time of the instant offense, the defendant was out on bond at the time of the instant offense, and there have been prior attempts at rehabilitation that have been unsuccessful.

The Court finds the aggravating factors outweigh the mitigating factors.

The Court having considered the written pre-sentence report and argument of counsel sentences the defendant to the Indiana Department of Correction for a period of *fifteen (15) years* [emphasis added] on Count I, a Class B felony. The defendant shall execute twelve (12) years at the Indiana Department of Correction followed by three (3) years on supervised probation. As a condition of supervised probation, the defendant shall serve the first year on house arrest with the Tippecanoe County Corrections Program. The defendant reads, examines, and signs Court's Order of Probation. The defendant affirms in open court that he agrees to abide by said terms and conditions of probation.

The Court finds the defendant shall be given one hundred and fifty-two (152) days credit toward the sentence of imprisonment for time spent in confinement as a result of this charge.

The defendant's driving privileges shall be suspended for a period of 180 days.

It is ordered that the defendant shall pay the costs of this action.

The defendant is remanded to the custody of the Sheriff of Tippecanoe County for execution of the foregoing sentence.

The Clerk is directed to forward a certified copy of this order, together with the abstract of judgment and a copy of the pre-sentence report, to the Sheriff of Tippecanoe County to be transmitted with the defendant to the Indiana Department of Corrections [*sic*]. The Clerk is further directed to issue a certified copy of this order by certified mail to the Indiana Department of Corrections [*sic*]. Copy to counsel, Probation, Community Corrections, and Bureau of Motor Vehicles.

Entered this 16th day of September, 2002.

Although Fabian was sentenced to fifteen years on September 16, 2002, he was scheduled for release on May 14, 2008. In the state where he was sentenced, Indiana, prison time served is half the prison time ordered as a result of an automatic good-time credit that cuts the sentence by one day for each day the person fails to lose good-time credit. In other words, good time is not "earned"; it is only "lost." Social scientists who find that rewards are more effective than punishments for changing behaviors may question why good-time credit should not be earned (Lindquist, Krebs, and Lattimore 2006; Wilson, Gottfredson, and Najaka 2001).

A UNIQUE FORM OF MATH

Let us do the math: Fabian received 152 days of credit for the 76 days he was in jail awaiting his plea and sentencing hearings (for every day in jail, he eared 2 days of credit to be deducted from his prison stay). While he was in prison, he completed the GED and therefore earned a six-month time cut. All told, although Fabian was sentenced to 15 years, he was scheduled to serve an actual 5.58 years (or 2,038 days). But wait—his sentence was modified, and he was released from prison on June 13, 2006. Anyone who looked at the local newspaper could read that on September 16, 2002, Fabian was sentenced to fifteen years. That person could conclude that his release date would be September 15, 2015, when, in fact, he was scheduled to be released on May 14, 2008, and actually was released on June 13, 2006.

At times, especially when a heinous crime attracts widespread media coverage, the general population calls for "truth-in-sentencing" laws (Anon. 2005b; Frase 2005; Turner et al. 2006). A truth-in-sentencing practice would put the sentencing courts in a no-win situation. Either the actual time sentenced would be minimal, for example, five years as opposed to fifteen, and elicit a call for punitivity fines (Barkow and O'Neill 2006; Benedikt 2003; Bennett 2008), or prisons would become even more overcrowded than they are today, with a greater percentage of the general population behind bars than is the case today. The United States currently incarcerates a larger percentage of its population than any nation on the globe (Gottschalk 2008; Wacquant 1998; Webster and Doob 2007). Although there is no ready solution, it is important to understand and interpret the state's sentencing laws and the state courts' sentencing practices when law or policy makers attempt to render appropriate systems for delivering just punishments or measured justice.

Generalizing across states to predict the time served for felony offenses is a hazardous endeavor, but researchers and community residents can be certain that, sooner or later, most of the persons sentenced to prisons will come home. It is difficult, however, to predict or explain success and failure: why do some persons return home *for good*—to do good and to stay at home—while others return quickly to the prison system?

THE SURGE IN INCARCERATION

The surge in incarceration over the decades in the United States (Franklin, Franklin, and Pratt 2006; Useem and Piehl 2008), the persistent social problem of drug abuse (Burdon et al. 2001), and changing laws that identify the behavior warranting conviction and incarceration (Engen and Steen 2000;

Feld 2001; Frase 2005; Griset 2002) make transition programs from the prison to the community imperative (O'Connell et al. 2007; Visher and Travis 2003). No reasonable state, county, or city would expect even the majority of inmates who return to local communities, without appropriate community transition programs, to avoid repeated acts of crime, arrest, and incarceration within three years (Herinckx et al. 2005; Kubrin and Stewart 2006; Lovell, Johnson, and Cain 2007; Miller 2007; Pager 2006; Schrantz 2007; Stafford 2006).

It is imperative to visit evidence-based practice principles in criminal justice to understand that only a small percentage of returning inmates need a comprehensive, highly structured, reentry problem solving court program. One-size-fits-all actually fits no one. If an ex-felon returning home is at low risk to reoffend, an intensive reentry court program will impose too many requirements and programs, requiring too much of the person's time. As a result, the low-risk offender may be more likely to reoffend. The low-risk offender may need a particular service to avoid reoffending (drug-abuse counseling, for example) but she will not benefit from being overserviced or overly monitored within the community (DeMatteo, Marlowe, and Festinger 2006; Marlowe et al. 2006).

We and others call this the "small is best" principle for comprehensive reentry court programs that are expensive for the participant and include deliberate methods for transforming master status. It is analogous to selective-incapacitation principles. Identify, with accuracy, the small number of persons who are likely to be responsible for the majority of crime committed in an area and incapacitate them (Auerhahn 1999, 2004; Bernard and Ritti 1991). It would be foolish to incapacitate all those who committed a single theft or act of domestic battery, never to steal or hit again.

The issue of surging incarceration is not readily discussed at the dinner table. Imagine what the general population would think (and fear) if they understood the consequences. Of all those thousands and thousands of persons incarcerated over recent decades and sentenced to protracted prison terms, most are angry, frustrated, and ill equipped in terms of human capital, social skills, and social connections to return to the community without strong criminogenic needs. Simply put, they have been in prison too long.

All of these men and women (with the exception of those who die in prison or are executed) are coming back; yet, few are properly prepared to survive in a society that has changed dramatically while they have been in prison. Few are prepared to resume family relationships, to acquire meaningful and well-paid employment, to locate clean and affordable housing. Few know how to maintain their own schedule. After many years of incarceration, when prison regulations determined daily routines, including times for breakfast, personal hygiene, and lights-out, returning home is difficult. Who will tell Brian when to go to his twelve-step meeting? How will he find transportation? How long can he survive on the $75 he was handed as he left prison, with no job and no home?

Community transition programs vary widely, from those that take a step-down approach, bringing long-term inmates from maximum-security prisons to a reentry prison prior to release, to those that provide transitional housing and employment, arranged by probation or parole officers or a local social service agency. Some transition programs focus on one dimension, such as employment, while others attempt to provide multidimensional services, or "wraparound programs," to reduce the likelihood of repeated criminal behaviors and to increase the availability of resources persons need to thrive in society (Birgden 2002; McGuire 2002; Ward and Brown 2004).

How can states and local jurisdictions prevent repeated crime? To say "it depends" does not communicate the complexity of the challenge of preventing recidivism. Consider the following dimensions of the problem: some inmates are released from prison with either no job or employment opportunity, no home, or no family to support. In addition, nowadays, a known percentage of inmates suffer from mental illness or have been diagnosed with mental illness related to their criminal behaviors (Diamond et al. 2001; Earthrowl, O'Grady, and Birmingham 2003; Hartwell 2003; Harty et al. 2003; Kupers 2008; Lovell 2008; Lovell, Gagliardi, and Peterson 2002; Metraux 2008; Renneville 2004; Rotter et al. 2002; Smith, Sawyer, and Way 2002; Wexler 2003). A high percentage of offenders can be classified as addicted to drugs or alcohol, and their addictions are related to their criminal offenses, especially burglary, theft, and fraud committed to make money for drugs, drunk driving that results in injury, and robbery associated with drug transactions[3] (Room 2005; Taylor et al. 1997).

Transition, or prisoner reentry, programs are necessary to prevent recidivism. In some states, prison facilities themselves offer community transition programs (McBride, Visher, and La Vigne 2005; Petersilia 2004; Wilson and Draine 2006). We wonder, however, how useful a prison program can be in preparing the inmate to cope in a social world that is not structured like a prison. A person on the inside can anticipate what life will be like after his or her release. But the anticipated reality may differ radically from that experienced.

Rhoda, a graduate of the reentry problem solving court, experienced the disjuncture between what she anticipated and what she experienced. Convicted of an A-level felony drug-dealing offense, she went to prison with a promise from her boss that he would preserve her job as a trucker for her. Rhoda entered prison following years of drug abuse that left her emotionless.

When Rhoda began reentry on July 24, 2006, she was sullen, walked with her head down, and spoke so softly that the judge often asked her to repeat her responses. On one occasion, the judge inquired about education, and Rhoda stated that she had no interest in pursuing the GED because she did not need it for her job. When ordered to enroll in and attend GED classes, she went to the Adult Resources Academy and cussed at the workers. She demanded that she be given special hours because she had been ordered to class.

The following Monday, the judge confronted Rhoda and told her that she was on her way back to prison if she could not learn how to appreciate all that the community was helping her to achieve. Rhoda, without telling anyone what she was going to do, returned to the academy and apologized to each and every worker. She also did not disclose that she attempted the GED before completing the preparation class. Much to her surprise, she passed!

Rhoda returned to court dressed in new clothes (from Goodwill) and wearing makeup. When called to approach the judge, with her head held high, she looked him in the eye and smiled. From that day on, she was different. Without being asked, she disclosed that she was working on how to take private time for herself. And most importantly, she announced that she had lost her job—the one preserved for her while she was in prison.

In response to the good-news, bad-news disclosure, the judge initially scolded her: "What are you going to do now? I thought that was the job of your dreams. You told the team that your boss was holding your job for you." Rhoda calmly explained that she was fired because she had chosen not to sell her car to her boss. She also said, quietly, that her boss was "giving her trouble" at work. Later, she disclosed to the case manager that her boss had raped her prior to her incarceration and demanded sex from her following prison in exchange for employment. Once Rhoda stood up to him and said no, she lost her job and gained her dignity. Rhoda quickly became employed full-time by another local trucker. Soon thereafter she brought her daughter and her infant granddaughter to court. She wanted them to meet the judge and the reentry team that helped her "discover a new life."

The judge responded to all the information about Rhoda that unfolded over the months she participated in the reentry court program. In an e-mail message to the team, he shared his thoughts.

> As I observed Rhoda walk the twenty-five steps from her seat to the podium with microphone, I saw that she appeared stressed over having to answer my question about her attitudes and beliefs. Rhoda's way of viewing the world is being challenged. Every Monday morning at 9:00 a.m. she stands in front of the judge, an authority figure, who represents her community and lets her know how

she is measuring up in the reentry program. During that hour she also sees her fellow participants sanctioned and rewarded for their progress in the program.

I remember how Rhoda, a few weeks ago, went to the reading academy demanding that she be put in a program so she could get prepared to take her GED because the judge was unhappy with lack of preparation; she felt she was on the cusp of failing and going back to prison. I remember the negative response of volunteers at the reading academy who faced this forty-year-old woman making demands on them, asking them to adjust their working hours, and to make policy changes so she could get in her weekly six hours of study after work. After all, the judge was upset about her lack of progress in preparing for her GED; she was pushing the volunteers hard to get her way, leaving behind hard feelings.

I recall how Rhoda saw no need for a GED because she drove a truck and that is all she wanted to do; besides, it had been a long time since she was in school. I can still see Rhoda's look of surprise when I asked her if she realized how she was coming across to other people and if she realized that she had offended volunteers at the reading academy. No, she had not considered how her attitude affected other people.

I considered whether Rhoda actually has any friends and if she has a strong relationship with her family. I also considered that Rhoda does not trust other people in the community. Today she readily admits that she really does not have a friend in whom she can confide and that she likes to keep to herself at work because she does not want to get into trouble. I thought about the possibility that she has a tendency to isolate herself and could very well be at risk for relapsing into her illegal use. Rhoda has been out of prison for about four months; I am wondering if she has continued with a prison attitude of not trusting anyone; an attitude that is not conducive to becoming a good citizen.

As I questioned Rhoda today, probably for the last time I asked her about her relationship with her fellow employees who are also truck drivers. Rhoda said that she works in a man's world and that trusting men has gotten her in trouble and they took advantage of her. I asked her about how she can work with others and yet set social boundaries to protect her. Rhoda volunteered that she hates to get greasy but she does not mind cleaning the inside of trucks. She worked out an arrangement at work with a couple of other men who are also truck drivers that if they will change the oil and grease her truck that she will clean the inside of their trucks because she does not mind cleaning. I told her that she is "job sharing" and that she is trusting her fellow workers to do their part of the bargain and that I was proud of her for setting work boundaries and that she was not putting herself at an unfair advantage because each worker was happy with the arrangement. . . .

As I asked Rhoda what she wanted to do in the future, she replied that she wanted to own her own truck and said her parents would help her. I asked her about her relationship with her family. Her biological dad lives in Illinois and they do not get along. The man who married her mom and raised her kicked her out of the house when she got in trouble with the law. This week she told me that they are now closer and getting even closer.

Rhoda has always paid her financial obligations, owing no money for her drug treatment; she is passing her drug screens; she is going to work every day as a truck driver; she has a sponsor and home group in the 12 step program; however, she is not engaged in the 12 step program because she really does not trust others and is reluctant to share her feelings with others. It is my duty as a judge to measure progress and to hold Rhoda strictly accountable for her behavior and to administer the sanctions and rewards. It is Rhoda's obligation to become a good citizen, and it is the judge's duty to reinforce that process in order to protect the community. What this reentry program is not prepared to do is respond effectively to a rape victim and to a sexual harassment victim. We don't have anyone on the team who can address these issues either. Suggestions? (July 24, 2006)

Problem solving courts, which use the power of the judiciary to order persons to treatment and other services, can stop the revolving door for persons released from prison who need services and treatments to reduce criminogenic needs, a return to crime, and reentry into the criminal justice system (Bozza 2007; Fulton Hora 2002; Terry 2004). PSC programs, nonetheless, cannot readily grasp all the needs that each participant either brings to or withholds from the case manager, the judge, and the team.

Convicted felons who also suffer from mental illness or have been traumatized are best served by diversion or reentry programs that use the power of the judiciary to increase their effectiveness (Wexler and Winick 2003; Fisler 2005; Stefan and Winick 2005; Watson et al. 2001). Together, diversion and reentry programs, both implemented within the court system, provide powerful tools for preventing repeated crime and responding effectively to a persistent and widespread social problem across the United States.

VIRTUAL IMPRISONMENT, HIGHLY STRUCTURED DAILY LIVING

It becomes obvious to researchers and analysts who study the widespread implementation of problem solving courts that they can turn community-based services into virtual imprisonment (O'Donnell 2005). Arguably, reentry programs organized by PSCs (Grudzinskas et al. 2005; Hartford, Carey, and Mendonca 2006; James 2006; Winick 2003) create levels of social control that are comparable to incarceration. The critic is quick to remind the PSC team of that reality. Imagine, however, that a PSC structures life for a person who needs that structure as he or she returns from a long term of incarceration—removed from the opportunity to act freely in ways that are helpful or hurtful. Morgan, for example, was incarcerated in 1992 and began the reentry PSC on September 11, 2006, after having his sentence modified. (He successfully completed the reentry PSC program on December 3, 2007.) While he was in prison, he earned a baccalaureate in political science and maintained a lucrative drug-trading business for more than ten years. He willingly explained to the reentry court how he transported his stash, undetected by authorities, from prison to prison as he was moved through the system of incarceration.

When Morgan came out of prison, he entered a world with cell phones, bank machines, and electronic search procedures for finding library books; eighteen was the voting age, and there were personal computers on nearly every desktop. The free world seemed more like science fiction than reality to Morgan, a theme he addressed in court on many occasions. He came home (on electronic home detention) to elderly parents who drove him to court-ordered appointments, drug-abuse treatment sessions, daily check-ins at the community-corrections facility, and employment services. Life outside of prison was exhausting. Completing all the reentry PSC requirements left him with no leisure or downtime. How could Morgan possibly succeed without a structured program to help him make the transition to a free and unstructured life?

For Morgan, the reentry court program was, at times, nearly overwhelming. He admitted to having difficulties doing things on the outside that he was not required to do while incarcerated. Shoveling snow was one example. He often spoke of how he looked forward to meeting new friends and doing social things with them. But that never happened. Instead, Morgan often expressed how frustrated he was with the highly structured program that left him little, if any, free time. It was not like being in prison, where he watched the snow from the windows without being responsible for removing it. He had not returned to the free world he remembered or envisioned. Morgan's whereabouts and activities were drastically structured and confined. In prison, he readily acknowledged, he had too much free time.

The community-based PSC program needs to provide a level of structure to an ex-offender's life such that he or she faces few opportunities to commit crime while having ample time and opportunity to receive the necessary services to prevent repeated criminal acts. Those services may be drug-addiction treatment, parenting classes, adult education, job training to increase human capital, or offending-behavior programs aimed at psychological well-being (Birgden 2004; Birgden and Ward 2003; Freeman 2003; Hjalmarsson 2008; Martinez 2006). All programs must be evidence based; that is, they must incorporate practices that researchers have shown to work effectively and efficiently (Basile 2005; Chandler et al. 2004; Friedmann, Taxman, and Henderson 2007; Hartford, Carey, and Mendonca 2006; Henderson, Taxman, and Young 2008; Mears et al. 2006; Needels, Jarnes-Burdurny, and Burghardt 2005; O'Connor, Lovell, and Brown 2002; Osher and Steadman 2007; Pager 2006; Saxe et al. 2006).

If court-run programs are evidence based, critics must withhold the claim that they have no purpose, are not effective, or are "soft on crime." Evidence-based practice principles require the court program to assess the needs and the responsivity of the participant (Birgden 2004). By responsivity, we mean that the participant is amenable to the specific program, such as a GED preparation course. If a person's ability will preclude the ability to pass the GED, it can only waste time and frustrate the participant to require that particular program within the PSC. Regardless of the mission and goals of the PSC, each participant is unique, with a unique set of abilities and emotions, a unique criminal history, and unique work, education, and family histories.

Those who look at the problem solving court movement in the United States take positions on whether the PSC is or is not a progressive response to the social problems of criminality and recidivism. The positions are more likely to be political than social science positions. Arguments include those that focus on legal procedure and tradition in the United States as well as those that examine the revolving door problem and see that it keeps moving, even with problem solving courts (Miller 2007; Fulton Hora 2002; Kushel et al. 2005; Nolan 2003; Weiman 2007).

PSCs require a heavy reliance on community-based programs, such as mental-health or drug-addiction treatment programs, which have been empirically tested and shown to be effective. They also require the court to continuously evaluate all the programs they use to prevent crime or repeated crime to ensure the best probability of success. Without the continuous evaluation, a "failure"—such as a drunk-driving event that causes injury—can devastate and close down a PSC program. If the PSC willingly commits to constant evaluation and communicates its findings to the community, failures, although tragic, may not have terminal consequences for the PSC.

THE JUDICIARY

What role does the judiciary play in the reentry problem solving court? Trial court judges, accustomed to monitoring a criminal or civil case through final disposition, represent the exemplar of repeat players (Galanter 1974) in the courtroom work group. The judge plays anything but the traditional judicial role in the problem solving court (Arkfeld 2007; Berman and Lane 2000; Eaton and Kaufman 2005; Gravier 2004; Wolf and Colyer 2001). The courtroom work group (i.e., the prosecuting and defense attorneys and the judge and his support staff) take on dramatically different responsibilities in the PSC. The judge must be willing to innovate yet must remain systematic. While the judge has the authority to sanction a reentry PSC participant with jail time or to expel the participant from the program and return him or her to prison to serve out his or her sentence, the most important dimension of the judge's job in the PSC is to talk with the participant over, and over, and over again. The judge is the courtroom leader who assumes responsibility for determining which social and personal problems will be addressed within the court and thus made public. The nontraditional role makes the PSC judge different from bench judges and different from therapists who work to maintain confidentiality. Some welcome the difference while others resist it forcefully. Nonetheless, the American Bar Association and other professional associations eagerly tackle new issues raised by judges taking on the work of the PSC (Arkfeld 2007; Berman and Lane 2000; Eaton and Kaufman 2005; Kaye 1999; Siobhan 2004). The judge is not an impartial person, wearing a black robe, looking down on participants. The PSC judge works to achieve justice and public safety while solving participants' problems, such as homelessness, drug addiction, or back child support. Finding solutions to such problems takes time and continuous participant-judicial interaction. It is anything but business as usual.

WHAT REENTRY PROBLEM SOLVING COURT PARTICIPANTS NEED: STAYING HOME OR COMING HOME "FOR GOOD?"

Problem solving courts across the United States work to respond comprehensively to the needs of troubled families and to disputes within the community (Braude and Alaimo 2007; Burton 2006; Maze and Hannah 2008; Rivera 2008; Wolf 2008). They work to prevent or divert a person who suffers from serious behavioral-health problems or drug or alcohol addiction from leaving the community and going into the prison system, and they strive to meet the needs of prison inmates who are returning to their home communities so that they may come home and stay home "for good."

"Home for good" has two meanings here. On the one hand, it implies that persons will succeed within the community and not need to be institutionalized or returned to prison. On the other hand, it implies that social actors, participants in a PSC, "do good" for the community. They care for family members, they are employed in meaningful jobs, they volunteer, and they pay taxes rather than depend on tax revenues for food and shelter. Simply put, they contribute to the economic and social well-being of a community. They build up their strengths and resources as contributing citizens.

One of the more effective methods for guiding reentry PSC participants toward coming home for good is to encourage volunteer work (Boezeman and Ellemers 2008; Casciano 2007; Chinlund 2004; Garland, Myers, and

Wolfer 2008; Planty, Bozick, and Reginer 2006; Prouteau and Wolff 2006; Ren et al. 2006; Weisz, Lott, and Thai 2002; White et al. 2008), not to be confused with community service, a sanction for minor offenses. Volunteer work introduces participants in the PSC to new relationships and new ways to value work, appreciate others and self, and avoid antisocial activities, such as abusive drinking or illicit drug use.

The reentry PSC in Tippecanoe County, Indiana, encourages participants to volunteer in a homelessness-prevention project. Week after week, men and women help set up apartments, move furniture, and perform other chores to establish permanent housing for a chronically homeless and disabled population. There is never a shortage of volunteer help, especially on weekends, when participants bring their teenage children along to volunteer and "feel good." The men and women in reentry court talk about their volunteer experiences. The work reminds them how well-off they are, compared to the homeless. They realize they have skills and abilities, such as setting up a home, which they were forced to put aside in prison. They interact with persons in the community who express appreciation for what they do.

A review of the published research and essays on the problem solving court movement can easily bring the oft-quoted opening stanza from *A Tale of Two Cities* to mind.

> It was the best of times, it was the worst of times, it was the age of wisdom, it was the age of foolishness, it was the epoch of belief, it was the epoch of incredulity, it was the season of Light, it was the season of Darkness, it was the spring of hope, it was the winter of despair, we had everything before us, we had nothing before us.

Indeed the reentry problem solving court movement is revolutionary. It is anything except business as usual, and it did not evolve gradually from rehabilitative programs in prison or mental-health systems. Under some circumstances, a PSC approach seems ideally suited for working out a community's social problems; yet, under other circumstances, the general population soundly rejects the possibility of using it. In response to certain issues, such as prison inmates returning home, it is the only reasonable program that, with the authority of the court, can deliver housing, employment, and family services. Is the PSC movement our best hope in criminal law and criminal justice, or is it a social and legal movement that ought to leave us in despair? Responses require the full disclosure of what works and what does not. It is our collective responsibility to examine approaches that fail, along with those that succeed.

6

Blended Social Institutions

ROSEMARY

Something had to be done for Rosemary. She was irritable, frustrated, and physically aggressive. Sometimes she was silent; other times, she became too agitated for anyone to control. When she was a child, her parents and caretakers could control her behaviors, but no one was able to do so as she grew into a teenager. Neither boarding school, nor tutors, nor the Catholic convent offered solutions. Tragically, in the 1940s, her father chose to have her lobotomized. Contrary to his hope for and expectation of a happy and well-adjusted adolescent, the results were horrific. Rosemary became but the slightest shadow of herself, and all the progress that her mother and others had made vanished to the point where she no longer even knew who she was or remembered her name. Lifelong institutional care became the only option for her (Goodwin 1987).

Rosemary's story illustrates how, in the 1940s, a person with unmanageable behavioral-health problems went through a maze of independent or autonomous social institutions—religious, educational, and medical—in a struggle for mental health and a productive life as a contributing member of society. In contemporary U.S. society, persons with anxiety and mood disorders similar to Rosemary's can remain within the community, taking medications and seeking therapy to control symptoms and aberrant behaviors. Yet, persons who suffer from a mental illness and call attention to the police with their behaviors, especially if they occupy positions in the working class, are likely to be jailed or, worse, charged with a criminal offense and incarcerated in state prisons.

HOSPITALS AND PRISONS

In 1961, Erving Goffman published the startling book *Asylum*. The psychiatric hospital was as much a prison as a hospital: patients had no more autonomy or independence than prison inmates. Patients, like inmates, were controlled twenty-four hours a day by staff whose primary responsibilities were to maintain social order. As a result of his ethnographic study of St. Elizabeth's Hospital, Goffman conceptualized the total institution as one in which custodial maintenance of the population was no less salient an organizational mission than psychiatric treatment of the patients.

State prisons now are the largest mental-health providers in the United States (Earthrowl, O'Grady, and Birmingham 2003; Konrad 2002; Renneville 2004). The prevalence of mental illness is dramatically higher in prison than among the general population. Researchers have documented well the parallel growth and convergence of the psychiatric hospital and the prison population. Observe a sentencing hearing and expect a judge to request treatment for the "patient" he orders to a term of incarceration (Abramowitz 2005; Gravier 2004; Lamb and Weinberger 2005; Redlich, Steadman, Robbins, et al. 2006). A civil commitment (Perlin 2003) can result in confinement for a lifetime.

In what we call blended social institutions in the twenty-first century, a patient in a hospital is likely to respond to the expectations most appropriate for prison inmates. It is not a matter of illness as much as it is the need to avoid sanctions or consequences for unacceptable behaviors. Likewise, an inmate in a state prison is likely to manifest symptoms of mental illness, either because the person entering prison was already ill or because imprisonment leads to behavioral problems that are a function of living within a total institution. In the blended social institution, the primary goal is control of the client population, and job tasks for staff members, whether working in prisons or state psychiatric hospitals, are quite similar (Adams and Ferrandino 2008; Arboleda-Florez 1999; Cohen 2008; Diamond et al. 2001; Dvoskin and Spiers 2004; Earthrowl, O'Grady, and Birmingham 2003; Hartwell 2003; Konrad 2002; Lamb and Weinberger 1998; Lewis 2000; Lovell, Gagliardi, and Peterson 2002; Lovell and Jemelka 1998; Metraux 2008; O'Connor, Lovell, and Brown 2002; Poythress, Edens, and Watkins 2001; Renneville 2004; Rhodes 2000; Rotter et al. 2002; Rutherford and Taylor 2004; Smith, Sawyer, and Way 2002; Toch 2008; Wexler 2003).

The overlapping populations served by prisons and psychiatric hospitals illustrate the dominance of blended social institutions in contemporary American society. The hospital, once designed to treat the ill, includes a forensic unit to control and keep the criminally insane. The local county jail contracts with a provider to administer psychotropic drugs to control symptoms or violent outbursts. The state prison may, as it does in the state of Ohio, for example, maintain a psychiatric hospital on its campus. The typical state prison will include special units for the mentally ill for the purpose of optimal control over inmates (Cloyes 2007). One of the most prominent features of blended social institutions is the organizational mission of social control. Whether it is the state psychiatric hospital or the state prison facility, the blended social institution must make the mission of maintaining order central. Sadly, an unintended consequence is stigmatization for "patients" as well as "inmates." It no longer matters so much to the general population that those who are ill are distinguished from those who are criminal. Communities do not accept the threat posed by the mentally ill any more than they do that posed by the inmate returning from prison.

Blended social institutions host the same types of staff. Social workers, psychologists, and consulting psychiatrists are as likely to be found in the contemporary prison as they are in the typical psychiatric hospital or community mental-health center. Blended social institutions are organized by similar goals. They should be charged with the responsibility for caring for persons in ways that will diminish harm or the probability of harm to the person and to the community. They are charged with improving the quality of life for individuals to help them develop strengths as citizens in their communities.

Blended institutions represent the way we do business in the United States and elsewhere. There is no evidence that the state prison's mission will ever differ dramatically from what it is today, considering the prevalence of mental illness. Nor is there any reason to project that psychiatric hospitals will become less concerned with social control than they are nowadays (Kupers 2008; Markowitz 2006; Prince 2006). Although we make no moral judgment about the status quo, we ask, What happens in the community, in the small town or in the large city, when a person, perhaps suffering from a mood or anxiety disorder, needs social intervention? What happens to the person, as well as the community, when he or she is released from the blended institution? Clearly the individual will need community-based support systems. Thus, it is imperative for social-control agencies, including problem solving courts, to address the consequences of the widespread acceptance of the blended institution.

COURTS AS CORRECTIONS

Persons returning from prison or hospitals, as well as those diverted from blended institutions, remain in or return to communities with clusters of problems. Few could reduce the possibility of harm to self or others without psychotherapy of

some sort, drug-addiction treatment, medical care, and services to support housing, employment, and family relationships (Anon. 2005; Alleyne 2006; Arditti
and Few 2006; Hammett, Roberts, and Kennedy 2001; Hartwell 2003; Jamieson
and Taylor 2002; Kubrin and Stewart 2006; Messina et al. 2004; Naser and La
Vigne 2006; Pager 2006; Petersilia 2001; Pettus and Severson 2006; Pogorzelski
et al. 2005; Ritter 2006; Stafford 2006; Weiman 2007). Differences in needs
based on gender, social class, ethnicity, and race must be acknowledged.

An older, man, Morgan, who spent fifteen years in prison for multiple
felony convictions, returns to his home community to a place he does not
recognize. When released from prison, he does not know how to obtain a
state-issued photo ID. He cannot imagine driving a car in crowded traffic,
dressing appropriately for job interviews, or working in a trade or occupation
other than drug dealing.

Kathleen, on the other hand, is a young woman incarcerated for three years.
She left her disabled child as she entered prison to serve time for conspiracy
to commit armed robbery. Although she was unarmed, a drug deal that Kathleen arranged went bad, resulting in a shooting death. While in prison, Kathleen refused to participate in any programs, such as drug-abuse treatment,
education, or job-skills classes. She turned down the parenting program that
would have allowed her extended visits with her son.

Kathleen is the younger daughter of a university professor. She dropped
out of high school when she got pregnant at age sixteen. She blames herself
for her son's problems because his disability was inherited from his biological father. While in prison, she claims, she understood for the first time that
she could have been shot and killed over drugs. Why did the shooter not
kill her? Kathleen came out of prison early, on a modified sentence, to live
with her mother and stepfather, the guardians of her child. For the first few
months, Kathleen soaked in every moment of freedom. She got a job, enjoyed
the drug-treatment program, enrolled in a GED class, and hoped to attend
community college the following semester. Her aspiration was to become a
drug-treatment counselor so that she could help other young girls avoid the
problems and despair she had experienced. Thus, she volunteered to intern at
a residential recovery house. There, she hit the wall.

Instead of being "high on freedom," as participants tend to be for the
first few weeks or even months in a PSC program, Kathleen, like others,
eventually got discouraged. Hitting the wall, or becoming discouraged, is
predictable, although it can take varied forms. Some participants will show
less enthusiasm; others will violate program regulations. In the worst case, a
participant will return to drug use or other criminal activity.

Kathleen showed that she had "hit the wall" when she began missing appointments, arrived late for work, dropped out of class, and got pregnant. The

problem solving court team expressed disapproval of Kathleen's internship on the premise that persons in recovery need to establish new and pro-social interpersonal relationships. At the recovery house, her only friendship opportunities were men and women addicted to alcohol or drugs. Perhaps she got discouraged because she witnessed too many persons struggling with addictions. The judge addressed Kathleen's hitting the wall on August 27, 2007.

JUDGE: Now, Kathleen, when you first came into the program, your scores on alcohol, drugs, legal problems—those sorts of things—were pretty high. Then, after six months, all the numbers went down. Since then, nothing has changed. I'm worried that your scores are not going down. Have you thought about that?

KATHLEEN: No, I haven't ever thought about that.

JUDGE: Can you talk to your case manager about that?

KATHLEEN: Yes, but it won't do any good.

JUDGE: I'm concerned about your family and social aspects of your life. There's research out there that says who you associate with, in terms of recovery and staying out of trouble, is very, very important. Could you talk to me about that when you come back to court?

KATHLEEN: Yes.

JUDGE: I want to know what you're thinking. Are you thinking through these issues?

KATHLEEN: Yes.

JUDGE: I know you're doing a good job at work. You're going to school and being responsible. But I'm concerned about the social domains of your life. So, will you think about that and talk to me when you come back to court?

KATHLEEN: Okay.

Most unusual for the loquacious Kathleen were her one word responses. Indeed, she had hit the wall and no longer actively participated in court dialogues or conversations with problem solving court team members or her case manager. In subsequent conversations, she expressed frustration over not gaining custody of her first-born child. Eventually, she moved into her own apartment, gave birth to her second child, and completed the reentry problem solving court program without any negative police contacts. She continues to live in rent-assisted housing with her second child's father. She perseveres in her struggle to regain custody of her first child, a topic for vivid discussion throughout her time in reentry, prior to when she hit the wall.

Other participants, Holly, for example, are working-class mothers who come out of prison without acknowledging their children. Holly had been in business with her mother, prostituting and cleaning houses, before serving her prison term on a drug-dealing conviction. While she awaited a sentencing hearing on bond, a surveillance officer from community corrections visited her home. She was living in her mother's basement, with the ceiling too low for her to stand upright. Out of prison, Holly was beyond shy, her eyes constantly gazing at the floor, even as she spoke with the judge. Her slouch made her appear older than her chronological age. In all her life, she had never earned a paycheck. Once established in the reentry problem solving court, she obtained a full-time job, with benefits, in a manufacturing firm. Although she did well at work, her speech was too soft for most in the courtroom to hear. After participating in the reentry court for approximately seven months, she disclosed, on February 19, 2007, that she was a mother.

JUDGE: Okay, Holly. Tell me what you're planning on doing now.

HOLLY: I'm going to go to my appointment [at the community college].

JUDGE: And tell me what you're going to accomplish.

HOLLY: I'm going to figure out for sure what I'm doing, I guess, for the classes I want to take. Then I'll probably set up an appointment with the academic advisor.

JUDGE: And why do you think community college is good for you? Why are you making the decision to go in that direction?

HOLLY: Because I want to go back to school. I want to do better things with my life. I want to further my knowledge.

JUDGE: Education can change your life, and it will. Have you always wanted to go back to school?

HOLLY: Yes, for a few years now. But it wasn't my first priority when I was using. Now I made a list of goals for myself.

JUDGE: What's the most important goal for you? Is there something really important to you?

HOLLY: Eventually I want to have my son living with me.

JUDGE: Now, this is the first time that I remember you mentioning your son.[1] Why is that?

HOLLY: I don't know. I've always felt that way. Keep it to myself. I just have to get on my feet before I can get to that point.

JUDGE: Is this a priority for you, getting your son back?

HOLLY: It's a priority. I see him once a week.

JUDGE: And how old is he?

HOLLY: He's a year and four months.

JUDGE: Is he walking?

HOLLY: Yes. He's walking. And he lives with my dad.

JUDGE: What is your relationship with your dad?

HOLLY: Okay. It's okay. It could be better, but it probably won't be.

JUDGE: Does he have a wife?

HOLLY: Yes. She hates me.

JUDGE: Okay, we're going to talk about this later—is that alright with you? How about that paper you are supposed to read today?

HOLLY: [She reads a "one-pager" to the court.] "Since starting the program, I've learned many things. Most of my gained knowledge has been about myself.

In the past there was a lot of things I was unable to envision myself doing due either to my anxiety, lack of self-confidence, my drug use, or maybe all of the above.[2] Sobriety has opened my eyes and allowed me to see what I want my life to be like and also what I don't want to go back to. Reentry has given me a second chance. . . . On the subject of what kind of job I'd like to have, I've been looking into computer graphics. I know that my passion lies with express- ing myself through being artistic and creative. I feel that a job that involves me doing those things would be best. . . . I have established goals for myself. These goals are being able to find better employment, attend classes, attain my driver's license, work toward getting my own place, and once I'm on my feet, having my son live with me. I feel these are reasonable goals for me. I believe they will get me to where I want and need to be. But for me the real success will lie in the journey."

Holly's family struggles remain complex. She lost her job, she turned to her mother for income, and she continues to fight with her father over child custody and child-support payments. The court ordered her to find employ- ment and arranged for her to enter rent-assisted housing. Holly and Kathleen face similar problems with child custody, but their solutions are remarkably different due to their social-class backgrounds. Kathleen's father is helping her to hire an attorney. Holly's father is battling her for child-support pay- ments, and Legal Aid is her only resource.

THE PROBLEM SOLVING COURT AND ITS JUDGE*

The problem solving court is a blended organization, a smaller version of a blended social institution. The judge is an advisor, a coach, and an advocate for participants in a PSC. Nonetheless, he remains a judge and orders par- ticipants who violate program regulations to work crew, jail, or community service work. In many ways, the court (the judge) blends with corrections in a problem solving court. He begins each new relationship with a participant with trust. The participant does not have to earn trust because the judge has the authority to deprive liberty. However, the participant can lose trust, which leads to termination from the program or expulsion. As a consequence the participant is ordered to serve in prison the amount of time stayed for partici- pation in reentry court and the amount of time the person would have served on probation.

Kyle, a forty-eight-year-old black man, provides a vivid illustration of how to lose trust and therefore personal liberty. For more than one year, Kyle was a participant in the reentry problem solving court. At the begin- ning of the program, he and the only other black participant at the time both missed appointments or check-ins at community corrections on a routine basis, resulting in sanctions or consequences. At one point, the judge asked the reentry court team to consider whether their race was associated with identifying the black men's violations. In court, the judge talked with the black participants about race and asked them if they thought the program was racist. From that day, Kyle began courting a closer relationship with the judge. He asked to speak at public meetings, in schools, at the university, and before a state housing agency with the judge. The judge asked him to help new participants get jobs and generally trusted him.

Kyle's was chronically in trouble, in and out of jail, due to a drug and alcohol addiction. When not incarcerated, he claimed he was homeless. When asked to complete the GED at a local adult resources agency, he claimed he could not read. When records suggested otherwise, he claimed he needed reading glasses. During his participation in the reentry court program, he once tested positive for alcohol consumption and claimed someone gave him beer-coated fish on the street. Being poor and hungry, he ate it.

Once he began making progress in reentry, he became the model participant, until the day that the director of a residential drug-treatment program accused Kyle of showing up at their place in a limousine, soliciting women for sex in exchange for money. Kyle was scheduled to meet with the judge and a group of families seeking housing assistance. The meeting took place in a church at 11:00 a.m. In the sanctuary, the judge asked the residential program director to tell Kyle what he had told the judge. Kyle made close eye contact with the judge and denied the accusations. He agreed to be drug-tested. Results of urine, blood, and hair tests were uniformly positive for cocaine and alcohol.

While he was in the reentry program, he gave an interview to researchers studying the retirement process, claiming that he had "retired from crime." The following are excerpts from the interview conducted on September 1, 2006, approximately one year before his relapse:

INTERVIEWER: What did you do prior to "retirement?"

KYLE: I don't know what a title would be. Not thinking in a positive state of mind, you know . . . letting my addictions rule my human chains of thoughts, you know.

INTERVIEWER: So what did you do?

KYLE: Whatever it took. Stole from people who I thought had more which was banks. I never had a burglary charge, no stick up, nothing like that because even in my active addiction, I was still a nice guy. It's just that banks had more money to offer than everybody else did so that was my target. That's who I targeted the most.

INTERVIEWER: Did you do anything else to make money?

KYLE: No, never sold drugs. I was a thief.

INTERVIEWER: How long did that go on?

KYLE: Oh, probably a course of ten, fifteen years.

INTERVIEWER: How do you define retirement?

KYLE: I define retirement . . . based on the time that I spent incarcerated and the time frame it gave me to get my chain of thoughts together about whether I wanted to be in society or be incarcerated for the rest of my life and . . . I took being incarcerated not being institutionalized but I took it as a learning experience and it gave me time to sit back and figure out who I was . . . you know, who I really, really was, and I steered myself away from a life of crime inside the prison walls because there is a life of crime inside the prison walls. You have access to just as much wrongdoing in there as you do outside in society.

INTERVIEWER: I've heard that was true.

KYLE: Oh, it's very true. I mean that includes sex, money, drugs, you know . . . it's like you can steal . . . get whatever you want and I just kind of got tired. There comes a time . . . I don't know how to really explain this, but to me it's explainable from my point of view. I was a different kind of drug addict than a lot of people that I've seen in active addiction. I only did it as a follower, and not a leader, and I let that following, that following got me ran up in the life of crime, and drugs, and alcohol . . . but I had to be one of the nicest—excuse me—[expletive] crack heads that you could ever meet. I never was disrespectful to nobody, even inside of the prison I had to be one of the kindest gentlemen, you know, I was born and raised in a wonderful family, so I have nothing bad to say about my family's background for what I did. It was a life that I chose to lead.

INTERVIEWER: And you actually supported yourself?

KYLE: Yes, I did, and I still do, through crime.

INTERVIEWER: And that's primarily theft?

KYLE: Well, primarily, it was. That's what it was, and I've never been a person that . . . .

INTERVIEWER: . . . you weren't incarcerated for burglary?

KYLE: No. It was checks. I had 142 cases of forgery at Bank One. That's how I stole. I said the bank had more money to offer.

INTERVIEWER: How did you get the checks?

Kyle: The story is wild. I went into the bank one day to cash a $5 AT&T refund check and this teller kept badgering me about why don't you open a checking account. "Lady, I got $5." She says, "Well, today is your lucky day because we have a special going on." And I'm thinking to myself, lady I don't want a checking account, okay?

INTERVIEWER: Why didn't you want a checking account?

KYLE: Because I knew . . . it was going to be tempting. I knew exactly what it was I was getting ready to do with these checks. Wait until the bank closed, and these were checks that I, that I had . . . you know how you get the starter checks? I probably wrote $60,000 in starter checks. You got to fill out everything on this check. . . . I mean I was staying at Fairfield Inn for a month and I was living expensive. But that was a case of check deception and then it started with credit cards, and I was getting people's credit cards, I was teaming up with other people who had got checks from somewhere else. . . . "Just sign it over to me. I'll put my correct name on it. Just cash it." I don't care. I just want to get some money so I can get high, so I ended up doing that.

INTERVIEWER: You got away with that for a long time?

KYLE: A long time. Then I was working at _____ and we got paid one Friday. When I opened up my check there were two checks inside of it. One check was mine which was for $300 and some change. The other check was for $10,750. It was a check that belonged to _____, and they accidentally put it into my envelope.

INTERVIEWER: And you thought?

KYLE: Oh boy! It is my lucky day. . . . I said that. I looked at that and said, "This ain't my money," but then that light bulb went off in my head that said, "It is now. If you get away with this, it is yours." So I went and dressed up in a suit . . . business suit, I walked into the bank. I cashed my $300 check, and then I sit and talk to one of the managers at the bank. And I gave him this outstanding story. He says, "Okay, well, wait just a minute." He took the check back. I'm thinking to myself, Well, I'm going to jail now anyway for attempted forgery . . . theft. He came back and said, "Mr. T, how would you like your bills?" He says, "With this amount of money, we give a brand-new briefcase with a pair of handcuffs and a key, so that you can put it to your wrist and leave here safely." He says, "How are you traveling?" I says, "I got a car outside." He says, "How do you want it?" I said, "Hundred dollar bills would be just fine." He put the $10,750 in a briefcase, shook my hand.

INTERVIEWER: Do you mind me asking what kind of story you told him?

KYLE: I told him that I had a business and that I had some stock inside of [the company] so a part of bonus that I got was from the stock.

INTERVIEWER: So, is that the one that landed you in prison?

KYLE: No, I continued going back to the bank until one day, I walked into the bank, and there was probably fifteen to twenty people standing in there, and all I heard was "click . . . click . . . click . . . click." They locked me in. So I knew. . . . I said, well, this is not a game we're playing, and these people don't seem to be looking around as if there's something wrong. I'm the only one with this petrified mind right now. That it's got to me. The end of the road. So I went and sat on one of those little concrete slabs . . . those little brick things. I went over and sat down. They came over to me. They said, "Mr. T_____?" I said, "Yessir, that's me."

INTERVIEWER: You used your real name all that time?

KYLE: All that time.

INTERVIEWER: So what do you do now? What do you do on a daily basis? First, how long were you in prison for that crime?

KYLE: My original sentence was fifteen years, do seven and a half. I spent five and modified out into the reentry program.

INTERVIEWER: So what do you do now on a daily basis?

KYLE: I work at _____ third shift. I work at the _____ [part-time]. I go to different places, recovery houses mostly.

INTERVIEWER: So a lot of your work is volunteer work?

KYLE: Yes, I do a lot of volunteer work—you could call it that I guess.

INTERVIEWER: Okay . . . do you think the term "retirement" best describes this phase in your life? Why or why not?

KYLE: I think it best describes me right now because I want a new life, you know. I want to be able to share my experience with other people.

INTERVIEWER: You said earlier that when you got into the reentry court you read something to the judge about retirement. Tell us about that.

KYLE: Yes, I wrote a paper . . . a retirement, or a resignation from the life of drugs, alcohol, and crime. I told the judge while being incarcerated in the DOC [Department of Correction] that I took the incarceration as a university, a learning experience instead of being institutionalized and living a life that they thought I should live under their guidance and rehabilitation to where . . . I don't really see a lot of rehabilitation unless a person wants it themselves because their job is to keep you there . . . keep you focused on the things that's going to keep you doing wrong because they're going to come at you with that attitude. So you can't get mad . . . but I steered myself away from just that type of atmosphere.

INTERVIEWER: So when you came into the reentry court, you thought that it was a time to sort of actually put that into an official statement. Why did you do that?

KYLE: Because there was like six or seven white hats. . . . White hats are the big people that's in the prison. . . . They wrote me letters of recommendation to the judge, to the reentry team . . . saying that I absolutely do deserve a chance to be out there because of my conduct reports with little if any write-up . . . . You get a short form. It's like ten hours extra duty or something like that. . . . Uh . . . I think in the five years I was locked up, I think I lost like ninety days total [in good-time credit]. I stayed on the honor roll . . . you have to be conduct free . . . I stayed on the honor roll and that, that helped my modification as far as . . . when they view it, that's how they do it. I sent probably twenty-five certificates back with my modification showing that I'm just not sitting here doing nothing. And our court system, they don't want to just see you go and say that you done some time. They want to see some progress while you're there, you know . . . so that helped my modification and upon admission to reentry to the program of reentry, I viewed it different. I wasn't expecting it to be as extensive as it turned out to be. I was out of the state of mind of prison, but I was back into a lockup situation and I still was incarcerated, and I'm still incarcerated right now in a way. I'm still in the system. . . . This reentry program has really helped me to build a solid foundation. It's helped me to build balance in my life, structure. It has given me a guideline to follow.

INTERVIEWER: How are relationships impacted by you being in different . . . you've retired from crime, so how does that impact relationships?

KYLE: Well . . . I can say that I have networked many different areas while being back into the world through the blessing of the judge who has given me the opportunity to travel with him to conferences and speak in behalf of the reentry

court program . . . talking to, as he called it, "the suits," right? [Laughs.] And
you know . . . it helps you to be able not to be afraid to voice your opinion at
these "suits" when they ask you a question about how did you get there? What
made you do it? . . . I've always been a people person . . . have that attitude to
be able to just . . . communicate. My job at _____ is one thing that
I really, really love the most because . . . you have to sell yourself to sell that
product. And when you sell yourself to them people, the people appreciate
the fact that being able to come into that place, have a joyous conversation
with the cashier . . . and you know, they feel comfortable parting with their
money.

Persons released from blended social institutions to a blended organization, such as reentry court, can benefit from the power of the court to attend
effectively to the cluster of problems they encounter when trying to live and
work within the community. The problem solving court judge can order an
individual to drug-abuse treatment, psychotherapy, and family classes, into
supportive housing, and to a nonprofit agency that specializes in adult literacy
and the development of employment skills. The judge (i.e., the court) can also
monitor progress and impose consequences if the person fails to go through
intake or enroll in a GED class.

Critics of the problem solving court approach find problematic the boundary spanning work that judges accomplish as they try to keep persons within
the community (Nolan 2003), while proponents argue that it takes the power
of the court to change business as usual into what works for solving problems
within the community (Berman and Feinblatt 2001; Wexler and Winick 2003;
Eaton and Kaufman 2005; Fulton Hora 2002; Grudzinskas et al. 2005; Kaye
1999; Maze and Hannah 2008; Mirchandani 2005; Winick 2008). As Kyle's
retirement interview indicates, although he lived within the community, he
still lived "in the system." Reentry court is much like a virtual prison, or
a blended organization, controlling the participant's place of residence, a
home-detention status, and the participant's opportunity to seek work, treatment, and education.

The research literature pays little attention to the fact that the problem
solving court judge may sit "on" the bench, but he works "in" the corrections, mental-health, and drug-abuse-treatment business. The judge orders
drug and alcohol screens, sanctions the problem solving court participant
with work crew or even jail time, and ensures treatment is delivered. In the
more comprehensive problem solving courts, the judge can also be the housing, employment, education, and family specialist. Although the judge does
not become a "therapist," he or she does transcend the boundary of the court,
becoming an advocate for the problem solving court participant while also
directing the work of corrections and other social organizations (Barton 1999;

Casey and Rottman 2000; Eaton and Kaufman 2005; Hafemeister 1999; Lurigio et al. 2001; Petrucci 2002; Schneider 1999; Winick 2008). It is possible that the problem solving court is the social space that best represents the blended social organization within the community.

NEW PRIVATIZATION

The blended social institution returns its clients to their home communities, sometimes through a transitional program, sometimes with nothing except a $75 check and a bus ticket home. A person released from prison is more likely than not to have a behavioral-health problem. Some states, to ensure that the person is stable before prison release, require prison inmates to forego medication during their last months of incarceration. This research was conducted in such a state. One reentry participant, Ned, had been diagnosed with a severe bipolar disorder prior to incarceration. During his years in prison, he was medicated; yet, once his sentence modification was approved so that he could begin the reentry court program, he was taken off medication. As a consequence, Ned's first few months in reentry were difficult. It took more than six weeks to get the community mental-health center to schedule a clinical interview, followed by a visit with the psychiatrist. Once he was stable on his medication, about three months into the program, Ned began making progress.

Persons like Ned return to their communities and depend on the same group of nonprofit or public agencies to help them adjust to life outside the confines of the hospital or the prison. They need medical care, often they need drug-treatment therapy, and they need homes, employment, and family connections. As a result, unless they return to a well-to-do family, they must approach the public health clinic, the nonprofit drug-abuse treatment center, a public adult-resources center for education and employment skills, and a nonprofit agency that specializes in family therapy and family-unification practices. All the agencies are public—partners of local, state, and federal governments—or nonprofit and dependent on some combination of grant money, United Way funds, and government dollars (Medicaid, for example) to survive as organizations.

State-community partnerships are important for a community to take care of social problems and those in need. A sentencing or problem solving judge may order a person to drug treatment and twelve-step meetings, anger-management classes, and a family-therapy program designed explicitly for noncustodial parents. Representing the state, the judge forms a partnership between the government and a community organization, be it public or nonprofit, and brings together a network of organizations and social actors with interests in the participant's and the community's well-being. The judge forms state-community partnerships that are necessary for public safety and for the development of the participant's sense of belonging to a community (Birgden 2002; Ward and Brown 2004). Are these partnerships ideal or preferable under the circumstances of blended social institutions and blended social organizations? Certainly, they are necessary, or as some policy analysts state, they are here to stay (Kelly 2004).

It is imperative to examine the state-community partnerships carefully and critically. As communities demand the use of evidence-based practices, or programs proven to work, in education, medicine, and community-based corrections, both private and public agencies are held accountable on the same themes and metrics. Are the programs effective? What do the performance measures indicate? Are the programs efficient? Does it cost the taxpayer more to house a state prison inmate or to provide the necessary services and programs in the community to prevent repeated crime?

Nancy Jurik conceptualizes "new privatization" to describe the need and the demand to scrutinize public and nonprofit organizations in ways similar to how for-profit organizations measure success. New privatization refers to the "discursive and programmatic restructuring of public sector organizations . . . to become more like businesses" (Jurik 2004, 4–5). New privatization means that communities expect or demand results from the nonprofit community mental-health organization or from the community health clinic. It means that a public agency can be criticized for spending too much of its resource base on developing outcome measures and too little on delivering services to clients. Ultimately, new privatization implies that the financial bottom line is as important to the public or nonprofit agency as it is to the for-profit organization. It is imperative to produce effective and efficient services and products.

Contemporary societies cannot ignore the new privatization movement. Communities want solutions to social problems and depend heavily on public and nonprofit agencies to find remedies for economic, health, mental-health, educational, and correctional problems. Although the accountability associated with new privatization can be valuable, it is important to ask questions about the focus on performance measures, strategies, and outcomes. How does this new way of doing business affect the well-being of clients and the community? Is the community well served by the culture of new privatization? Or does new privatization put a community at risk by, for the purpose of saving money, delivering less than a drug-treatment program is supposed to deliver (Jurik 2004)?

The new privatization movement corresponds to the emergence and transformation of problem solving courts. The first generation of drug courts brought a new method to local communities to respond to drug- or alcohol-abuse issues. Drug courts rely heavily on a small number of social actors in the public sector to care for and monitor a small number of participants. The new generation of problem solving courts tackles substantial problems that require expensive and extensive resources to improve the person's and the community's quality of life. Reentry court participants have lived through daunting periods of adolescence and adulthood that resulted in the commission of serious crime, followed by incarceration. Life-changing resources, especially for persons who cannot afford to pay the bills as they return home from prison, are necessary but unaffordable. Public agencies now have case loads that swell beyond the numbers they are prepared to manage and surpass the treatment levels that public dollars support. New privatization raises important questions regarding the appropriate boundary between governmental and private organizations. Both types of organizations need to pay the electricity bills, and both types face the moral obligation to contribute to the well-being of all residents in all communities.

7

The Community

What It Needs and What It Deserves

MEASURE FOR MEASURE

In Shakespeare's *Measure for Measure,* Isabella begs Angelo for mercy, to save her brother's life.

> ANGELO: The law hath not been dead, though it hath slept;
> Those many had not dar'd to do that evil
> If the first that did th'edict infringe
> Had answer'd for his deed. Now 'tis awake,
> Takes note of what is done, and like a prophet
> Looks in a glass that shows what future evils,
> Either new, or by remissness new conceiv'd,
> And so in progress to be hatch'd and born,
> Are not to have no successive degrees,
> But ere they live, to end.
> ISABELLA: Yet show some pity.
> ANGELO: I show it most of all when I show justice;
> For then I pity those I do not know,
> Which a dismiss'd offence would after gall,
> And do him right that, answering one foul wrong,
> Lives not to act another. Be satisfied;
> Your brother dies tomorrow; be content.

Justice and equality are the hallmarks of American law, much as Angelo tells Isabella about English law. To aspire to achieve them, along with mercy, is laudable, but to realize them simultaneously is impossible. In contemporary societies, such as the United States, communities are challenged to decide what social-control agents should emphasize, knowing full well that mercy precludes equality, and justice precludes mercy.

Isabella invokes the Bible in her attempt to persuade Angelo: "He that is without sin among you, let him cast the first stone." Only those without sin should judge and punish the others? Angelo, unimpressed, provides a practical response: obviously, the lack of sinless police or judges does not justify letting murderers, rapists, or burglars remain unpunished. Clearly, if the agent of social control commits crime, he or she also is subject to the rule of law and merits punishment.

What a community deserves and needs to promote quality of life and public safety challenges lawmakers, policy makers, and social scientists alike. Communities, yours and ours, tend to face persistent social problems such as illegal drug and alcohol abuse, pockets of poverty, racial- or ethnic-group conflict, unemployment, fear of crime, delinquency, high school dropout rates, and family abuse and violence. The community without social problems is both fortunate and unusual. In most metropolitan areas, a similar cluster of problems affects quality of life and public safety (Chiricos, McEntire, and Gertz 2001; Edwards and Hensley 2001; Eschholz, Chiricos, and Gertz 2003; Farole et al. 2005; Miller and Knudsen 2007; Purvin 2007; Room 2005; Taylor and Covington 1993).

The courts are not designed or intended to be community problem solvers; yet, the emergence of problem solving court programs, beginning in 1989, signals a sea change in the work of the state courts. The community in any jurisdiction that supports a PSC expects the judge "on" the bench to be a member "of" the community, willing to address social problems while supporting the rule of law. Yet, the PSC is different. The presiding judge is supposed to deliver justice tempered by mercy.

CAROLINE

Caroline, a young female participant in a reentry PSC, presented the judge with a dilemma that reversed the roles of Angelo and Isabella in their dialogue on justice and mercy. Caroline was presented to, and rejected by, the reentry team due to her criminal background, which showed numerous arrests and convictions for fraud and drug dealing. The team found the mercy argument, presented by the judge, unconvincing. Although considering the team's objections, the judge scheduled a sentence-modification hearing to bring Caroline into the reentry problem solving court.

Caroline is articulate and could outwit and outtalk treatment providers and reentry team members when her drug-use patterns were brought up for discussion. She has a history of heavy cocaine use and association with two of the well-known drug dealers in the community (who were imprisoned at the time Caroline became a participant in the reentry PSC); she also comes from an intact middle-class family in the local community that supports her emotionally and in material ways. While Caroline was incarcerated, her parents contacted the sentencing judge numerous times in an effort to obtain an early prison release. He became convinced: "She is a high school graduate and highly motivated to become a good citizen in the community"[1] (personal correspondence, April 13, 2008). Once he concluded that she should be in the reentry PSC, he also became convinced that she faced a fork in the road and needed his guidance. She could either return to her old ways or, with his supervision, become a productive member of society.

Caroline entered the program on February 1, 2008, and within ten days produced two diluted drug screens, which, following lab analysis, allowed the reentry team to conclude that she was deliberately covering up her drug use. The following week, police officers conducting a traffic stop found Caroline in a car with a female driver and a well-known cocaine-addicted man. The reentry rules precluded her being in the company of those not approved by the team. She clearly set a bad example for other participants who were aware of her violations. The prosecutor and the police officers on the team argued to expel her and return her to state prison as she had breached the team's faith in her to become engaged in the treatment process. In this case, contrary to the dialogue in *Measure for Measure*, it was the judge who advocated mercy and the PSC team members who argued for justice. Caroline, they claimed, should not remain within the community. She had violated laws and the terms of the participation agreement (see appendix B) and should be returned to prison to serve time like others who committed similar offenses. Moreover, Caroline had given birth to a cocaine-addicted child, and her supposedly supportive parents were encouraging her to have the troubled child adopted. The team concluded that if she remained in the community, Caroline faced an unacceptably high risk of having a second cocaine-addicted child. The merciful judge wanted her to get another chance. After all, he argued, Caroline was an addict with a high risk of reoffending, and relapse is a part of recovery.

The presiding judge in the reentry PSC thought that they must find a way to balance justice with mercy. Caroline must face consequences for her use of illegal drugs and attempts to cover up that use, her false claims, and her failure to associate only with those individuals approved by the PSC team. Nonetheless, he remained convinced of his duty to make merciful decisions within the context of the PSC. He felt he must remember that Caroline had been in the program for only a short period and might have undiagnosed but treatable mental-health issues. Yet, the team was advising him to weigh the mounting evidence that she could not succeed in the reentry PSC. She showed signs of an antisocial personality. Cocaine dealing is a serious criminal problem in this particular community. If appropriate punishment were not administered quickly and effectively, other PSC participants would see a green light to use drugs.

The judge concluded that putting Caroline in jail for a week, while retaining her in the PSC, was appropriate as a just yet merciful response. It would be Caroline's wake-up call, as well as her last opportunity to work her way back into the program and avoid a return to prison. Caroline spent a week in jail, returned to the PSC, and within one week again tested positive for cocaine use. The judge, realizing he could not make a decision premised on mercy outweighing justice, returned Caroline to prison at the end of April (three months after she began the PSC program).

We relate this case not to argue against mercy but to demonstrate the problematic nature of protecting the community while working to keep persons returning from prison home "for good" in a problem solving court program. PSC programs face challenges that traditional criminal trial courts do not. Judges and teams know they are working with persons who, if not for the PSC, would be in prison or jail. A continuous justification is demanded, explicitly or implicitly, for decisions that are ostensibly based on too much mercy and not enough justice.

Our example of Caroline comes from an extremely successful PSC. Most persons who start the program complete it and have no further contact with the police or any other criminal justice agency. We compare it to two distinctive PSC court programs, located in the same Midwestern metropolitan area as Caroline's PSC. All three represent blended social organizations.

A TALE OF THREE PROBLEM SOLVING COURTS, ALL IN ONE CITY

The reentry problem solving court is a dramatically successful program, the forensic diversion problem solving court is at best moderately successful, and the third program, a reentry court for returning sex offenders, failed completely after three attempts at initiation. Two judges presided over the three distinctive problem solving court programs. One presides over the very successful program and presided over the failed PSC. A second judge is responsible for the moderately successful PSC. We chose to focus on these particular PSCs and not two others convened in the same jurisdiction in order to present information that covers the continuum from what works to what does not.[2]

REENTRY COURT

The reentry PSC is continuously evaluated with input, output, and outcome data. A total of 158 potential candidates were reviewed for the 58 slots filled by participants at the time of data analysis. Those not taken into the program were rejected by the prosecutor, did not fit the profile of the preferred participant (a history of drug abuse and symptoms of behavioral problems or mental illness), or had too little time left to serve in prison. The program is a four-phase program with goals and milestones for each phase (see appendix D). The number of persons who progress from one phase to the next is monitored, and the outcomes for graduates are measured continuously using the number of police contacts, employment records, housing records, and family and community-activities records. For participants, graduates, and graduates on probation, actuarial-type risk instruments are administered to measure progress in the program. The risk-to-recidivate measures and whether or not a participant is arrested are the two key outcome measures analyzed in quarterly reports.

The program was modeled on other evidence-based programs, or what the research literature shows "works" to prevent recidivism while ex-felons are treated in the community, and it was modified to account for the local community's needs (Adams and Ferrandino 2008; August et al. 2006; Austin 2001; Basile 2005; Bushway 2006; Eskridge 2005; Evans 2005; Freeman 2003; Friedmann, Taxman, and Henderson 2007; Grudzinskas et al. 2005; McClure 2004; Miller 2007). The special needs or issues that characterize this particular community include a concentration of social problems in a small downtown area, a persistent cocaine and methamphetamine problem, a large homeless shelter that temporarily houses and feeds persons from an eight-county region, and inadequate treatment facilities for behavioral-health and drug-addiction problems. Because the county has the only residential safe shelter for battered women in an eight-county region, its juvenile and adult general-jurisdiction courts adjudicate a disproportionate number of cases involving family abuse and violence.

The reentry PSC (McClure 2004; Miller 2007; Weiman 2007) takes persons out of prison at least two years earlier than their scheduled release date. The target population for this particular program includes those who, when returning from prison, face a disproportionately high risk of recidivism because of their drug addictions and co-occurring behavioral-health problems. Prison case managers and community-corrections case managers identify candidates for the program. Once a written and comprehensive summary of the potential candidate is prepared, it is presented at the reentry team's weekly staffing meeting. If the team votes to accept the participant, a sentence-modification

hearing is scheduled, an intake process begins, and the participant is transported from prison to the county jail for assessment and case planning.

The incentive package for participants includes a modified sentence, supportive housing, and a structured program to facilitate a transformation of
the person from "ex-felon" to "productive member of society." Only persons
from the local community are considered. In exchange for the incentives, the
participant signs a legal agreement to follow the rules of the program, which
typically lasts for one year to eighteen months. The agreement spells out the
expectations of each of four phases of the program, the regulations of the
reentry PSC, and the possible sanctions for violations of the rules.

Once admitted to the reentry PSC program, participants undergo a clinical interview in the local jail that is conducted by a trained specialist from a
community-corrections facility. Along with the clinical interviews to assess
needs, two valid and reliable measurement instruments are administered; both
are used in the United States and other nations to indicate the severity of drug
or alcohol addiction and the various needs that must be met to discourage
a person from committing crime. A community-corrections case manager
(not the interviewer) uses the results of the Addiction Severity Index (ASI)
(Joosen et al. 2005; Leukefeld et al. 2007) and the Level of Services Inventory (LSI) (Spohn et al. 2001) to plan a course of action for the participant's
first ninety days in the program. Every six months, the LSI is administered to
measure a reduction in the risk of recidivism. Once the participant completes
a drug-treatment program, the ASI is administered again to measure severity
of addiction to alcohol or drugs. The changes in the LSI and ASI indicate
program progress or lack thereof.

Following the clinical interview and preparation of a case plan, participants are moved from the jail to the local community-corrections facility,
where they complete a number of tasks, all aimed at initiating a transition
into the community. In principle, participants are expected to complete all
tasks within one week. In practice, reality kicks in, usually in the form of a
participant's not being able to secure a photo identification because he or she
has no birth certificate available, and the tasks of community transition can
take as long as three weeks to one month to complete.

Most participants in the reentry PSC are required to complete a sixteen-
week group-therapy outpatient program called the Matrix Model. Two hour-
long group-therapy sessions are held during each of the sixteen weeks. Those
who complete the program are required to meet for hour-long aftercare sessions once a week for thirty-six weeks. Family members are encouraged to
attend the aftercare sessions. The Matrix Model treatment program is targeted
toward those addicted to any substance other than marijuana, especially those
whose drug of choice is cocaine or methamphetamine. Along with the Matrix

Model program, reentry court participants must attend ninety twelve-step meetings in ninety days. They must select a home group and a sponsor by the end of that period.

The case plan may call for additional program elements, such as Dads Make a Difference for noncustodial parents who need to pay down accrued child support and reestablish parental relationships. Anger-management treatment, cognitive behavioral classes (called Thinking for a Change), and medical and dental care are necessary for most participants.

Random drug and alcohol testing are essential. Participants carry a limited-use cell phone provided by community corrections and must report for a urine screen within one hour of receiving a call. A failed test will not necessarily result in expulsion from the PSC, but it will guarantee a one-week jail term, a sanction specified in the legal agreement all participants sign upon entry to the PSC and in the participant's handbook (see appendixes B and D).

The reentry PSC uses a "step-down" approach for housing and a "step-up" approach for employment. Initial housing is in the work-release program at community corrections. Participants obtain passes to leave the facility to seek jobs and attend twelve-step meetings and drug treatment. Once employed, they are moved into supportive scattered-site housing on home detention (i.e., with an electronic monitoring device). Surveillance officers make unannounced visits, inspect housing, and report their findings using a standardized form. If the participant remains employed and demonstrates appropriate care for the apartment for at least three months, he or she is released from home detention and begins a daily-reporting requirement at community corrections.

Housing is a key component of the reentry PSC (Cooke 2005; Cooper 2007; Galster et al. 2002; Petersilia 2001), supported by a competitive grant awarded to the reentry PSC by the Indiana Housing and Community Development Authority, a quasi-state agency. The grant provides tenant-based rental assistance for one year for each participant. The level of rent paid is based on income (participants have virtually no income upon leaving prison), and the rent payment is fixed for one year on the premise that the participant will pay down bills and fines and prepare for financial independence. A group of participating landlords cooperates with the reentry program, making clean and safe apartments available and terminating leases if a participant is returned to state prison or otherwise expelled from the reentry PSC.

The "step-down" housing approach is complemented by a "step-up" employment approach, known as the ABC program for employment. The reentry PSC recognizes the importance of employment for preventing repeated crime (Butzin, Saum, and Scarpitti 2002; Dalessio and Stolzenberg 1995; Goldstein 2005; Leukefeld et al. 2004, 2007); thus, new participants are expected to obtain an "A" job, that is, "any job," within two weeks of release from prison. Fast-food and other service-type jobs, such as hotel housekeeping, are the typical "A" jobs. Once a participant develops and demonstrates appropriate work habits (sometimes called soft work skills), such as punctuality, a good work attitude, and no missed workdays, he or she is encouraged to find a "B" job, or a "better job." These positions generally include benefits and are in occupational fields such as light manufacturing or maintenance work. Eventually, a participant seeks a "C," or "career," job. A group of chief executive officers met to make C jobs available to reentry court participants. Generally, these positions are in advanced-technology manufacturing firms that require a highly skilled labor force. The C jobs pay well (on average $20 per hour plus overtime) and provide generous benefits packages, including health insurance and retirement pay.

A case manager employed full-time by the community-corrections facility to work for the reentry PSC interviews participants each week and checks on program progress. Weekly summary reports are distributed to the team members to prepare for staff meetings. At such meetings, rule violations and sanctions are discussed, as are possible promotions to a higher phase of the four-phase program. When participants are likely to be promoted or graduated from the PSC, they are scheduled to be interviewed by a police captain or a deputy sheriff. Certificates are handed out in court sessions to recognize promotion or graduation.

Sanctions for program violations vary in severity as a function of the seriousness of the violation. For instance, if a participant is five minutes late for an appointment, she may be required to write an essay to read aloud in court the following week. If a participant fails to show up for an appointment and makes no effort to notify the provider, a punishment of eight hours of work crew is typical. Most participants violate rules, but most successful participants are in total compliance with all the regulations by the time they are in the fourth or fifth month of the program.

This PSC is designed to use sanctions wisely: the stick is but a painted carrot. If an essay is read aloud in court, it is also given to a reentry volunteer, who meets with participants to improve their written communication skills. The essays become polished documents that are assembled in a keepsake booklet. In addition to the traditional program components, all participants engage in a reading program—Changing Lives through Literature—with weekly reading assignments and meetings convened by a volunteer. As participants attend the reading and writing programs, they also begin to understand the importance of volunteer work. Consequently, participants volunteer to participate in hunger walks, church programs, neighborhood cleanup programs, and other local activities. While most of the reentry PSC components are evidence-based programs—such as Thinking for a Change, Changing Lives through Literature, or the Matrix Model—some components work well within the community served by the persons who come home from prison "for good."

Weekly court sessions are held following the staffing meetings. Participants get advice and suggestions from the presiding judge, whether the advice is sought or a reminder of what to do. On October 9, 2007, Joanie and the judge had the following dialogue.

> JUDGE: In terms of getting through this program, as we look at the big picture here, the first part of the program is talking about engagement, getting engaged in recovery and so forth. And the second phase is gaining the tools to deal with your substance abuse and whatever other problems you have. And there's kind of a commitment to the law-abiding life. And then restoring your rights to society. So there's goals in each one of these phases. And so when we're looking at you, we're looking at you making some progress. . . . If things aren't working out in the first phase, we look at things a little differently because we wonder, Are you engaged? If you screw up on Phase 4, we look at the nature of the screwup and a penalty you might have gotten in Phase 1 will not necessarily be the same as Phase 4. And we're looking at you individually. We want every one of you to make it. And we want you all to keep working hard and making progress. And I know it's going to work out. And you might think, Geez, I don't have any free time. Well, as time goes on, we'll give you a little more space for you to be who you are. And then in the end you're going to make your own decisions in life, in terms of what you're going to do with it. . . . So good luck to everybody. Joanie. Where are you? We've got a certificate here for Joanie in recognition of completing Phase 2. Let's give her a hand. [Applause.] Joanie, in terms of getting moved to this phase, what have you accomplished in this program that you're proud of, that you think is important to you?
>
> JOANIE: Getting reacquainted with my family. That's a big accomplishment for me because they looked down on me for a long time. So having the relationships that I have with them now means a lot. My ex-husband likes me. We plan to reunite with my son, but I don't want to rush things.
>
> JUDGE: And what is there about you that they're looking at you differently-now?
>
> JOANIE: The change, the things that I've gone after and accomplished. I have a full-time job and that helps support the family. I did exactly what you told me to do. And now it's all working out better.
>
> JUDGE: Okay. Well, congratulations.

Joanie is an example of those who succeed in reentry. She reconnected to family members, completed all the treatment programs ordered by the reentry court, progressed in the jobs program, and eventually landed a full-time, permanent job on the second shift in an automobile manufacturing company.

Life was tough—she needed overnight child care for her son, for instance—
but Joanie put problems and accomplishments in perspective and worked
hard to avoid a return to drugs or crime. Joanie clearly developed a sense of
pride and citizenship. She watched the political process carefully, somehow
finds time to volunteer at her church, and has allowed the judge to interview
her before public meetings for the purpose of recruiting other corporations to
hire reentry participants or landlords to house them.

Among reentry participants who entered the program between January
2005 and December 2008, 82 percent completed the program phases or
graduated and have had no negative criminal justice contacts. They are true
successes. The remaining 18 percent failed either because they were expelled
by the reentry court judge and returned to state prison or because they were
arrested for the commission of a new crime.

Although the reentry court is highly successful, it is not funded directly
by the state or the county. Participants must pay their bills, whether for drug
treatment or home detention. One source of state funds does support a full-
time community-corrections case manager. The state has a community transition program (CTP) that pays local counties $18 per day for thirty days to
provide transitional support for persons leaving prison. After the first thirty
days, CTP funds are reduced to $12 per day for A- and B-level felons who
return to the county and remain under supervision by the county's community-corrections agency. All CTP funds terminate within three months.

The reentry court's success has received local and state media attention.
News releases were prepared and circulated as participants were scheduled
for graduation or engaged in community volunteer activities, such as neighborhood cleanup projects. Television, radio, and print media coverage at-
tracted the attention of a quasi-state housing agency to invite the reentry court
to submit a competitive proposal for a tenant-based rental-assistance program
for reentry participants. A one-year pilot project was funded that supported
up to thirty participants for up to one year in reduced-rent housing. Among
all those who received rental assistance, one was arrested for stealing, and he
was returned to prison. It is worth noting that he did not live in the county but
returned to it only because it was the county in which he was convicted and
sentenced to state prison. Clearly, housing matters.

No additional funds support reentry, but participants are encouraged to
take advantage of the no-cost programs, such as adult-literacy and job-train-
ing programs, that are available in the county. A binary logistic regression
analysis showed that full-time employment, housing assistance, and completion of the Matrix Model program are statistically significant predictors of
success or failure in reentry. A participant's race, gender, and marital status
are not significantly related to success. One very important family indicator,

however, is significantly related to success. Participants who are custodial parents, either fathers or mothers, are more likely to succeed than those with no children or those who have children not living with them.

In summary, the formula for success in reentry is drug-treatment therapy, individual counseling when necessary, housing, employment, and responsibility for children. The formula is no different today than it ever was. We knew in 1959 that those with "stakes in conformity"—conforming life styles, characterized by employment, family responsibilities, and connections to the community—tend to avoid crime (Bredemeier and Toby 1960; Toby 1964). What is different nowadays is the mechanism for getting persons, once incarcerated, to develop stakes in conformity. Rehabilitation in prison does not work as effectively as rehabilitation within the community. We know with certainty that a well-designed and comprehensive reentry problem solving court builds on participants' strengths and helps to provide the stakes that participants can use to anchor themselves in conventional society.

THE FORENSIC DIVERSION PROBLEM SOLVING COURT

The forensic diversion (FD) problem solving court is a moderately successful program designed and implemented in 2004 by its presiding judge, who attended a National Judicial College conference on how to respond effectively to co-occurring mental-health and drug-abuse problems within the community. Potential participants have all been convicted of felony-level drug offenses and are awaiting a sentencing hearing as they are considered for the FD PSC. In the case of the FD PSC, the prosecutor is the official gatekeeper, identifying candidates to present to the FD team by locating them on the sentencing calendar. Defense attorneys contact the prosecutor's office to urge admission for their clients. The purpose of the program is for the problem solving court, a blended social organization, to collaborate with a community mental-health center to provide treatment within the community and divert appropriate participants from serving time in prison.

In most cases, the participant has served one or more terms of incarceration prior to placement in the FD PSC. The FD program, unlike reentry, has state funding. The money, from the Department of Correction, pays for a case manager at community corrections, a case manager at a community mental-health center, and most of the programs that participants are required to complete.

In the program's first eighteen months, the FD team considered fifty-four potential participants and decided to admit thirty-nine to the program. Fifteen applicants were denied due to their prior criminal histories. Nine persons admitted to FD were quickly expelled for continuous program violations. An expulsion from this PSC, as compared to the reentry court, means that the participant is returned to jail to await a sentencing hearing.

At its peak performance level and at the time of data collection in 2006, the FD PSC enrolled thirty participants: thirteen women and seventeen men. The youngest was twenty-three, the oldest was sixty, and the average age for all participants was thirty-four. Of this group, 60 percent had attained either a high school diploma or the GED certificate. Seven had not yet completed the GED, and four had completed some college. The sociodemographic profile of the FD participants was not statistically different from the profile of reentry court participants.

By 2008, the number of participants had dropped to seven. Only one case manager (at community corrections) continued to work in the program, and less than 50 percent of all the participants admitted to the program had avoided arrest and a prison sentence. This may be considered a moderately success-ful program, one that struggles to keep participants coming in and a PSC that struggles to deliver the services its participants need to succeed.

The first person to graduate from the FD PSC in 2005 was Beth, who en-tered the program as a convicted cocaine dealer and exotic dancer. In 2008 she was married and the owner of a successful house-cleaning and pet-sitting company. She participated in the FD program for eighteen months. She com-pleted an intensive outpatient program for drug abuse, a relapse-prevention class, a goals-setting group, a women's empowerment class at the YWCA, and the Thinking for Change program (a cognitive behavioral therapy). She received one sanction for violating a program regulation.

FD participants, as a group, tend to commit more program violations than do reentry PSC participants. We speculate that prison time serves a specific deterrence function for reentry participants, one that does not operate for FD participants. The FD program, like reentry, uses the LSI[3] (it does not use the ASI) to measure program progress and risk of criminal activity.

Consider these LSI score ranges (with risk levels adjusted slightly to ac-count for gender differences):

- A score of forty-one or higher indicates a high risk of reoffending.
- Scores in the thirty-four to forty point range indicate a medium to high risk.
- Scores in the twenty-four to thirty-three point range indicate a moderate level of risk.
- Scores in the fourteen to twenty-three point range indicate a low to moderate risk.
- Scores in the zero to thirteen point range indicate a low risk of reof-fending.

Beth began the FD program with a total LSI score of twenty-seven. The risk of her reoffending was moderate. When she was interviewed as she was graduating from the program, her total LSI score was twelve, placing her in a category of low risk to reoffend within twelve months.

On average, the thirty FD program participants in 2006 scored 29.10 on the LSI as they began the program. Scores ranged from fifteen to forty-three. By the time they had been in the program for eighteen months, the average score dropped to twenty-one points. Although they made progress, they did not make enough progress to call the program an unmitigated success.

The LSI instrument gives case managers opportunities to identify the services that participants need to make progress in crucial dimensions of their lives that will reduce the risk of reoffending. Nine dimensions[4] that can be addressed are

1. education and employment
2. financial problems
3. family/marital relations
4. accommodations or residential stability
5. leisure/recreation activities
6. companions
7. alcohol/drug problems
8. emotional/personal issues
9. attitudes/orientations or pro-social versus antisocial thoughts and beliefs

Each of the nine dimensions is weighted by the LSI scoring rules. For example, the education and employment dimension is scored on a ten-point scale, and companions are scored on a five-point scale. While each dimension has a different weight in determining the overall LSI score, all the dimensions are scored in the direction of decreasing need for services. Lower scores for the total LSI and its separate dimensions indicate progress.

To examine progress, the percentage of total possible points for each of the nine dimensions is computed. Comparisons are made at two points: time 1 scores represent the participants' LSI scores as they enter the program, and time 2 scores represent LSI scores one year later. There are statistically significant differences on five of the dimensions measured. Participants who have been in the FD program over the recent year face decreased levels of difficulty in the following areas:

- education/employment
- leisure/recreation

- companions
- alcohol/drug problems
- attitude and orientation

Unfortunately, there are no statistically significant differences between time 1 and time 2 scores for four of the nine dimensions of information measured by the LSI instruments. Participants face similar levels of financial, family/marital, accommodation, and emotional/personal problems across a twelve-month period.

Financial and family problems can be "treated" by problem solving court programs. The acquisition of job skills and employment and family counseling or reunification programs should help participants succeed. Although the differences in accommodation are not statistically significant, there is a trend in the data toward improved residential stability. Likewise there is a trend toward improvements in the participants' emotional/personal problems.

Why did participants not make the progress hoped for them on these dimensions? Unlike the reentry problem solving court, forensic diversion has no tenant-based assisted-rent program. Each participant was at the mercy of the mental-health case manager to locate housing. At one team meeting, the case manager made it clear that she did not know how to direct a participant toward applying for a housing voucher (in the United States, a HUD Section VIII voucher). Other team members needed to tell her the location of the office. A few months after the first participant, Donna, moved into a Section VIII housing unit, she wanted to move out to be with her boyfriend. The case manager presented the scenario to the team and asked the team to approve Donna's holding onto her housing voucher but moving into another apartment with her boyfriend. An attorney on the team needed to explain to the case manager that she was proposing a violation of the law.

Participants' emotional problems were not eased in the program. This issue is critically important to address. Participants had access to a community mental-health center but depended on their case manager to direct them to services. The case manager told the team that she did not like working with the mentally ill, which prevented the participants from getting the help they needed. On occasion, she argued for imprisonment of a seriously mentally person—in a program designed to get the mentally ill treatment and keep them in the community—because she could not make progress with him. This case points to an issue that all problem solving court programs must face: personnel do indeed matter.

In forensic diversion, a fully funded, specialized case manager did not accept the value of retaining persons within their home communities. Though it was not apparent until too many participants had failed, she undermined the success of the program and the participants' opportunities to succeed as individuals. Although she eventually chose to leave her job, her decision was made too late to save the program. In 2008, only seven participants remained in the program. Plans are underway to build the program or move the remaining participants out of the forensic diversion PSC and into another drug court (a program not discussed in this book).

We would be remiss to end this section on a downbeat. Although as many participants failed as succeeded, there were remarkable and noteworthy success stories. One, a young mother named Haley, talked with the presiding judge on May 30, 2006. Before joining the FD PSC program, Haley had never held a job for pay.

JUDGE: Haley, are you still working at Caterpillar? [The firm hired her through a temporary employment agency.]

HALEY: Yes, sir.

JUDGE: How are you getting along?

HALEY: I'm great. I feel on top of the world.

JUDGE: Your boss still thinks a lot of you, I would guess.

HALEY: Yes, sir. She wants to get me a raise soon.

JUDGE: And are you still giving your boss extra help, help with the disabled people who are on cleaning duty?

HALEY: Yes, I do whatever she asks me to do. I like to help the other women.

JUDGE: You amaze me. You went all those years when you never had a job— not any job—and now you've got a job where you have to show up for work every day. And you're going the extra distance. What's the toughest thing about having a job like this, and not just hanging out every day and fiddling around?

HALEY: I like my job actually. I like the people I work with so it makes it easier on me. I get along with everybody.

JUDGE: And how often do you see your little one? [Haley had temporarily lost custody of her baby and was in the process of reunification under the guidance of the Division of Children and Families.]

HALEY: I see him on every weekend now. As soon as I can move into my own apartment, he will be able to live with me. [She was living in a transitional housing complex at the time.] And my mom will take care of him while I am at work.

JUDGE: Well, Haley, I think it's time for you to move out [of transitional housing] and into your own apartment. Next week I want to hear how you and your mom and your son are getting along.

Haley completed the program with a new GED in hand and reunited with her child; she continues in 2009 to hold onto her permanent job, which pays her a living wage and provides medical and other benefits for her and her child. She is medicated for a generalized anxiety disorder and has never had a negative police contact since she began the program.

Generally speaking, the women in forensic diversion were more likely to succeed than the men. The following exchange between Rick and the judge on August 21, 2006, illustrates how some participants do not engage in the program and, as a consequence, fail. (Rick was eventually sentenced to serve prison time.)

JUDGE: I'll release you today. Is that all right?
 RICK: Yes.
 JUDGE: We need to be able to trust you. How can we trust you?
 RICK: I had time to think about that. I kind of backslid, that's all.
 JUDGE: The team decided that you should go back to [drug treatment at] the Dales. Let's try it again, okay?
 RICK: Yes.
 JUDGE: Well, we'll be sure to see you every Monday for a while, okay? [He was scheduled to appear in court every two weeks.]
 RICK: Yes.

Rick is a single, never-married, thirty-four-year-old man with an unstable work history. He told the forensic diversion court that he has no family in town and very few friends. As in reentry, one of the key factors related to success is having a child or children to care for. Those women and men with children succeeded, with one exception, and those without children ended up in prison.

What remains perplexing is a financial question. The FD PSC was supported by the Department of Correction with an annual $50,000 budget to provide mental-health and drug-addiction counseling. The reentry court is not funded. Participants are financially responsible for all the services they receive with the key exception of housing.

What accounts for the different levels of success across two problem solving courts? Both programs are similar along the following dimensions:

- Case plans are developed and implemented by case managers dedicated to the problem solving court program.
- Risk for relapse or recidivism is continuously assessed.
- Evidence-based treatment programs to develop cognitive skills or avoid drug or alcohol relapse are delivered.
- Participants are carefully monitored in the community.
- Participants are randomly screened for drug or alcohol use.
- Participants engage in twelve-step meetings.

- Participants routinely appear in court to disclose their recent problems, challenges, and goals.
- Participants are routinely rewarded, and they are sanctioned when they violate program regulations.

The key differences across the two problem solving court programs include the following:

- Reentry participants have spent time in state prison; forensic diversion participants, if incarcerated, were in county jail.
- Reentry is a self-pay program, whereas the FD program pays for treatment and services.
- Reentry provides housing; forensic diversion does not.
- Reentry includes a formal employment program; forensic diversion does not.
- In this state, reentry is authorized under a statutory title that defines court programs; forensic diversion is authorized under a title that defines drug-treatment programs.

We end this section of the chapter with some comments on language. In both of the programs analyzed, the reentry and FD PSCs, two agencies are crucial: a community mental-health provider, called the Dales, and community corrections. The Dales delivers therapy for behavioral-health problems and drug- and alcohol-addiction treatment. Community corrections is responsible for monitoring participants (on home detention or day reporting), surveillance, and drug and alcohol testing.

The Dales and community corrections both use "case plans" to refer "participants" to the "programs." The same words are used to refer to very different activities. The same words mean different things to mental-health and community-corrections organizations.

- A "case plan" at the Dales may have the purpose of identifying appropriate treatment plans.
- A "case plan" at community corrections may have the purpose of ensuring compliance with court-ordered sanctions and procedures.
- A "participant" at the Dales is a client who is referred to treatment programs or who is participating in treatment programs.
- A "participant" at community corrections is a person under community supervision.
- "Programs" at the Dales include individual or group-therapy programs or relapse-prevention programs.

- "Programs" at community corrections include work crew, day reporting, home detention, community service, and work release.

The "case plans" for the "participants" enrolled in "programs" are different at the Dales and at community corrections. Yet, the two organizations and their staff are partners in the PSC programs. There should be strong reasons for aligning them in response to community problems. The second-generation PSC programs have experienced success on account of the partnership between mental health and corrections as well as the valuable alliances formed with community and state organizations and volunteers who work to improve the quality of life for the citizens of the county and city. It is imperative to look carefully at the valuable partnerships that account for program success; it is no less important to recognize the differences in principles and practices that characterize mental-health and corrections agencies using the same terms and language to describe notably different concepts and practices. For PSC team members to understand each others' languages, it is important to operationalize what terms means to all organizations or agencies participating in a problem solving court program.

A FAILED PROBLEM SOLVING COURT: TITLE 33

We conclude this chapter with a description of a failed problem solving court. Called Title 33 to avoid sounding the alarm within the community, it was a specialized reentry court for sex offenders returning to the community. The prosecutor named the program because its statutory authority derives from the state's laws governing court programs. The program was designed and submitted for funding to the Office of Justice Programs, U.S. Department of Justice, Bureau of Justice Assistance. The title of the proposal is "A Problem Solving Court Approach: Sex Offenders Returning from State Prison." A $168,000 three-year grant was awarded (2007-WP-BX-0025). It provided all the ingredients necessary to operate the problem solving court program: a full-time case manager, a sex-offender cognitive-restructuring treatment program, surveillance, sex-offender-specific polygraphs, and housing vouchers for participants. The program was designed in consideration of the containment perspective for treating sex offenders within the community (Kokish, Levenson, and Blasingame 2005; La Fond and Winick 2003; McGrath et al. 2007). Nonetheless, it failed. After three start-up attempts between 2007 and 2008, the presiding judge closed down the program and cancelled the Department of Justice grant.

The curious reader probably wonders if the problem solving court dialogues were somehow unusual for the Title 33 PSC. Did participants fail to engage in the program? Were they reticent and dominated by their denial? The following exchange from May 12, 2008, took place between Len (a person who returned from prison having served time for the rape of an adult woman) and the presiding judge.

> JUDGE: Len, step up here. Okay, Len, I missed you last week because I was out of town. What have you accomplished? What are you doing?
>
> LEN: I've been to Work One [a state employment service]. Got that taken care of. I've got a disability appointment for rehab vocational, or whatever it's called. I applied for health insurance. I have medical right now. I have shots coming up [for a back problem] again this week.
>
> JUDGE: So it looks like you've got a lot of medication needs and you're getting this taken care of, right?
>
> LEN: Well, my old health insurance will run out soon. That's why I need to apply for new insurance.
>
> JUDGE: So what's going on in the big picture here?
>
> CASE MANAGER: He's applied for Medicaid as well as the Healthy Indiana Plan. And we've put some job applications in. And he's reading a lot. I've also made some contact with the Salvation Army, different places, to help out with his medication expenses.
>
> JUDGE: And, Len, where are you living right now?
>
> LEN: [Specifies street address.]
>
> JUDGE: Are you having someone visit with you from time to time to see how you're doing?
>
> LEN: Oh, yes. Every day. And I go to church. And I see [the case manager] twice a week. She goes with me to check out library books. And I see [the therapist] on Wednesdays.
>
> JUDGE: Okay, we have the housing, we have the medical covered. How's he doing in terms of his therapy and the polygraphs?
>
> LEN: I'm doing good in therapy. I take the polygraph on Saturday.
>
> JUDGE: What kind of polygraph is this? A maintenance polygraph?
>
> LEN: I think it's maintenance. But I don't know for sure. It's Saturday.
>
> JUDGE: How do you feel you're going to do on the polygraph?
>
> LEN: I should pass it. I don't see problems.
>
> JUDGE: I'll see you next Monday then. Tell me about how the polygraph went. I'm still worried about your leisure time. I want you to get some new friends; I want to know who you associate with, and so on.

The Title 33 PSC did not fail because the participants repeated their crimes or were arrested or failed the program. It failed because the program, a blended social organization, could not elicit the community support enjoyed by the other PSC programs.[5] Partnerships with agencies did not emerge. Criminal justice agencies made no attempt to hide turf battles. Team meetings were often attended by only three or four members of the fifteen-member court team.

The therapist, probation office, and parole expressed strong resistance to the program. Representatives expressed aloud the following sentiments, recorded at a team meeting held in 2008:

> "We already are taking care of the sex offenders. We don't need another program."
>
> "No one wants sex offenders in our county. Let's move them to another county. That's my idea for how to contain them."
>
> "Don't let the press find out that we're doing this. That would blow up all the other programs."
>
> "Parole doesn't get it. They need to let the therapists do their jobs."
>
> "They're scum. That's all they are. Scum. The worst kind."
>
> "I will not agree to one day less in prison than what the offender's sentence calls for."
>
> "He had a Swiss army knife on his dresser. That's a knife, right? I want to violate him. I want him back in prison. He violated parole regulations."
>
> "He's suicidal? What business does anyone have to treat him? You were supposed to notify me, not get treatment for him. If he had really done it, I'd lose my job."
>
> "They're all alike. Who wants all these child molesters living in our county?"

General-jurisdiction trial courts and problem solving courts developed within them take responsibility for delivering public safety to the community (Austin 2001; Fisler 2005; Lynch 2006; Petersilia 2001). The community that endorses a PSC expects reduced recidivism and reduced crime as a consequence of the court's monitoring ex-offenders carefully within the community. The community may, as it expresses sentiments in letters to the editor of the local newspaper and calls for public forums, demand more public safety than any court or law-enforcement agency can deliver. Moreover, community members often express the expectation that criminal justice agencies will respond effectively to all public-safety issues.

The Title 33 team participated in two, two-day training programs, both focused on forming alliances across agencies and developing an appreciation for the persons returning home from a term of incarceration for a sex offense. The training programs seem not to have changed anyone's perceptions. As a consequence, team members' values and attitudes truly undermined the program. The Title 33 problem solving court had no opportunity to survive because service providers and criminal justice personnel strongly resisted any community-based treatment for ex–sex offenders.

Communities affected by high rates of crime, recidivism, or incarceration are justifiably (or not) fearful of crime and its consequences. Residents are likely to perceive themselves as potential victims of violent or property crime. They become concerned about safety for themselves and for others, especially their partners and children, in their neighborhoods (Cates, Dian, and Schnepf 2003; Chadee and Ditton 2003; Roh and Oliver 2005; Walklate and Mythen 2008; Wiles, Simmons, and Pease 2003). This community was not prepared to launch a problem solving court for sex offenders. Other states (e.g., New York) have implemented highly successful programs to model. Public sentiment, nonetheless, must be considered for a PSC program to succeed. In this case, the sentiments expressed by representatives from therapeutic and criminal justice agencies were negative, and their strong resistance to the program prohibited its implementation. It would be impossible to hope for a tolerant sentiment on the part of the general population for the Title 33 PSC. What does this attempt and failure illustrate? It shows that public and professional attitudes regarding the problem that the problem solving court attempts to address are critical. Until the community and its criminal justice system are educated and prepared to address the sex-offender problem without misinformed attributions, stereotypes, and ignorance, no PSC program should be designed or implemented. The issues and the consequences, for the participants and for the community, are too serious to ignore. What can this community hope for as a result of this failed program? It can count on "business as usual." The moral panic about sex offenders, like other moral panics, will subside in time (Kruttschnitt, Gartner, and Hussemann 2008). Of course, then we will not need a sex-offender reentry court to increase perceptions of public safety and the quality of life for the community and all its residents.

8

Words, Words, Words

Distinctions and Differences

*Jeralyn Long Faris, JoAnn Miller, and
the Hon. Donald C. Johnson*

THE IMPORTANCE OF BEING DIFFERENT

While attending a state judicial conference meeting held to promulgate standard rules for implementing and sustaining problem solving courts, we were handed a list of "problem solving courts" in operation across the state. Because we had visited many of these court programs to learn what they do and how they run, we were anything but surprised when a Tower of Babel problem emerged as six state court judges engaged in six different forms of judge-talk. While one judge discussed his "specialty court," another complained about the hundreds of "offenders" for whom he is responsible. Yet another spoke about the problem of getting nonprofit agencies to the table for the purpose of delivering comprehensive services to the seriously mentally ill within the community. A staff attorney for the judicial conference kept asking what the state's definition of a problem solving court should be? In a discussion of supposed rules for problem solving courts, no social actor could understand the others. The distinct jargons used to discuss issues characteristic of compliance, drug, and problem solving courts made it impossible for one judge to understand what fellow judges were saying.

It is important to differentiate between compliance courts, drug courts, and problem solving courts. According to the National Drug Court Institute, there are at least fourteen distinct types of problem solving courts and no fewer than twenty-five hundred unique problem solving courts operating within U.S. state court systems, a claim the more contemporary Center for Court Innovation would not dispute. It is likely that the only common feature among the PSC types and the separate court programs is the use of some version of behavior modification, or carrots and consequences (Birgden 2004), to motivate

119

participants, elicit desired behavior, and discourage substance abuse or crime (Bozza 2007). Some problem solving courts will pass out movie tickets or impose work crew, a reward-and-punishment scheme that brings Pavlov's dogs and classical conditioning to mind. The more comprehensive courts will order a person to a cognitive-behavior class or therapy program and offer rewards and consequences mostly in the form of judicial praise and criticism.

Differences in problem solving courts are valuable. Without them, communities would be faced with a one-size-fits-all model that can only fail (over and over again). If a person with no prior criminal history is arrested for a relatively minor marijuana-possession offense, it would be a grave error to place the first-time offender in a diversion program that could provoke subsequent criminal behavior (Bernburg, Krohn, and Rivera 2006). Likewise, if a convicted offender commits a large number of nuisance crimes, such as loitering or public intoxication, because he or she is chronically homeless and mentally ill, it makes little sense to place the offender in a court program that lacks the necessary intervention and supportive services, such as therapy and housing, necessary to prevent repeated crimes.

Without making explicit the relevant distinctions among types of courts, appropriate judicial programs cannot be designed, and evaluations of ongoing programs can quickly blow up because the wrong questions are being asked. Expectations regarding the process, output, and outcome of court programs can only be specified when the researcher or judicial officer responsible for the program knows what constitutes a success or a failure, based on the mission and the purpose of the court program (Gottfredson and Exum 2002; Hartford, Carey, and Mendonca 2007; Burton 2006).

COMPLIANCE COURTS

In some important ways, compliance courts, or court-compliance programs, have the longest history across the states. Lawrence Sherman (2000), known for his innovative criminal justice solutions to numerous social problems, called for the expanded use of compliance courts to respond to the dramatic consequences of the surge in incarceration related to increasingly punitive responses to crime and deviance. Diversion programs, designed to prevent incarceration of accused youth or adults with serious behavior problems, can be compliance court programs: follow the court's orders, attend an anger-management program, for example, and avoid a criminal conviction or a criminal sanction (Butzin, Saum, and Scarpitti 2002; Redlich, Steadman, Monahan, et al. 2006; Weisz, Lott, and Thai 2002).

Modeling successful compliance programs, domestic violence and family court programs, especially those concerned with a parent's complying with visitation orders or counseling sessions prior to a divorce hearing, emerged long before the drug court movement took hold in the United States (Maxwell 2000; Sherman 2000; Tsai 2000). The compliance court approach to domestic violence tells the batterer to comply with the judge's order to complete a batterer's program, return to court to show proof of completion, and avoid subsequent court intervention (Gondolf 2000). A teen court, focused on responding to school truancy and dropout rates, orders the juvenile to attend school daily, attend remedial education classes, and avoid certain types of classmates. Even some contemporary drug and prisoner reentry courts are, by definition, compliance courts. A drug or reentry court that depends almost exclusively on the participant's following the judge's orders and appearing in court merely to show proof is a compliance court. The court may use urine screens to ensure abstinence from alcohol and drug use, but the program remains a single-dimensional compliance court.

DRUG COURTS

The generic drug court phenomenon swept the United States (and other nations) with the support of government dollars and the promise of a solution to the widespread substance-abuse problem. By 1980 it was apparent that something different needed to be done: mandatory minimum sentences did not deter drug offenders, and voluntary treatment programs did not seem effective for or available to a large number of self-defined addicts. The states witnessed dramatic failures when relying upon police and prosecutorial practices to diminish drug abuse. The 1973 Rockefeller drug laws (Spunt 2003) are merely an extreme example of failed attempts by the legislative and executive branches of government to ameliorate a widespread and persistent social problem. The infamous War on Drugs did more to increase than decrease the drug problem throughout the United States (Campbell 2005; Corva 2008; Martin et al. 2004; Saxe et al. 2006; Wermuth 2000; White 2002).

In 1989, a drug court was initiated in Miami–Dade County, Florida, setting the stage for the emergence of the drug court movement throughout the state courts. With Attorney General Janet Reno's support, a federal office responsible for funding pilot and implementation projects was established. A national association of drug court professionals held annual meetings, which often took on the characteristics of theatrical performances (Nolan 2001, 2003). Trial court judges had access to training sessions and online documents, and many quickly memorized the ten key components of reputedly successful drug courts (Bureau of Justice Assistance 1997, 2004).[1]

All this activity took place before an evaluation research literature was produced to demonstrate that the drug court was an effective and efficient method for responding to convicted substance abusers within local communities (Goldkamp, White, and Robinson 2001; Gottfredson and Exum 2002; Listwan et al. 2003). In general, early studies of drug courts produced mixed results: some programs worked to prevent recidivism while others did not. Relapse was as common among drug court participants as it was among alcohol- or drug-treatment populations. Although some outcome studies could show effectiveness, many struggled to identify what accounted for success or failure. The Tower of Babel emerged: Which output or outcome measures matter in determining if a drug court is effective? How can we know without an experimental research literature (Sherman 2000)? Only the more recent studies specify the characteristics, or key independent variables, that account for favorable outcomes (Bouffard and Smith 2005; Krebs et al. 2007; Wolfe et al. 2004). The best studies are based on at least a quasi-experimental design for the purpose of determining the cause-and-effect relationship (Banks and Gottfredson 2004; Broner, Mayrl, and Landsberg 2005; Marlowe 2006; Rodriguez and Webb 2004). Nonetheless, three clusters of questions remain and invite empirical inquiry.

1. Is the judge-participant relationship the most important feature of the drug court? Is the traditional judicial role compromised (Mount 2007)?
2. Do random drug tests really work? How important is the substance-abuse-treatment component of the court program (Banks and Gottfredson 2003)?
3. Will drug court participants stay sober and lead law-abiding lives once they graduate from drug court (Alemi, Haack, and Nemes 2004)?

PROBLEM SOLVING COURTS

Whereas the U.S. Department of Justice spent $50 million annually to support the planning and implementation of drug courts, thanks in part to the newsworthiness of the 1989 Miami drug court (Belenko 2002) and in part to the federal dollars spent on drug courts, new problem solving courts, whether focused on substance abusers, the seriously mentally ill within the community, or prisoner reentry, tend nowadays to rely on local government funds and participant fees to sustain programs. Contrary to the judicial conference discussion we mentioned earlier, a prevailing definition of "problem solving courts" is used. It can apply to comprehensive drug, prisoner reentry, domestic violence, family, mental-health, and community courts:

> Problem solving courts address the individual participant's and the community's problems simultaneously. They are judge-run programs, in general-jurisdiction courts, that facilitate long-term behavioral and attitudinal change among participants and their communities. Each participant's unique circumstances are addressed, and the court's response is comprehensive. The purpose of the problem solving court is to reduce the probability of repeated criminal acts among those who have been arrested or convicted, thus increasing public safety and the quality of life for all residents within their communities.

Five key characteristics (unlike the ten characteristics used to identify drug courts) define, distinguish, and drive the problem solving court (Berman and Feinblatt 2005). First, problem solving courts take a tailored approach to justice: small is better. Each participant receives all the resources he or she needs. This is in stark contrast to adopting an "uncrowd the jail or prison" model that marches all defendants or participants through a compliance court. The tailored approach to justice is analogous to selective incapacitation. Based on the earliest cohort studies, especially the famous Philadelphia study, social scientists know full well that a small number of highly productive offenders is responsible for the overwhelming majority of criminal events that affect a neighborhood or city (Auerhahn 2004; Bernard and Ritti 1991). To reduce crime, it is most effective to identify and incapacitate the worst offenders.[2] Likewise, in a problem solving court, it is most effective and most efficient to identify the small number of persons in a community who will likely be responsible for a disproportionate share of crime and deliver the services of a problem solving court to them.[3]

Second, creative partnerships deliver the resources a participant and community need. A good problem solving court judge is resolute in getting nonprofit organizations and public agencies to the table. The PSC is a blended social organization that works to deliver services that can bring about long-term personal and social change. The PSC, nonetheless, is a court and not a housing agency, a mental-health provider, or a college. Community agencies and organizations, of course, benefit because many of their clients come from court systems. Partnerships between police agencies, the prosecution, and the public defender's office emerge as the problem solving court is implemented[4] in order to ensure public safety and participant success. Criminal justice system partnerships must be connected with networks of community agencies by the PSC leader.

Third, while following governmental and other regulations that ensure the confidentiality of medical and patient records, problem solving courts engage in informed decision making. The defense attorney, for example, may encourage her client to disclose medical or psychological records to make the most complete information known for the purpose of responding to all the participant's needs. Likewise, if the problem solving court is addressing substance addiction, it is imperative for the court to learn the etiology and best treatment options for those addicted to alcohol, cocaine, or heroin. Knowing what causes the problem and how to respond to it further requires the decision maker to know what is within the community and what is affordable to the participant for the purpose of addressing the specific problem.

The fourth characteristic of a problem solving court is accountability. Judges and courts can hold problem solving court participants accountable by continuous and consistent judicial monitoring. A problem solving court must hold frequent (weekly) court sessions to deliver accountability. The community is comfortable with a problem solving court for prison reentry or for convicted drug abusers if accountability is communicated to the general population. The participant, likewise, relies on accountability to learn how to build strengths and avoid habits, behaviors, and social relationships that tend to result in criminality, deviant behavior, or substance abuse. Effective problem solving court judges hold service providers accountable for delivering the programs they bring to the table for participants. What is the judge supposed to do, to protect public safety, if he finds that scheduled drug-abuse treatment was not delivered because the provider, in a climate of new privatization (Jurik 2004), refused to see a participant until prior bills were paid in full? Program service providers are no less accountable than participants in the problem solving court.

A focus on results is the fifth characteristic that distinguishes a problem solving court. A compliance court may satisfy the auditor who counts the number of persons served by a "drink-counting class" that teaches persons how to avoid the .08 alcohol-blood level that designates the legal limit for driving after drinking. Suppose ten persons have a DUI charge; they are all sent to the drink-counting class and then show proof that they completed the class. This type of information is not even relevant to the problem solving court that asks the basic question, Did it work? Did the class prevent the person from driving under the influence? A results-focused program demands empirical data at two levels of analysis. Data on each individual participant and how he or she progresses in the PSC program and maintains a crime-free life after graduating are imperative. No less important is an empirical comparison between groups of participants and groups of similar offenders not in the PSC program. Do reentry problem solving court participants, as a group, tend to avoid subsequent crime or relapse for a longer period compared to a similar group of persons released from prison but not enrolled in the reentry court?

The five characteristics of problem solving courts—a tailored approach to justice, creative partnerships, informed decision making, accountability, and a focus on results—were not created in a social and political vacuum. They emerged from lessons learned from the drug courts and the drug court studies that examined the evidence. The key problem solving court characteristics imply that evidence-based practice principles must be followed in the court program for it to succeed (Osher and Steadman 2007; Wild 2006).

Like the drug court movement, the problem solving courts represent a judge-initiated sociolegal movement. It is not the state legislature or the citizenry that thinks a particular jurisdiction needs a reentry or mental-health court. From the bench, the judge is well positioned to see who comes into court, over and over again over a period of years, and who becomes a repeat player, or a "frequent flyer," in the criminal justice system. It is the judge who demands that the door stop revolving (Fulton Hora 2002; Kushel et al. 2005) by initiating a problem solving court program. Because the sociolegal movement is judge led, there are problems associated with sustainability, or institutionalization. If a court system includes ten judicial officers, for example, and only two subscribe to the benefits of problem solving courts, the movement will not grow to address the most pressing social problems within a contemporary community. Moreover, if the two proponents retire and no newly appointed judge dares to challenge the conventional role of the general-jurisdiction trial judge, the PSC programs cannot be sustained. Simply put, the problem solving court movement depends on judges to initiate and implement programs and on the judiciary to foster them. Judges are individuals who may be more or less suited to a set of activities and responsibilities. The judiciary, however, is a social institution that can sustain programs and positions for purpose of maintaining justice and a quality of life in the community that social actors alone cannot deliver.

REENTRY COURTS: A TYPE OF PROBLEM SOLVING COURT

The purpose of a reentry problem solving court is to facilitate a participant's role-status change from "felon" to "contributing member of society," thereby preventing crime, or recidivistic behavior, among men and women who return from a term of incarceration to their home communities. Generally, they exist in various forms throughout the United States for four reasons. First, the drug problem in the United States, regardless of the effectiveness of the drug courts and the drug court movement, persists and results in high rates of incarceration (Bourgois 2003; Fulton Hora 2004). Dependent persons need substance-abuse treatment; yet, that is only one of multiple needs. The typical

drug court is not equipped to respond comprehensively to financial, housing, health care, educational, employment, and family needs within a community. Drug-dependent persons can drift into poverty, often at a young
age, and fail to develop the constellation of social skills or human capital
required to succeed as independent adults (Bourgois et al. 2006; Tenorio
and Hernandez 2005).

Second, the surge in incarceration that imprisoned the men and women
now returning home mandates the comprehensive response from the problem
solving drug courts, not compliance courts (Oliver 2008). Arrest, prosecution,
and imprisonment affect social groups throughout the United States differently. The populations most likely to experience high arrest rates are those
most physically and socially visible to the police and to the sentencing judges
(Cyrus 2007; Izenman 2003; Ulmer and Kramer 1998). While incarcerated,
many abusers can continue using and trading drugs (Kassebaum and Chandler 1994; Plourde and Brochu 2002; Shearer et al. 2006). A reentry court
judge should ask two related questions of all new participants: How long did
you use? How long have you been clean? It is not uncommon for a reentry
court participant to indicate that clean time is considerably less than the time
spent incarcerated.

Third, reentry courts proliferate as state sentencing laws and practices
change (Bjerk 2005; Diederich 1999; Engen and Steen 2000; Frase 2005;
Griset 2002; Helland and Tabarrok 2007; Roberts 2003; Sorensen and Stemen 2002). In a number of states, once the general population and legislatures
realized that drug abusers faced longer sentences than those convicted of
manslaughter in a number of jurisdictions, persons incarcerated as the War on
Drugs escalated were automatically eligible for a sentence-modification hearing. As the rule of law changed, so did the practice of imprisoning a person
for a protracted period. Three-strikes laws and mandatory-sentencing laws
are key examples of the legislatively created need to correct decisions once
based on the law itself. As persons were resentenced, the need for reentry
courts became apparent.

Finally, and perhaps most importantly, reentry problem solving courts
emerged as social scientists and the judiciary came to understand, theoreti-
cally and empirically, that crime and substance-abuse problems are highly
correlated with a host of additional social problems. Problems with behavioral
health, education, unemployment, poverty, homelessness, and public health,
as well as family problems, are the key factors that tend to co-occur with
substance abuse or addiction (Barnett and Mencken 2002; Freudenberg 2001;
Oh 2005; Room 2005; Wenzel et al. 2001; Wolf and Colyer 2001). It takes
more than a reentry program—without the authority of the court—which
focuses on a single dimension, such as unemployment or income, to respond

effectively to a population of prison inmates returning home. The quasi-experimental and powerful Transitional Aid to Released Prisoner studies, the earliest scientific studies on reentry and recidivism, found that a complex pattern of factors led released property offenders to recidivate (Rossi, Berk, and Lenihan 1980). Unemployment payments or weekly living stipends did little to prevent repeated criminal acts.

Today's reentry problem solving court cannot rely on housing, work, or substance-abuse treatment alone to prevent recidivism. It must deliver a unique package of services and programs that a unique individual needs to gain or regain the tools necessary to succeed as an independent adult within a unique community (Birgden 2002; Ward and Brown 2004).

POLICIES AND PROCEDURES FOR REENTRY COURTS

A typical reentry court subscribes to the five key principles of problem solving courts. Typically, it begins by formulating policies and procedures to admit participants and direct them through the maze of necessary services to reduce the likelihood of repeated crime. It decides on measurement tools to assess needs as participants enter programs and to examine the progress or success a participant experiences throughout a twelve- or eighteen-month program. It creates policies on admitting participants. Should all returning inmates go through a transitional type of reentry court program, or should the program focus on high-risk offenders or those with specialized or high levels of needs? Although the small-is-better approach is always preferable, some jurisdictions insist on putting all persons returning from prison into some form of community transition—a prisoner reentry program.

Policies and procedures specify how participants will be monitored and supervised within the community and what sanctions or punishments can be imposed for violation of program regulations. The reentry court judge uses the influence of the bench to aggressively pursue an interdisciplinary team of experts in criminal justice and the community who agree to meet regularly to discuss participants' and their needs. Law enforcement is an especially important part of the team. Not only do police officers influence participants, but they provide reassurance to the general population that the reentry program is increasing public safety within the community. Service providers in the community tend to approach a successful reentry problem solving court to offer what they deliver—and to ensure a steady stream of clients for their organization.

A regularly scheduled, preferably weekly, reentry court session is held in a public courtroom. The session's length and who appears before the judge are functions of the program's size, the participants' needs, and the judge's willingness to engage in meaningful dialogue with participants. The court sessions are also used to impose consequences for persons who violated regulations and to reward persons who engage in the transformative process of becoming a contributing citizen within society. All told, problem solving is the court program's key activity. The participant's problems are addressed as the court works to respond to the most pressing problems within the larger community.

AN EMPIRICAL EXAMPLE

Unlike compliance courts, problem solving courts address simultaneously many or all of the issues that social scientists show reduce the risk of repeated crime, deviant behavior, and substance abuse (Bozza 2007; Cho 2005; Grudzinskas et al. 2005; Rivera 2008; Terry 2004). Described and analyzed here is a three-year-old reentry court that works on three major principles of evidence-based practices (Friedmann, Taxman, and Henderson 2007; Henderson, Taxman, and Young 2008). First, the reentry court program is designed to treat persons returning from state prison who face the highest risk of repeated crime or recidivism. Persons incarcerated for serious drug abuse or showing symptoms of a serious mental illness are preferred. Second, only those intervention programs that have been studied by other researchers and found to be effective are implemented. Third, the participants and the reentry program are continuously evaluated to ensure program effectiveness and efficiency.

In the reentry court, a cluster of programs—substance-abuse treatment, cognitive behavioral therapy, education and employment assistance, and housing services—are delivered to the participants. The exact mix of programs, or the treatment, and the intensity of the treatment, or the "dosage," are determined by administering two structured instruments, the Level of Services Inventory (LSI) and the Addiction Severity Index (ASI). Progress in the reentry court program is measured by readministering the instruments.

Those interested in reentry petition the court for a sentence modification. The preferred and typical participant has been incarcerated for two years or longer and has two or more years left to serve at the time of the application for reentry court. Potential participants are brought to the attention of the prosecutor, who may object to an early release from prison.

New participants live in work release while completing requirements for Community Transition Week (CTW). During CTW, participants register to vote because empirical study shows that participating in the political process reduces recidivism as it increases a person's stakes in conventional society (Manza and Uggen 2006). Based on an initial case plan, the participant is responsible for initiating all required treatment programs and applying for entitlements, such as food stamps and Medicaid. Before leaving work release, a participant must hold a job for a minimum of thirty days.

A participant's progress is monitored weekly by a case manager who is responsible only for reentry participants. The case manager schedules drug and alcohol tests and reports each participant's progress or setbacks to the reentry team each week. The reentry team convenes and meets with the presiding judge for a staffing meeting on Mondays at 8:00 a.m. Team members include representatives from police agencies, probation, and the prosecutor's and public defender's offices, as well as treatment providers, employers, and education and housing personnel. As the meeting concludes, the judge begins a special one-hour court session, during which time individual participants and the judge engage in dialogue to ascertain the need for additional services and the timing for promotion to a more advanced phase of the program. If a participant has violated a reentry court program regulation during the week, the judge imposes a consequence, which might be four hours of work crew for being late for work, an essay on the importance of being organized, or jail time if the infraction is relatively serious (such as getting fired from a job for cause). All reentry participants witness court dialogues and the distribution of rewards and consequences.

What does the reentry problem solving court look like? Asked differently, what happens during the Monday morning courtroom sessions to contribute to the participants' reentry back into the community?

AN OBSERVATIONAL STUDY

Observing the details of events and interactions in the reentry court is important, and researching the participants requires vigorous recognition of the complexity of human social interaction and culture. We make every effort to portray the world of the reentry court from alternate vantage points in this section, which briefly summarizes an observational study.

The objective in researching the reentry problem solving court from an observational perspective is premised on the imperative to understand what it is like to be a participant, to be within the problem solving court scene, using the social actors' own words and stories. We want to observe participants—not be a participant observer (Strauss and Corbin 1990). That is, we attempt "being there" to understand but not to become like the participants or to "go native." The objective is to get close enough, but not too close, to participants' realities in order to view the procedures that they use to create and sustain their sense of reality.

The research intention is to record with as much accuracy as possible the rich textures of the social location of reentry court and to provide a vivid description of the lived experiences of participants. The approach asks the "how" question, aiming to understand how the various social actors in the courtroom produce their realities. Specifically, we attempt to understand how the social order is created through talk and interaction, how participants in reentry court develop the will and the way to live constructive and productive lives (Birgden 2004).

The data presented here were collected using mostly observational methods over a protracted period in various locations, such as community corrections, the court room, and the jury room in which the reentry team meets weekly. Our identities and interests were not disguised in any way for the team or the reentry court participants. A university institutional research board approved the study prior to its commencement. Before notating systematic observations, we participated as team members for eight months.

Persons present in the courtroom during the weekly public reentry problem solving court sessions are the subjects of this study. These subjects can include, but are not limited to, the judge, his staff members and intern, community-corrections case managers, probation officers, public defenders, prosecutors, police officers, social service workers, and other members of the reentry court team. Additionally, participants who are offenders returned to the community from prison, their family members, and others who support them are in the courtroom. All of these social actors are involved in the scene that occurs in the weekly court sessions; therefore, all are included in the observational descriptions. No one in the courtroom during the public court session was purposely omitted from the study.

Members of the reentry court team advise the judge and provide wrap-around services to the participants who need assistance transitioning back into the community. Some members of the reentry team observe and participate in the public court session at approximately 9:00 a.m. every Monday with the formerly incarcerated participants. Social service team members, a program evaluator, and representatives from all criminal justice agencies sit in the jury box. Reentering participants stand behind a podium a few feet in front of the judge's bench as the judge interacts with them individually; their personal supporters remain seated in the gallery behind a railing. The back area of the courtroom is usually flanked by one or two uniformed officers or bailiffs.

During the time of the observational study, public court sessions averaged about an hour and a half. Extensive field notes were taken during these hours, reconstructing the activities and interactions of the persons present in the courtroom in as much detail as possible. Notes were taken openly during the hours of observation, and because the participants and the team members were aware of the observational study, everyone expected to see note-taking activities.

To provide methodological triangulation, additional methods of collecting data were used to achieve a convergence of meaning (Lindloff and Taylor 2002). Brief interviews were conducted before and after the court sessions, focusing on questions that clarified various expressions being used. Written essays, prepared by participants, were collected. The essays, or thought papers, are typically sanctions read aloud by participants to the judge during the problem solving court session. Students attended some of the court sessions, and their written impressions of what occurred in court were included. A transcription of a radio broadcast was obtained; this was a public forum in which one of the reentry court graduates spoke about his experience in the program. The combination of these data-collection methods enables a detailed view of the complexity of the reentry court scene.

The data include hundreds of pages of typewritten field notes, essays written by the program participants, personal observations written by students, court transcripts, and a transcription of the radio broadcast. We used a grounded theory approach, using the constant comparative method (Strauss and Corbin, 1990). As we analyzed the data inductively, we organized them into four categories of social interaction for analytic purposes: (1) giving or receiving support, (2) exercising control over another, (3) demonstrating submission, and (4) voicing personal responsibility or agency. Analytic themes emerged as analysis continued, and the findings are framed with a general dialectical perspective.

THEMES FROM A REENTRY COURT: SUPPORT AND CONTROL

The weekly public courtroom sessions of the reentry problem solving court reinforce the realization that a person's successful transition from prison to the community does not occur in a vacuum. It became clear that a central feature of the reentry court is the contradictory interplay of elements of support and control by members of the reentry court scene. The social interactions that occur in this environment serve dual communicative purposes. The judge and reentry court team members offer support to the participants while providing necessary social control through an accountability structure. Simultaneously, participants receive a venue for giving evidence of their lawful exercise of personal agency and self-control. Thus, we chose to frame the results of this ethnography with a dialectical perspective to focus on "support-versus-control" themes that explain the social interactions of the reentry court scene.

The social support offered to the participants takes three forms: emotional, informational, and tangible (Cohen, Underwood, and Gottlieb 2000; Uchino 2004). Our observations of the activities and interactions in the courtroom provide clear witness to these three forms of support. We also observed the control exercised by others and the self-control exercised by the participants themselves.

Emotional Support

Probably the most important and consistent form of support witnessed in the court sessions is emotional support. The theater aspects of the courtroom scenes are realized regularly as all the social actors in the reentry court celebrate the successes of fellow participants. As men and women progress through the four stages of the reentry problem solving court program, the courtroom is the location of public recognition and congratulation. During the period of observation for this study, some participants were graduated and others promoted to the next phase of the program. Two of the graduates are middle-aged African American men who had entered the program together. Each, dressed up for the occasion—one in a shirt and tie, the other in a sports jacket—was called individually to the podium in front of the judge's bench. In both cases, the judge immediately announced the team's unanimous vote to graduate the men from reentry.

The first man, Kipp, let out a loud cheer as he approached the judge, who had come down from his bench to greet him. With a hearty handshake and a warm smile, the judge handed him a certificate of graduation. Nearly everyone in the courtroom applauded enthusiastically, and the judge instructed Kipp to address the current participants. The graduate spoke of the need to persevere, of the times when he "didn't think he would make it," and of having "put his wife and kids through a lot." He seemed proud of the judge's continual admonishments to "suck it up." The audience laughed in agreement when hearing the familiar phrase.

Kipp stated, "I'm proud of me," and the judge responded, "I'm proud of you, too." As Kipp returned to his seat, he hugged his wife, who was seated with him in the back row of the gallery. Near the end of the court session, she stood and explained how much the program had meant to her. "Thank you!" she said. "My husband changed due to this program. He's the person I fell in love with. He used to be an asshole!" Her comments were greeted with laughter and applause.

The second man to graduate, Kurt,[5] was called forward, and the same ritual unfolded with the judge's greeting and presentation of the certificate and the audience's applause. However, Kurt, a humble man, turned to those seated in the jury box (the team members) and thanked them for their help and support. When the judge asked Kurt if the program had been easy, he replied emphatically, "No! I wanted to play horseshoes, and the judge wanted to play hand grenades!" He was referencing an earlier illustration the judge had used with another participant: "There are different kinds of games where 'close' counts, some misses being more painful than others." The graduate acknowledged that though the program was difficult, he "was treated fairly."

Even during these moments of celebration, references are made to the important aspects of control used to assist the participants in their reentry process. The emotional support demonstrated in these scenes can be viewed as a lauding of the successes achieved from the lessons learned during times when control and accountability were deliberately communicated. The graduates spoke of the times they endured consequences for violating minor program regulations. They expressed pride in communicating dimensions of self-control that they claimed they learned in reentry.

The promotions to the next program phase witnessed during the court sessions observed were similar to the graduations in terms of the rituals enacted, but with a lower degree of celebration. The men and women were called to the podium individually, and in each case, the judge announced that the team had unanimously voted to transition the person to the next phase of the program, meaning visits to the court would be required less frequently. The judge stepped off the bench and approached the open area in the middle of the courtroom, greeting each participant with a smile, a handshake, and a certificate. Usually, the judge said something private that those of us in the courtroom could not overhear. Most members of the courtroom scene applauded in congratulation, and in each case the judge returned to his bench and began a dialogue with the next participant on his list.

The judge asked one participant being promoted, Jack, "Where are you making your greatest progress?" Jack replied, "I feel more confident in caring for my children." The judge had instructed him to write a "one-pager" about plans he was making for the tough job of providing structure for his teenage children during the upcoming summer. He read the following:

This summer I plan to be a very active father to my children's lives. I plan to structure theirs in a way that gives them a well-balanced lifestyle, not to overburden them with responsibility but to incorporate responsibility with leisure time. My son is going to be 17 in June. We just got his learner's permit to drive. This will be one focus of his summer vacation, and along with that he is going to get a part-time job. My daughter is going to go to summer school and participate in a sports program at school. . . . We will spend much of our summer together, planning and cooking meals together, doing household chores together. I will continue to encourage and praise them for a job well done.

At the conclusion of his reading, the judge said, "Let's give him a hand," and members of the courtroom scene joined together in applauding Jack's words. This ritual, played out regularly, is a means of offering emotional support to the participants as they think through and discursively construct the reality of their daily experiences. The emotional support was earned, given in response to the participant's successful reply to the judge's exercise of control. Jack had shown progress in meeting the requirement to put plans in writing for his teenage children's summer activities. In his essay, he communicated his plans to replicate what he learned in the courtroom, that is, to deliver emotional support with a healthy dose of social control for his children.

A radio broadcast addressing the issue of teenage substance abuse was used for this study because a reentry participant, Charles, was a member of a panel of young people speaking at a town forum. An elected state official in the audience asked Charles, "What has been the greatest help for you in reentry?" The important tension between support and control is evident in his response.

I think the greatest thing has been the structure in my life. The reentry court affords me the opportunity to have someone watching over my shoulder at every moment which is something I really needed . . . in my first year of sobriety. You know, I'm kind of volatile and it's the whole thing that I'm powerless over alcohol and drugs and if I don't have somebody . . . just guiding me along and giving me that push that I need. That's an excellent opportunity but also I had caring and supportive people there to back me up. . . . My dad and mom have both been there for me and with me through everything.

Charles's mother died during the time he was enrolled in the program. The judge had released him from home detention, against the advice of the reentry team, to allow him to travel to another county to be with his mother before she died and to attend her funeral. Charles earned more trust and respect from his fellow participants as he was held accountable for returning to the program and as he disclosed the emotional difficulties he experienced, feeling guilty that he had been incarcerated when his family needed him. At the time of his arrest, he was a university student, majoring in mathematics. The reentry court, which encourages education, made it possible for him to return to a community college on full scholarship to complete the associate's degree. He is now reenrolled at the university.

Informational Support

The judge and members of the reentry court team frequently offer the participants informational support. For example, the women were told to go to Planned Parenthood for educational sessions. One participant, Susan, asked if she was required to attend because she had had a tubal ligation and could not get pregnant. The judge informed her that she needed to be aware of and informed about problems other than unwanted pregnancies, such as "STDs that need to be guarded against. Also, Susan, it's a good idea to learn about responsible relationships." We note that the women were not given an option; they were ordered to use this means of educational health support. Once again, we observed support and control meted out simultaneously.

Most of the participants need help with budgeting and financial matters. During one session, Randy was telling the judge that he wanted to attend the local community college in the fall but needed $350. The judge asked, "How do you plan to save the money?" His answer was to use the food pantry. Knowing that this person needed more information and understanding to reach his goal, the judge referred him to a member of the team seated in the jury box who agreed to counsel him on ways to save for school expenses. The judge's control was again evident in that the person was told to seek this counseling; it was not stated as an option.

Information related to "good citizenship" is often provided to the participants. Educational presentations are made during the half hour preceding the court session. Topics include voting, the use of the public library, how to obtain a driver's license, and volunteering in the community. The judge follows up on these presentations by asking the participants specific questions about what they learned or directing them to write a "one-pager" about the learning experience.

In one such situation, a program participant, Ned, came to court with the "one-pager" in hand, and when called to the podium by the judge, he read the essay. The lengthy report to the court explained how to register to vote and detailed the locations for voting in the upcoming primary elections. The judge and the reentry court team directly controlled and monitored the participant's actions in this informational and educational activity. Participants demonstrate accountability for the informational support they receive by writing and reading essays in the public courtroom or by being prepared to answer questions about their learning experiences.

At times, informational support takes the form of explaining the evidence-based practices used by the reentry court team. The judge explains that the team expects to see ASI scores drop as the tests are administered periodically. When Carter's scores were not changing, the judge entered into a discussion with him: "The scores haven't changed, but I know you're not the same person." He went on to explain that the tests indicate the risk level for substance abuse. However, Carter needed to retake the test so that the scores could be checked because "something could be wrong here" in how the last test was administered. The judge then ordered the community-corrections case manager to have a different person administer the test to the participant. In this situation, the judge exercised control over the community-corrections workers. They are held accountable for reporting test results to the team and meeting the demands placed on them by the team and the judge.

One aspect of support that can be seen as both emotional and informational is the required attendance at twelve-step meetings, either Alcoholics Anonymous (AA) or Narcotics Anonymous (NA). Although no reentry team member attends meetings or attempts to achieve disclosures from sponsors, careful meeting-attendance records are kept. The judge questioned a participant, Marlon, about his meetings: "Are you doing your ninety meetings in ninety days?" Marlon acknowledged the requirement and said, "Yes, your honor, I am attending the meetings at [a local meeting site]." The judge then asked, "Do you have a permanent sponsor?" "No, sir, I'm working on that." The judge continued the conversation by asking, "What step are you on?" When the recovering addict responded that he was on step two, the judge asked him to explain what that step means in the AA twelve-step program. Unsatisfied with the answer he received, the judge then instructed Marlon to come back with a "one-pager" next week with a better explanation.

Charles, who spoke at the broadcasted town forum, attested to the value of the support he received at the required meetings:

> There've been many wonderful mentors who have had many years of sobriety that have showed me the way of how I have to live in society and, you know, just to kind of immerse me in the whole recovery culture and society gave me an opportunity to stand on my feet and just get a little grounding before I had to face the world and all it temptations.

In the required AA/NA meetings and individual meetings with sponsors (who are recovering addicts), the participants receive informational and emotional support. The reentry court team and the judge exercise control by making sure the participants access this means of support.

Other programs within reentry offer both informational and emotional support. Dads Make a Difference, the Matrix Model for drug-abuse treatment, and Thinking for a Change are structured programs offered through local mental-health and family service agencies with representatives serving on the reentry team. A mental-health counselor is usually seated in the jury box and often referenced by the judge. For example, the judge asked one young woman, Caroline, a new participant in the program, if the Matrix program was helping her "focus on relationships." "Yes," she replied, "relationships with others and myself. It's a lot of emotional work, and it helps to talk to [the mental-health counselor seated in the jury box]. I've had treatment for depression in the past."

The judge then asked what her drug of choice had been; she explained that she began using cocaine after her daughter was born, and "it destroyed my life."[6] In a follow-up question, the judge asked, "How do you protect yourself from your old friends, the cocaine users, and at the same time develop new and pro-social relationships with others?" She answered, "I have to be proud of myself and vocal," indicating that she plans to accomplish that goal by starting school and registering for fall classes at the local community college. The conversation concluded as she agreed with the judge that she feels a tremendous amount of guilt and struggles with feelings of unworthiness. The informational and emotional support afforded by the mental-health and family service programs has obvious benefits. The reentry court's control and accountability structure in requiring participants to access these services is also clear.

Tangible Support

The provision of tangible support is integral to reentry participants, most of whom have returned from prison with no job prospects, no permanent living arrangement, and a lot of financial debt. The judge, team members, and even fellow reentry court participants help individuals find jobs and move into apartments. The judge explains the ABC (any job, better job, career job) program to new participants. Several members in the courtroom we observed were eager to help the new participants find "A" jobs. One of the more veteran members of the program, for example, assisted two new members by talking to his boss at McDonald's about their applications. One participant had been job hunting for over three weeks and was on the verge of being sent back to prison, but more senior participants helped him get an A job at Wendy's.

Court discussions center on the difficulty of getting a job when a person has a felony conviction and how it is necessary to depend on others for support in gaining full-time employment. However, it is important to note that the judge and the team exercise control by insisting that participants find work quickly, expecting that they will find A jobs. The threat of a return trip to prison is used whenever a participant claims, "I can't find a job. I'm trying, but I just can't get hired." The judge typically says, "You cannot be a good citizen if you do not work. You must get a job to stay out of prison."

When deemed ready by the reentry court team and judge, participants are allowed to seek a "B" job that will require more responsibility. The control message is crystal clear. The judge instructs a participant to give two weeks' notice when a better job has been found. When one young woman told the judge she did not like the environment at the restaurant where she was working, he gave her permission to look for another job with the caveat that she had to give her present employer two weeks' notice. In another instance, the judge began his courtroom conversation with Albert by asking, "What's going on with your job?" Albert reported having a third-shift job at a local meat-butchering plant. The judge asked, "Do you think this is a B job?" Albert replied, "Definitely." The judge followed up by asking, "What do you like most about the job?" The participant replied, "It has good hours, pay, benefits, and I'm able to carpool." A fellow participant helped Albert get his job, and he in turn helped others get jobs at the same plant.

A "career" job is a goal for all reentry court participants. It is not a requirement for graduation from the program, but the judge and members of the team work continuously to give direction and assistance so that participants at least have a future expectation of a "C" job. The judge reported to the participants that "someone from [a local manufacturer] will be here to talk about how the jobs program will work for those who can get hired for factory jobs." He went on to explain that the participants chosen for employment "will be watched to see who they are associating with during breaks and lunch" and warned the participants to "be careful." This discussion is an example of how the reentry court offers support in preparation for "career" employment that can enable participants to become "productive members of society" (a commonly used phrase in the reentry court). However, it also illustrates the control that the court has over the participants who benefit from such employment.

Housing is the second form of tangible support made available to all reentry participants. Once employed, each person is moved from work release to home detention and an apartment with rent subsidized by a tenant-based rental-assistance program. The initial rent payment is determined by income and remains fixed for one year to encourage each participant to pay down bills. The tangible support is worth thousands of dollars, and the deliberate tension between support and control is clear.

The judge often asks new participants, "How are things going at work release?" One participant, Bob, echoed the replies of predecessors: "I'll be glad to be out of there." The judge then said, "It's time to move you to an apartment." A reentry court team volunteer entered the conversation and offered to help Bob move. Although in his own place, Bob faces a highly structured living environment that involves curfews, home detention, and unannounced visits by surveillance officers who check out the condition and cleanliness of the apartment.

One young mother, Audrey, had demonstrated stability and responsibility in her job and her living arrangement at the halfway house. The judge told her to "talk with the housing guy here" because "it is time for you to be out of there [the halfway house] and in your own place." The housing support is clear, but also evident is the control and accountability that the court program retains as it delivers tangible support.

Other means of tangible support include health-related assistance such as dental care. The judge asked Joe, "How are your teeth?" He quizzed the man about his use of methamphetamines and what effect the drugs had on his teeth. Although the man spoke with a whistle because of missing teeth, he expressed thanks to the judge for requiring him to undergo the weeks of free dental care that the team arranged. He did not receive the support for his dental care voluntarily but eventually appreciated the judge's insistence on it.

In some reentry court sessions, forms of support are far less obvious than mechanisms of control. During one session, as we entered the courtroom following a team meeting, we noticed immediately the unusual presence of four uniformed officers. By the end of the session, three women had been put in handcuffs and ankle shackles. One at a time, they stood before the judge. One woman who could or would not account for a diluted drug screen was told she was going to jail where she would be given a polygraph. A second woman had been reported as "complaining and whining about the requirements of the program" at some of the meetings and programs she was attending. The judge told her, "We can't have that. I'm sending you to the jail for a week. I'll see you next Monday. Keep a journal of what you are learning." The young woman began crying as the officers cuffed her. The third woman was asked, "Are you engaged in the program?" When she answered the judge with a firm yes, he explained, "The team feels you are not engaged. You might not make it because you are not focused. You are going to jail for a week. Keep a journal."

The three women were seated by the officers in the back corner of the courtroom, across from the other participants and behind the table where the case manager from community corrections was seated. Later during the session, Dan, who has been in Phase 1 longer than most of the reentering participants, addressed the women. While responding to the judge's queries about his times of "hitting the wall" in the program, Dan said, "Like the girls in the back, I want them to know that I've been there [in shackles] three times." The judge then stated that there had been many graduates from the program, and he asked the program evaluator, seated in the jury box, what that meant. She keeps quantitative data for the court and explained that "one year was the average time in the program for the graduates, and none of them have been in trouble with the law." She then addressed the women in the back and asked, "Are you getting discouraged? Think about it. It's well worth your effort. Stick to it."

The ultimate sense of being controlled and losing all autonomy obviously affected the women, who demonstrated indicators of sadness and frustration. If they heard the words of the other participants and the program evaluator, they knew they had an opportunity to start again. From a different perspective, team members understand that they and the judge exercise control to fulfill the responsibility to protect and support the larger community and all the reentry court participants.

The Dialectical Relationship between Support and Control

These data suggest that the events of the reentry court involve negotiating dialectical tensions in the individuals' lives. Indeed, the Monday morning court sessions can be conceptualized as a time in which participants are pulled in multiple and often conflicting directions as they confront what they want and what they need to do while they search for structure and meaning. Drawing from research on dialectical tensions (Baxter 1990, 1992; Baxter and Montgomery 1996, 1997, 1998), we respond to the assertion that "the social scientific enterprise needs to focus more concertedly on the complexity and disorder of social life, not with the goal of 'smoothing out' its rough edges, but with a goal of understanding its fundamental ongoing messiness" (Baxter and Montgomery 1998, 3).

The fundamental assumption in a dialectical analysis is that social life is a dynamic knowledge of contradictions, a ceaseless interplay between contrary or opposing tendencies (Baxter and Montgomery 1996). Further, social life exists in and through the communicative practices in individuals' lives, and people give voice to the opposing tendencies by relating to others. In observations of reentry court, the fact that members of the team are in the courtroom scene both to control the actions and activities of participants and to provide emotional, informational, and tangible forms of support is an example of a dialectical tension. Participants return to the courtroom knowing that they must demonstrate an appropriate level of submission, but they also may exercise personal agency, grow in self-control, and earn access to the community as productive members of society.

The tension between support and control in the reentry court is not an issue or problem to resolve. Rather, it is an ongoing reality that participants in the courtroom scene encounter and that may either present exciting challenges or be somewhat depressing. Graduates of the program return monthly and praise the benefits of the highly structured and controlling program, claiming it is necessary for success in making the transition from prison to the community.

On the other hand, a participant may have a difficult time when he or she "hits the wall" and experiences consequences for rule violations. At these times, the participants may become discouraged and start wondering if they made the right decision in opting to enter the program rather than completing their sentence behind prison walls.

The dialectical tension of support and control should be addressed with a process of critical self-reflection, not only for the reentering ex-prisoners but for all members of the reentry court team. Every social actor has agency, or personal autonomy, yet is controlled. In reentry court, participants are controlled by members of the team and the judge. Team members are controlled by their employers. A process of critical self-reflection, for all persons associated with the reentry court, is useful for dealing with issues that are seemingly at odds with one another.

III

PERFORMANCES AND TRANSFORMATIONS

9

Transforming Master Status

FELON: A MASTER STATUS

A woman in her mid-twenties, Monica, sits cuffed at the defense table in a courtroom. A month ago, she pled guilty to an A-level felony for dealing cocaine too close to an elementary school. Today, she can hear her own heart beat, and she knows the impossibility of relieving her fear. While she tries to comprehend fully the meaning of the criminal sentence she hears pronounced, it is too complicated. The judge has ordered her to serve some prison time and recommends that she enter a treatment program, followed by some community-corrections time, some term of probation, and a series of other requirements. As the judge details the split sentence, she can concentrate only on the reality that she will spend the next six years of her life in state prison, apart from her two children (who will take care of them?) and exiled from her friends and community. Her master status, that perception she holds of who she really is and the same perception that social actors attribute to her, could have been "mother" or "woman." Once she was caught dealing cocaine, everything changed. And now the sentencing judge has conferred on her a new master status: felon (Brownfield, Sorenson, and Thompson 2001; Frable 1993; Frable, Blackstone, and Scherbaum 1990; Hiller 1982; Huffine and Clausen 1979; Stiles and Kaplan 1996).

She knows she will someday return to her children and her community, to her family and friends. Will she always bear the master status of "felon?" Because she is in a state that returns her right to vote once she is released from prison, she could become a "citizen" again by registering to vote and doing volunteer work. She worries, however, that she may never get a job that pays her enough to care for herself and her children. Worse yet, she knows that her mother is unlikely to care for her children for more than a few months. They could get adopted. As Monica is escorted out of the courtroom by the bailiff, thoughts of returning to her hometown, of reentering society, make her wonder what life will be like then. What will change?

Shakespeare's Sonnet 121 claims it is not as horrible to be bad as it is to be labeled or considered bad by others:

> 'Tis better to be vile than vile esteemed,
> When not to be receives reproach of being,
> And the just pleasure lost, which is so deemed,
> Not by our feeling, but by other's seeing.
> For why should others' false adulterate eyes
> Give salutation to my sportive blood?

Contemporarily, social science and legal scholars speak of the master status attached to the felon, the discrediting attribution that makes everything difficult: getting a job, finding a safe place to live, feeling the respect of family and friends. Scholars document the difficulty of shedding the negative master status—deviant, felon, sex offender, criminal—due to a labeling perspective that posits that a negative attribution or stigma leads to secondary deviance, or behaviors that correspond to the negative label (Arneson 2007; Bernburg, Krohn, and Rivera 2006; Haldane 2008; Siennick 2007; Stiles and Kaplan 1996; West 2005).

OPPORTUNITIES TO DIMINISH THE CONSEQUENCES OF THE FELON STATUS

All convicted offenders, even if diverted from prison, and prisoners are labeled and stigmatized. The stigma may not be physically visible, evidenced, as in the past, by the old-fashioned, striped prison uniform, but it is socially visible to the employer or the landlord who asks about criminal history and to the extended family who must explain the absence of a person incarcerated.

Reentry of a stigmatized population is the inevitable consequence of incarceration. "With the exception of those who die of natural consequences or are executed, everyone placed in confinement is eventually released. Reentry is not an option" (Travis 2005). They all come home. Left unasked is the important question, How do persons return home, shed a stigmatized master status, and stay home for good—to do good for themselves, their families, and their communities? How can the person with a pejorative master status, if she cannot shed it, at least bracket it and to do good for the community?

Prisoner reentry programs, especially those focused on convicted drug offenders or those with mental-health problems, can take restorative approaches focusing on the positive contributions persons can make within communities and, as a result, reduce the likelihood of repeated or new criminal behavior that results in police contacts, arrests, or a return to prison (Maruna and LeBel 2003). Basically, a well-designed and -implemented reentry program, regardless of whether it is supported by a court, focuses on facilitating a positive future vis-à-vis educational attainment, employment, housing, drug-addiction treatment, cognitive-based methods for avoiding criminal acts, and, in some instances, family reunification. However, reentry provides social control with the virtual handcuffs necessary to guide a novice through the process of learning to successfully navigate family work, job seeking, employment, budgeting and saving, and the everyday tasks and interactions associated with social life.

Participants likely to benefit most from reentry (or a diversion program) are those who return from hospitals or prisons to their hometowns, earlier than their initial sentence permitted in the case of prisoners, and enter some type of community transition program (Gormsen 2007; Ritter 2006; Seiter 2002; Stafford 2006). The early work in reentry, circa the 1970s, showed that returning home to intact family support networks, by definition, included housing and thus discouraged recently released prisoners from resuming their customary habits of crime (Rossi, Berk, and Lenihan 1980). Contemporarily, however, reentry program policy makers and practitioners nationwide are quick to note that housing remains a challenging but vital component of a successful program (Cooke 2005; Hammett, Roberts, and Kennedy 2001; Naser and La Vigne 2006; Osher and Steadman 2007; Petersilia 2001; Pogorzelski et al. 2005). While some released inmates find that their families exceed their expectations for housing and financial support, not all families are eager to roll out the welcome mat for a man or woman returning from years of incarceration who requires, at least temporarily, affordable housing in the local community (Martinez 2006; Naser and La Vigne 2006). With the legitimacy of the court, however, families can reassure their friends and neighbors that "the judge is looking out for us. He won't let anything bad happen."

THE JUDGE'S JOB

Reentry programs situated within a court can represent the ideal solution for reintegrating formerly incarcerated persons into society (Miller 2007). However, reentry courts, like their drug court predecessors, pose challenges, especially with respect to the blurring of roles across prosecution, defense, and the judiciary within what we have called blended social organizations (Hartley 2003; Nolan 2001). Yet, empirical evidence demonstrates clearly that reentry, within the context of a problem solving court, can reduce recidivism dramatically (Galloway and Drapela 2006). Judges, rather than ending their involvement with a convicted offender at the sentencing hearing, retain control over persons returning from incarceration and manage their transition to a productive lifestyle (Arkfeld 2007). The judge can facilitate and monitor progress, especially with respect to housing, employment opportunities, mental-health and drug-addiction treatment, and activities within social service agencies necessary for successful reintegration. Moreover, the judge, and only the judge, can facilitate the transformation of a disvalued master status, "felon," to a socially valued status, such as "citizen" or "contributing member of society." We posit that the transformative status work that the judge does, with the support of service providers and criminal justice system actors, can significantly increase the likelihood of an ex–prison inmate's returning home for good.

SITUATING REENTRY IN PROBLEM SOLVING COURTS

In this chapter we continue our analysis of a problem solving reentry court by focusing on judge work. The presiding judge is a general-jurisdiction trial court judge who convenes reentry court session weekly, works to solve the problems of the reentry court participants as well as those of the community, especially those faced when large numbers of persons return from prison—one consequence of mass incarceration (Anon. 2008; Barker 2007; Clear 2005). Thousands upon thousands of problem solving courts are found in the United States, Europe, Canada, Australia, and New Zealand. Comprehensive PSCs, unlike social programs and arguably unlike the first-generation drug courts, are innovations that deliberately facilitate the transformation of a participant's most important social status (i.e., master status). A judge at one time pronounced, "You are a convicted offender and deserve to be removed from this community," thus attributing the status "felon" with its associated negative attributes. A judge must therefore facilitate the transformation of the status from "felon" to "member of this community." A therapist may reassure the participant, "You're okay. You can do this." But the therapist is not the party responsible for the attribution of the master status "convicted felon." In concrete ways, the felon must approach a judge for a modified prison sentence, or a hardship driver's license, or a court order to see his children. In more abstract ways, continuous involvement with a judge is a method the social actor uses to change status—from felon to licensed driver, parent, worker, and eventually contributing member of society. Ultimately, it is the community members and organizations that must restore the person's rightful place, and they are inevitably more willing or eager to do so when confident that judges are working to make sure their communities are safe and welcoming.

Transformation is a long-term process[1]: it changes a person's identity, what a person thinks, and how a person reacts to circumstances and situations in the community. It is qualitatively different from adapting to a situation. Imagine, for example, that two prison inmates, both having served ten years, are released from prison on the same day. They are transported to a county jail, where they are greeted by eager family members. In one instance, Will "adapts" to life in his hometown by adjusting to the technological changes of the past ten years. Will attempts to make no other changes. "I am who I am" is how he explains the situation to others.

In the other instance, Paul, also an ex-felon, begins a demanding yearlong process of becoming someone different. Through his participation in a reentry court, he enrolls in a program to teach him new work skills, the appropriate methods for presenting himself at a job interview, and how to prepare a resume. He joins a twelve-step home group, finds a sponsor, and goes to a Narcotics Anonymous meeting daily. He registers to vote and reads the newspaper each day. He works to reunite with his extended family and deliberately avoids old friends who, like him, got into trouble. He learns how to commit to an apartment for a full year and maintain it to the point where he is proud to bring his new work colleagues to "his place" for dinner. On a weekly basis, he talks with his sentencing judge and gets advice on how to take whatever next step is necessary to make progress. His narratives focus on his new identities and responsibilities and the person he can become rather than condemning over and over again his past actions (Maruna and LeBel 2003).

In the first instance, Will adapted to life on the outside. He learned quickly how to make the necessary adaptations, but nothing about Will really changed: his attitudes and dispositions, employment opportunities, and sense of himself remained the same. In the second instance, Paul engaged in the long-term process of transforming himself from a person who broke the law, lived off proceeds earned from participating in an underground economy, and enjoyed the moment. He began gradually to change who he was, what he could do, and what and who he aspired to become. What would one predict for Will and Paul? One adapted to life on the outside, and one worked on the future contributions he could make to his hometown and family. Based on the published recidivism studies, we know that within three years, Will is likely to be arrested and perhaps incarcerated once again. Paul, however, is likely to continue to transform. He is likely to maintain an apartment, stay employed, develop new pro-social relationships, and aspire to a future in which memories of prison will not be necessary to motivate him to avoid bad influences. Paul's transformation, although a lengthy process, paves a path forward. Will's adaptation to life on the outside does nothing to prevent his return to a prison cell.[2]

Reentry programs, generally premised on the importance of transformation, are designed and implemented by prisons or by social service or criminal justice agencies within local communities to increase a reentering person's stakes in conformity (Wooldredge and Thistlethwaite 2002) by engaging him or her in the multiple responsibilities inherent in a crime- and drug-free social life. If the program is embedded within a problem solving court, the ability to transform and create a pro-social master status dramatically increases the probability that a returning prison inmate will indeed come home for good. The judge is the key authority figure to preside over the reentry court, to distribute the rewards and the consequences, and to facilitate the process of shedding the felon master status.

Reentry programs, in- or outside prison walls, share a set of common characteristics. They begin with the recognition that an unprecedented rate of incarceration, which dominated the criminal justice process for more than two decades, now demands a social response that will protect the general population from a large number of released inmates who, without reentry programs, have no place to sleep, eat, or work, yet an ample supply of criminal opportunities. The rate of incarceration in the United States in 1973 was 110 persons for every 100,000 adults. By 2000, the rate had increased to 470, allowing Americans to claim justifiably that we incarcerate at a higher rate than any other nation in the world.

Further, reentry programs recognize that a graduated change, from institutionalization to independence, is necessary to live successfully in a community. Most importantly, program designers understand that providing well-researched services that meet ex-offenders' needs indeed reduce the rate of recidivism among returning inmates (Armstrong and Griffin 2007; Bushway, Brame, and Paternoster 1999; McGuire 2002).

The research of Christy Visher and Jeremy Travis (2003), a state-of-the-art study of reentry programs, takes a life-course framework to explain how (1) experiences prior to prison, (2) those within prison, (3) immediate postprison needs, and (4) experiences with postrelease social integration together affect the likelihood of a released inmate's return to prison. Successful social (re)integration depends on maintaining stable, legitimate employment, finding affordable and safe housing, and reestablishing family roles. Most importantly, the research shows that a status transformation to "responsible citizen" prevents recidivism. "Citizens" vote, engage in volunteer work, and give back to their communities.

Judge work in problem solving courts accounts for status transformation for a very obvious reason. It was a judge who pronounced an antisocial status, and it takes a judge to facilitate the transformation of the antisocial to a prosocial master status. Although a small percentage of the reentry population can succeed without community intervention and support, the majority of nonrecidivists have retooled their lives comprehensively and most efficiently with the social legitimacy of a problem solving court.

Without a master status transformation from felon to citizen, the most successful reentry program remains elusive. Some evidence indicates that without status change, employment matters (Dalessio and Stolzenberg 1995). A living-wage job can decrease recidivism by as much as 20 percent, as measured by rearrest rates. However, the very expensive Project Greenlight failure illustrates the cost of neglecting the master status transformation facilitated by courts and judges. Researchers used a quasi-experimental design to randomly select a group of returning New York State inmates and provided them with cognitive skills, employment, housing, drug-prevention, family, and other forms of training and counseling. One year postrelease, the intensive reentry program group failed at a higher rate than the control groups. No attempt was made to facilitate the transformation of status outside of prison. All the work of Project Greenlight took place in a prison facility. Prison inmates became employed ex–prison inmates. Researchers could only look to program design and implementation to explain the failure and never thought to measure or examine the master status of their experimental subjects: ex–prison inmates.

JUDGE WORK IN A PROBLEM SOLVING COURT

A reentry problem solving court was designed, redesigned, and eventually implemented by the presiding judge of a superior court in a Midwestern city in November 2005. The state's judicial conference approved this particular PSC as the first in the state following the enactment of a reentry court statute. To recruit participants for the program, the Department of Correction (DOC) posts flyers throughout its facilities and directs city residents to contact their DOC case managers for more information. An additional pool of applicants is assembled by various sentencing judges who receive requests for sentence modifications.

The judge and the interdisciplinary reentry court team use an explicit policy to bring participants into the program. The policy excludes violent offenders and prefers those with drug-dealing convictions and mental-health problems over inmates incarcerated for habitual property offenses.

The policy requires an examination of a complete prison record, gives the county's prosecutor veto power, and requires the team to examine each potential participant's background and educational or drug-treatment activities before and during incarceration. It is important to note that reentry team members sign confidentiality agreements before reviewing the file. Candidates sign release forms to allow the team to get a full picture of their background and circumstances.

ADMISSION TO REENTRY AND THE SUCCESS FORMULA

The problem solving reentry court takes a small-is-best approach and admits only a quarter or a third of applicants (29 percent). Persons from other states who return to this state only because they were convicted and sentenced in the county are automatically excluded. The county's prosecutor rejects or vetoes cases based on information he has, such as a candidate's connection to an ongoing investigation by local, state, or federal officials. All others who are rejected have (1) an insufficient amount of time left to serve, (2) violent criminal histories, (3) gang membership, (4) write-ups for violent behavior while in prison, or (5) an escape history.

Although participants tend to have committed drug-dealing and property offenses, according to the state prison system's classification scheme for preparing release and reentry plans, the participants accepted into the reentry problem solving court (with one exception) presented a moderate to high risk of reoffending within one or two years. The participants' offenses ranged from C-level to A-level felony crimes, and the actual time they served in prison ranged from two to twenty-two years.

In the beginning of the third year the problem solving reentry court, in contrast to the reports of every published recidivism study, no person had been arrested for committing a new crime. By the end of the third year, two persons had been arrested, one for shoplifting and one for driving under the influence (on a moped).

Graduates, on average, took fourteen months to complete the program. A total of eleven participants violated program regulations repeatedly and were returned to prison. Of those, only one person in the reentry PSC who received housing support was terminated from the program. The importance of tangible support received by participants cannot be overestimated.

In July 2008, twenty participants were in one of the four phases of the program (70 percent were men, 2.4 percent were black). Although absolute success is an unrealistic goal, we do know that participants in the reentry problem solving court have rarely compromised public safety. The formula for success, determined by examining reduced risk and comparing those who succeed with those who fail, entails undergoing drug-abuse treatment and having rent-reduced housing for one year, full-time employment, forward-looking discussions about work and family, and custodial care for at least one child. This formula is the same for women as men in this particular program, most likely because the women are single parents who need job training and full-time jobs to support their families.

Every six months, the reentry court judge receives process and outcome evaluation reports. They are distributed to state and county officials. The state's Department of Correction was sent an overview of the reentry court program's costs and benefits. The savings to state taxpayers are a function of the cost of state prison minus the cost of servicing a person within the community. The state (under)estimates an average annual prison cost of $21,552 per inmate. The annual cost for the problem solving reentry court, based on the salary and benefits for a community-corrections case manager, pay for a part-time surveillance officer, and housing, is $7,000 ($4,000 per year for community corrections and $3,000 per year for housing support).

The state saves a minimum of $14,552 for each person in the reentry problem solving court, or $291,040 per year for twenty reentry participants. These taxpayer savings do not include the additional cost of police, prosecution, defense, and court time to arrest, convict, and sanction persons who would have, if not for reentry court, committed crime. Nor do they include the dollars contributed to the local economy by the participant who works and consumes products and services. Most importantly, they do not reflect the social and economic costs associated with the imprisonment of a family's breadwinner.

The ongoing program process evaluation allows necessary changes to be made to the reentry court. For example, once it became apparent that the risk-to-reoffend assessment instrument used (the LSI) was not sufficient for measuring certain problems, such as psychological or family problems, the Addiction Severity Index (ASI) was added to the battery of tests and clinical interviews used to measure participants' progress.

Six months after it was introduced, the team assessed the utility of the ASI by examining the scores generated for three participants. All three had high legal-problem scores, merely reflecting the fact that they were convicted of serious crimes and had recently been released from prison. Two of the three showed higher than average drug scores because both continued using drugs while incarcerated.

One young white man, Jon, failed the reentry program because he refused to work. He depended on his father to pay his bills, including his drug-treatment bills, and thus showed high scores on the employment and the family dimensions of the ASI. He had a father who routinely bailed him out of trouble. That particular family relationship, which was ostensibly supportive, interfered with the participant's commitment to a normative lifestyle within the community. The use of the ASI confirmed what clinical interviews showed and allowed the team to confidently suggest changes to the comprehensive case plans prepared by community-corrections case managers.

Like all successful problem solving courts, this one treats each participant as a unique individual with unique strengths and needs. For example, a participant who has been in prison for two years has different needs than a person incarcerated for ten years. Women have different needs and problems to address than men (Arditti and Few 2006; Arnold, Stewart, and McNeece 2001; Earthrowl and McCully 2002; Kruttschnitt and Gartner 2003). Women tend to return home to the children they left behind and the need to collect child-support payments. Men tend to return home to a substantial child-support bill.

Moreover, women and men with unique backgrounds have unique needs. In this reentry court group of twenty participants, two women were prostitutes, another had been repeatedly raped by her boss (which started her down the path of drug abuse), and one never-married woman had a college degree. One man was a transvestite, one suffered from AIDS, and one began abusing drugs when his infant son died and his marriage dissolved. These are only a few examples of the characteristics that make it necessary to consider each participant's unique needs and (potential) strengths when developing a case plan based on clinical interviews and actuarial-type instruments that predict survival in the community or a quick return to state prison.

COURT SESSIONS

Participants in the first two (of four) reentry court phases meet the judge each week in an open court session. They are encouraged to bring friends, family members, coworkers, and twelve-step sponsors. In the later phases, participants appear in court on a biweekly and then monthly basis. All told, the judge speaks with twelve to fourteen participants each Monday. Court sessions, generally lasting more than an hour, tend to begin with consequences for program violations. Being late for an appointment is a violation likely to result in a "one-pager" (i.e., an essay writing assignment) on the importance of punctuality. Quitting a job without authorization may result in a week in the county jail. Court sessions proceed with unrehearsed, problem-focused dialogue. For example, Jack is a forty-one-year-old man who spent years in the Indiana Boys School. His adult record includes battery, operating a drug laboratory with a child present, and dealing drugs. He has three children and was sentenced to prison in 2000 for twenty years. He was brought into the reentry court in November 2006. During one session, he asked the judge, "How do I apologize to my kids for what I did? I really messed up bad, and I don't know what to say to them. I feel horribly guilty. Whenever I try to say something, nothing comes out." The judge instructed him to talk to a police captain who told Jack that he too was a dad and had messed up from time to time. He gave Jack his business card and cell phone number, telling him to call whenever he needed help. Later, Jack reported to the judge that he is "cordial" with his ex-wife and "close" to his children. His children know he will remain present in their lives.

IT IS NOT SOCIAL WORK

An interdisciplinary team of criminal justice and social service agency representatives advise the problem solving reentry court. Many sit in the jury box to observe the participants as they engage in dialogue with the judge each week. Also in the courtroom are an armed bailiff and a court reporter. Court sessions are recorded, and if a participant is taken to jail, he or she is handcuffed and transported at the end of the court session. The swift response to violations, coupled with the highly visible and audible ritual of being cuffed and shackled, has a specific deterrent effect on participants, who tend to avoid future violations, and a general deterrent effect on the group of participants sitting in the courtroom gallery, waiting to be called to a podium only a few feet away from the bench. We can argue (though not "prove") that a PSC for reentry participants deters recidivistic crime by delivering certain, swift sanctions very soon after a violation is committed (Chen 2008; Heckert and Gondolf 2000; Kleck et al. 2005). The sanctions are measured punishments—not too severe and not too lenient—to correspond to the seriousness of the violation.

A TEAM APPROACH

Every team member is held strictly accountable by the judge. Although consensus is sought, when bringing new participants into the program or when determining rewards or sanctions, the judge retains leadership and independence. Providers and team members occasionally resist the practices of the reentry court, saying, "That's the way we've always done it" or "It's confidential information that I cannot disclose." Since PSC programs are anything but business as usual, the team members must be as willing to change as the participants. Each team member is as accountable to the program as the participant. As a result, agency representatives tend to show up early—never late—for staff meetings. Reticence is inexcusable and never justified by invoking any client-confidentiality claim. The judge insists on full disclosure for the purpose of working effectively with the participants. When new program components are tried out, if they do not work or are inefficient, they are discarded.

When advising the judge, the team recommends consequences or rewards, phase moves or expulsions. But only the judge decides, from the bench, what a participant will experience in response to information disclosed at the staff meeting. When necessary, the team will be schooled on due process, the rule of the law, or the importance of reentry's being a court program and not a social service agency.

BLACK ROBES AND SPORTS JACKETS

In the traditional courtroom, the judge dons the black robe, which, according to a trial court judge who is also a problem solving court judge, helps

> on the bench to keep my "personality" from coming through. I think that a good judge wears a robe for that reason—not to let individual personality come through—but rather to be a kind of universalized, fair, dispassionate decision maker who cares and who does justice. . . . I think that a judge should not show too much personality because what is said in terms of irony, jest, or humor can be misunderstood or misinterpreted. I worry about these things.

Yet, when the same bench judge meets with reentry court participants, he wears a sports jacket, usually without a tie, and he shows a lot of personality, to which participants relate. Symbolically and culturally it matters. The robe is off; thus, the judge is free to be the problem solver, the person the participant can trust. His social roles are as numerous and varied as the participants in the reentry court. Nonetheless, he remains the judge, the authority who can order a week in jail for a program violation.

To one participant, the judge is like the older brother who advises a woman saving money to buy her own truck. To another, a younger woman who has never earned money except through prostitution, he is the stern father who warns her not to be late for work or she will face the consequence of "cleaning the cat cages [at the animal shelter]. Now would you like to do that again, Haley?" Of a man locked up for fifteen years, he asks, "You know you can vote, don't you? Now, I want you to register to vote, right here in the courthouse, before you leave for the day, okay? You can handle that." Of a participant who had become complacent, he asked, "Do you remember where you came from?"

Trial court judges favor certain verbal expressions, such as "Now, we're going to have a little chat," when addressing defendants or convicted offenders. In reentry court, he will tell a participant who has taken an appropriate step toward solving a problem but not yet succeeded, "That will be fine." He communicates that the participant is moving forward, and the judge has reasonable expectations for when a particular objective will be achieved. He often says, "I can handle that," in response to a participant's telling him that she has hit some road block, for example, not getting a return call from an attorney. The shortcut means that he will make sure the attorney contacts the participant before the next scheduled court session.

If a participant dares to complain about a program requirement, such as attending a political candidate's forum, she will hear, "Suck it up. Now, just suck it up." When the judge uses that expression, other participants seated in the gallery with their friends or family members tend to laugh quietly, but aloud. In some instances, a participant will anticipate the judge and say, "I know, Judge. I need to suck it up." Outside the court setting, at work for example, participants have been heard saying to those they supervise at work, "Just suck it up." They all know what the shortcut means: Regardless of what you think about what I am asking you to do or what your employer is telling you to do, just do it. Do not sit around and feel badly about things. Move on and be productive. Be thoughtful.

A participant told the judge about walking away from a confrontation with the night supervisor. The judge responded, "Do the right thing. Just do the right thing and move on." Two weeks later, the participant was telling a newly arrived participant, "Now, you just do the right thing. You'll stay out of trouble that way."

The verbal expressions are cues or shortcuts to communicate expectations about how to work and parent, why it is important to show up on time for an appointment, and how thinking about political candidates can help a reentry court participant become a "citizen." The expressions would lack use value if the judge wore the black robe to talk at, not with, a participant.

The verbal expressions help participants turn the corner. One hotheaded man, Mike, was inevitably ready to fight. His facial gestures, clinched teeth, gait, and stance with his arms firmly held by his side showed his attitude. Four months into the program, after two weeks in work release for showing disrespect to a service provider, Mike had internalized the judge's expressions. Now, when the judge calls on him, he approaches the judge, hands in his pocket, head cocked to one side, smiling. Usually, he repeats one of the verbal shortcuts that he has internalized, perhaps to remind the judge that he gets it now.

The reentry court judge facilitates participants' transformation from felon to citizen through unique dialogues that address their individual strengths, needs, and challenges. Although generally supportive, he is quick to express disagreement over a job choice or attitudes expressed in court. He is also quick to dispense consequences for program violations. In the city and county, he is known as the bluntest judge, who metes out the aggravated range of the sentence when he deems it justifiable and necessary. For eighteen years, his reputation as "Father Time" has never been challenged. While he wears no black robe in the problem solving court setting, he never stops being the judge. He is willing to expel someone from the program, send someone to jail, or make life either as unpleasant or as pleasant as necessary to bring about change in a person's social status and sense of the self. Being a "citizen" means contributing to the community, not taking from it; to the judge and the participants, it means being a good worker, a good family member, and a volunteer. When participants or graduates see the judge on the street, they stop to talk, to get one more piece of advice. What should I do about my job? Where should I apply for volunteer work now?

A recent graduate asked a group of six participants, all still in the program, what becoming a citizen or a contributing member of society again meant to them. A forty-year-old white man said, "Being a good citizen is important because I feel that I need to make amends to the community for the actions I have taken in the past. Also to make sure that I continue to be a good role model to those around me." A thirty-five-year-old black man said,

Who am I? I am a new man today—a husband, a father, a role model who's confident and will go through any obstacle that gets in my way 'cause I'm on a mission. . . . I've come too far to do wrong 'cause right is all I know now. I am living proof that people can change. I can contribute now. I can give back.

A forty-six-year-old white grandmother said,

All of my life I never thought about what I was doing to my family or myself. Only where I was going to get my next fix and how soon I can get it. I have made some definite changes in my life. I have this overwhelming desire to continue to move forward in my life and to be much more than I have ever been. I am a real member of society now. Sitting and talking with my children . . . rebuilding the trust and going above and beyond for them is the person that I've always dreamed of being.

MASTER STATUS TRANSFORMATIONS

We posit that a person's master status can be transformed through participation in a reentry problem solving court program. The master status concept
is most often attributed to Everett Cherrington Hughes, who in 1945 argued
that occupation, an exemplar of master status, carries a "set of expectations
concerning the auxiliary traits associated with many of the specific positions
available in our society. . . . The 'natural' combinations of auxiliary characteristics become embodied in the stereotypes of ordinary talk." Thus, the
popular conception of the Catholic priest was an Irish priest "who may punch
someone in the nose if the Lord demands it."

A master status can convey positive qualities, such as those associated
with "judge," "mother," or "president." Impartiality, compassion, and wisdom, for example, are typical attributes of such occupations or positions in
life. Master statuses, such as "gang member" or "ex-felon," however, con-
note negative attributes that, due to labeling or self-fulfilling prophecies,
can result in socially deviant or criminal activity. Thus, it is imperative for
the ex-felon to subscribe to a different master status—citizen or community
member—which can only be facilitated by a person in the social and legal
position (i.e., a judge) to pronounce status authoritatively (Arkfeld 2007; Berman and Feinblatt 2003; Berman and Lane 2000; Brownfield, Sorenson, and
Thompson 2001; Wexler and Winick 2003).

A young woman in the reentry court had trouble getting along with the
other participants and claimed that she was not like the others who had been to
prison. She is a young mother, age twenty-five, and the daughter of a professional. A person died during the commission of the felony for which she was
incarcerated. As a consequence of her complaint about the other participants,
she was asked to think about her attitude and required to write an essay on the
stigma she faced upon release from prison. For her assignment, she wrote,

> When a person is released from prison or receives a felony conviction they know
> that their life is forever negatively changed. They now have to face the closing
> of many doors. . . . Many employers look at felons as high risk, untrustworthy,
> unreliable, and sometimes dangerous people. During the years I spent in prison
> I saw repeaters, as we call them, stuck in a revolving door, in and out of prison.
> Most said the same thing, that they were unable to find a job quick enough or
> they did not have the means to provide for their family. In return they resorted
> back to what they knew to do to make ends meet. . . . When I was released I
> too saw how harsh it is. As I continued to look for employment I had door after
> door closed on me due to that little box I check saying, "Yes, I have a felony
> conviction." . . . Maybe some people need to see I am sincere and maybe they
> never will. Life is too short and can be taken too suddenly.

Reentry court programs tend to focus on increasing personal strengths, eliminating deviant behaviors, and increasing stakes in conformity on the premise that attaching the self to the community discourages criminal or deviant activity. Having stakes in conformity is necessary, but not sufficient, to prevent repeated crime. That fact we know from the volumes of criminological research examining behaviors ranging from partner violence to burglary. Indeed, it is the interaction of increasing stakes in conformity with the transformation of master status that is necessary to bring ex–prison inmates home for good.

10

Backstage Action

BEHIND CLOSED DOORS

Prior to a problem solving court session, a team of social actors meets behind closed doors, usually in a jury room, to discuss participants' progress and setbacks, learn new strategies, and consider necessary changes to procedures and practices. A layperson can walk into the public courtroom and witness the drama of the court session; however, as with the live performance of a ballet or play, backstage is the space for figuring out what will transpire front stage—or in court. Audiences generally have no access to the backstage action. For decades, social science and legal scholars have documented the backstage tasks associated with the work of the traditional criminal justice process, for example, negotiating guilty pleas. The backstage action of what we and others term the second-generation problem solving courts, however, is more likely inferred than observed systematically and analyzed.[1]

In the problem solving court, the key actors' roles and performances are different from, or even the opposite of, those that characterize the drama of the American criminal court trial. While sitting in the gallery of a courtroom to observe a trial, a person sees the adversarial system of justice at work. The defense attorney maintains anything but a collaborative relationship with the prosecuting attorney. One attorney represents the accused, presumed inno-cent, while the other represents the state and the need to protect public safety. The gloves are off at trial and also during the more routine court hearings scheduled to achieve criminal convictions or to impose a criminal sanction.

Courtroom work groups emerge, generally consisting of a judge, a pros-ecutor, a defense attorney, a court reporter, and a bailiff (Galanter 1974). The outcomes of hearings and trials are more predictable than the media and entertainment industry lead the general public to believe. The importance of the adversarial model is that it represents and symbolizes a model of U.S. justice. Jury trials, for example, occur rarely, but they retain and celebrate the core values of the criminal justice system. It matters little if a burglar is captured on security camera film. What counts is the protection of his rights as he experiences his day in court. He is presumed innocent until a jury of his peers finds him guilty.

If students or legal professionals from another country observed all the criminal trials held in a particular state court over a period of six months, then entered the same courtroom to observe a problem solving court program, they would probably fail to understand the action of the actors at team meetings and within the courtroom. Why is the prosecutor advocating for the convicted offender? Why is she arguing with the judge to keep the offender in the community and not in jail? Who are those people seated at the defense table? Why are they suggesting a court-ordered treatment program? Is that unethical or illegal?

In problem solving courts, the tables are turned. Roles are switched or reversed. The judge becomes the legal expert and the social actor who dispenses advice instead of prison sentences.[2] Advocates of PSC programs must never forget the rule of law and the ethics that apply to the legal, medical, mental-health, and judicial professions. Critics of PSC programs must also take the time to look at what the rule of law actually is, how it changes over time, and how the legal professions adapt to changing social problems.

Ann, a public defender, met a judge outside the prosecutor's office on Monday, following a forensic diversion court session. Before saying hello, she began a version of the refrain heard often regarding work in problem solving courts.

> You know, I don't know sometimes if I'm a defense attorney or a prosecuting attorney. I participate in teen drug court, in adult drug court, in forensic diversion, and in reentry. I keep thinking that I'm doing what's best for my clients. But sometimes I feel a lot more like a prosecutor than an attorney defending her clients. What's going on? Do you think this is appropriate? I know my clients need court-ordered treatment. Sometimes they even need a swift kick—a little jail time won't hurt them. But here I go again, sounding like a prosecuting attorney. (January 28, 2008)

In the traditional courtroom, the defender sits with the client at the defense table and takes an adversarial role that in many ways separates the client's rights and best interests from what the state, represented by the prosecution, argues is best for the community. The separation between the defense and prosecution tables keeps the parties apart, in part to ensure safety when the arguments heat up and in part to symbolize the separation between defense and prosecution in an adversarial system of criminal justice in the United States.

Turning from the defense to the state's table, it was the chief deputy prosecutor who argued in May 2006 for reentry problem solving court resources before the community corrections advisory board. He sent the following letter to community leaders to advance his plea:

May 11, 2005

Dear Community Leaders,

I am writing on behalf of the Reentry Planning Team to support the request by Community Corrections for a Program Manager dedicated to the Reentry Court Program.

The Reentry Court Program may be the most important innovation in years to advance public safety in our County. It builds upon this county's successful experiences with evidence-based practices and problem solving courts.

More than 100 offenders return to the city and the county from Department of Correction (DOC) facilities each year; yet, the county has had, until now, no comprehensive strategy for preventing the commission of new crimes. The recidivism statistics are grim. Of those returning from prison:

- 33% are rearrested in 6 months and 44% are rearrested within one year.
- 47% are convicted of another crime in the first year and 67% within three years.
- 51.8% will be returned to prison, with about half being returned for new offenses and half for probation or parole violations.

Reentry Court Programs, similar to the one implemented here, have been successful in reducing recidivism rates significantly. Not only does the Reentry Court Program notably increase public safety, it saves tax payers money that would be spent on the criminal justice system, our county jail, and our state prisons.

Reentry programs have only recently been introduced in Indiana. Allen County established the first Reentry Court Program in the state. An evaluation study shows that it has been very successful in reducing recidivism. A presiding judge leads a Reentry Court Team that recommends evidence-based practices for returning inmates. The judge convenes special court sessions to meet with all participants. Community Corrections and Police agencies take the responsibility to deliver programs and monitor participants.

A law will go into effect on July 1 that provides a statewide framework for Reentry Court Programs. They will take the shape of problem solving courts, exemplified by the Superior Court I Forensic Diversion Court Program.

Certification of new Reentry Court Programs will be done according to rules promulgated by the state judicial conference. Our county is the first in the state to submit a request for certification under the new statute. The Judicial Center has received the implementation plan and related documents. It already approved the

Court to continue its work and participate in the process of determining the uniform rules and regulations under which the future Reentry Courts will operate.

Our Reentry Court Program is organized by a presiding judge who leads a Reentry Court Program Team. It represents police agencies, the prosecuting attorney, probation, parole, Community Corrections, Home with Hope, public defenders, mental-health and addictions services providers, Work One, the Adult Resources Academy, Family Services, Inc., and other community agencies. The Team meets each Monday to review participants and fine-tune the program. It reviews the recommended evidence-based practices to which our county has made a strong commitment. It has the support of all our judges.

The presiding judge leads the team's planning and review of participants and the Reentry Court Program Team activities. His commitment to the program has been important for insuring the quality of the program.

The Team meets weekly and its value cannot be overestimated. It represents the agencies and organizations that make our county an ideal and safe place for families to thrive.

The use of evidence-based practices is the hallmark of a successful program for a correctional population. The Department of Correction favors our own Community Corrections because of its commitment to evidence-based practices. As applied to the administration of the Reentry Court Program:

1. Risk assessment will be determined using the best tools available including the Addiction Severity Index (ASI) and the LS/CMI (to determine the level of services needed).
2. Programs and services, especially drug-addiction treatment, educational, work, and family programs, will be determined by the needs of each participant.
3. Program evaluation will be ongoing. It will track costs and benefits of all the programs and services to which participants are referred. It will measure the commission of any new crime and the violation of any Reentry Court Program regulation.

The anchor to finance the program is money granted by the Department of Correction to Community Corrections. DOC allocations for our Community Corrections' "Community Transition Program" are sufficient to support a Program Manager for the Reentry Court Program. In addition, each participant will pay user fees.

Case management is an essential ingredient to make the Reentry Court Program successful. Without a case manager, dedicated to the Reentry Court initiative, returning offenders will not obtain the services necessary to prevent recidivism. I ask that you support the request of Community Corrections to contract a qualified case manager.

Thanks you for your attention,

John Meyers

AT THE TABLE

In a problem solving court, social and legal actors sit around a single table to decide on the best course of action to recommend to the presiding judge. Adversarial roles are put aside, although the arguments presented by attorneys and service providers are sometimes more emotional than they are in the traditional criminal justice setting. The judge, in his or her traditional role, is responsible for hearing the facts of the case and ruling on matters of law. In the problem solving court, the judge's purpose is to determine the right thing to do for the participant, who may suffer from a drug addiction, want to reunite with his siblings, or need a hardship driver's license to get to work and back home (Arkfeld 2007; Berman 2004; Berman and Feinblatt 2001, 2003; Berman and Lane 2000; Eaton and Kaufman 2005; Farole et al. 2005).

James Nolan (2001), in his critical and critically acclaimed book on the early drug courts, comprehensively addresses the fundamental shifts that take place in drug court. The umbrella under which a number of the changes in the criminal justice process are held together is a problem solving jurisprudence (or what he refers to as a therapeutic jurisprudence).

We acknowledge the potential conflicts and issues that Nolan presents in *Reinventing Justice*. Treatment is court ordered and indeterminate in length, decided by problem solving court judges. Programs are implemented with a time-to-completion standard that can range from nine months to two years (Freeman 2003; Friedmann, Taxman, and Henderson 2007; Fulton Hora 2002). The PSC judge is responsible for determining when the risk of relapse or recidivism is low enough to release the participant from the program. It is likely that the PSC court monitors a number of convicted offenders for a protracted period relative to the time an offender would have served behind bars.

Judges' decisions in a PSC are characterized by more discretion than are traditional courtroom decisions, which are highly structured by the rule of law, regardless of the variation in laws that characterize the states' substantive and procedural criminal laws (Barkow and O'Neill 2006; Ferrall 2004; Jacobson 2006). Typically, a participant signs a legal agreement that expands judicial discretion and judicial decisions to reflect treatment providers' suggestions.

Nolan cites critics of the early drug court movement who expressed concern over the constitutionality of discretionary "punishment," albeit delivered in the community and not behind bars, and the fact that participants (in diversion programs) forego the presumption of innocence and their trial rights. In addition, participants sign over their search-and-seizure rights. The prosecutor and defense attorneys are not adversaries; they are members of the same team.

Instead of operating in conflictual relationships, the various actors in the drug
court drama are to work together. Successful treatment-based drug court programs are built on collaboration. . . . The judge, prosecutor, public defender,
treatment providers, and others must work together as a team to promote rehabilitation by placing a high priority on the defendant's success. (Nolan 2001,
75–76)

The team approach (Draine et al. 2005; Simpson et al. 2006) is now accepted as the best practice to use in a problem solving court. It does indeed
imply that prosecuting and defense attorneys and judges take fundamentally
different positions than they would in a jury trial or a traditional plea or sentencing hearing (Mirchandani 2005; Wolf 2008).

It is no longer the case, as it was a decade ago, that the legal or mental-
health communities, including those devoted to treating the drug-addicted
population, are concerned about the role reversal or swapping typical of
social and legal actors in the problem solving court. The American Bar Association, judicial conferences, and psychological and psychiatric groups
endorse the nonadversarial problem solving approach to treating persons
with problems in the community. Appellate courts have tested and approved
the constitutionality of the PSC (Marlowe 2006; Nolan 2002; Siobhan 2004;
Wolf 2008).

CHALLENGING COLLABORATIONS

Nowadays, PSC team members understand the need to work together as well
as the difficulty inherent in their collaborative work toward the shared goals
of achieving public safety and enhancing quality of life for all community
residents, including PSC participants. In the three PSC programs analyzed in
this book, the teams showed continuous, yet varied, resistance to accepting
the "mental-health" or "criminal justice" model for delivering problem solving court justice. For example, social workers resist the use of actuarial-type
measurement tools to assess problems or progress, believing the clinical
interview to be a superior, holistic approach to understanding the participant.
Probation officers, on the other hand, think social workers do not understand
"criminal thinking" and how it can affect progress in a PSC program.

Ongoing education is an important component of all successful drug courts
or problem solving courts. The problems that the court program attempts to
solve must be understood. For instance, if the PSC program is designed to
treat participants suffering from serious mental illness and a co-occurring
drug addiction, all PSC team members need to understand both problems,
as well as the criminal justice system (Chandler et al. 2004; Osher, Stead-

man, and Barr 2003; Sullivan et al. 2007; Weitzel et al. 2007). Likewise, the team needs to understand the collaborative process. It is not "natural" for the mental-health worker to seek assistance from the correctional officer. It is a "strain" for the judge to refrain from adjudicating and sentencing participants in a problem solving court.

In the forensic diversion and reentry courts that we studied, the presiding judges asked the team members or subcommittees to read different books in search of the appropriate PSC team model. Should the team be like a jury and deliberate until a consensus position is reached? Should it be a team of managers, representing criminal justice and social service agencies, headed by an executive (i.e., the presiding judge)?

The judge responsible for the forensic diversion problem solving court worked on a jury-consensus model for approximately eighteen months, then decided that the divisiveness among team members mandated a change. Every week he faced what seemed like a hung jury, not one that achieved consensus in decision making.

The judge responsible for the reentry PSC took the executive-manager team approach. In both cases, judges initially asked team members to read the ever-popular *Who Moved My Cheese?* for the purpose of illustrating the difficulties and stress individuals experience when asked to stop doing business as usual (Johnson 1998). The forensic diversion judge, although he started the program with a jury model, was the first to take the executive-manager model to the team (Kotter 1996; Lencioni 2002) in an attempt to demonstrate the reasonableness of working collaboratively. Feeling frustrated but hopeful, on May 25, 2006, he distributed the following memo to the PSC team, reflecting on his own difficulties with accepting change:

> On a personal note, a few decades ago I attended a yearlong junior year abroad program at a Japanese university in Tokyo. I was rather surprised to see Japanese men and women removing their shoes and putting them in a designated place before entering a home. It was only later that I understood the symbolic importance of this simple act. The Japanese understand the idea that a line should be drawn between the inside and the outside of their homes; a distinction must be made between their personal lives where they relax and reflect and their public lives where they work and play.
>
> Imagine that the Third Floor Jury Room is a special space where we, the Forensic Diversion Team meet, generally on Mondays at 1:00 pm. As we symbolically take off our shoes to enter this special space we are aware that it will be necessary to tuck away a few of our most cherished workplace views. For this one-hour period of time each Monday we are prepared to open our minds based on evidence-based practices for the benefit of our participants. We truly value the different ways of thinking that each team member brings to the table, making decisions by consensus on the merits of the case. When each of us enters the

Jury Room we may share a work view that is different from what the Reverend thinks, and it is different from what I, the Judge think, and it is different from what the treatment team thinks. [The director of a residential recovery program] may ride the elevator thinking about "his residents," but when he enters the Jury Room he hears about a particular FD participant, and 100% of his professional work is focused on determining what's best for the participant. The same is true for [a social worker] or [a community-corrections case manager]. [The person responsible for the county jail] may have gotten out of her car concerned about a jail problem, but when she enters the Jury Room, her work view changes and her focus, like all the other professionals in the room, is on the FD participant and on the FD program. Together we enter a room and that space becomes special. It is different. It is a space where men and women fuss, fight, express frustration, trust each other, and exchange information. Together we deliberate what's best for each participant and for the Forensic Diversion Program. At 2:00 the shoes go back on. Let's think about these three lines by Kobayashi Issa.

The cloudburst
Scrubs it clean . . .
The old house.

What is the preferred model for problem solving court teams? Most important for the program is a representation from all the public and nonprofit agencies that serve the participants. In first-generation drug courts, teams were small in number, consisting often of only three or four persons, and did not necessarily represent all the community's stakeholders. As the PSC movement evolved and matured, as it tackled more complex problems and more serious offenses, and as it became a problem solver upon which the community could depend, the teams grew in size and scope. Nowadays, if the PSC program includes a housing dimension, the team needs to hear about housing needs and housing problems. If the reentry court program is comprehensive, the team should include a representative from a medical clinic or group, one especially sensitive to the need to treat HIV/AIDS and hepatitis C (Brunsden 2006; Needels, Jarnes-Burdurny, and Burghardt 2005; Rhodes and Treloar 2008; Rich et al. 2001; Werb et al. 2008). What the court program attempts to accomplish can be sketched out in a diagram, perhaps one showing nested programs within the PSC program, and a good team will have members for each component of the program (Braude and Alaimo 2007; Draine et al. 2005; Fisler 2005; Zaller et al. 2008).

Although there is no ideal or typical model to present, three points are important. First, a problem solving court team must continuously remind itself that all members have stepped outside their comfort zone—their work setting or silo, as it is popularly known—to participate in a collaborative effort to solve problems. Second, the team must be willing to continuously evaluate its work to make sure that only those programs and practices that are effective and cost-efficient are used. Third, the team must remind itself that the problem solving court must be anchored by the rule of law. A defense attorney is a team member, but the attorney must always protect the client's rights. A social worker is a treatment provider, but he or she is working within a court program. A judge advises participants and team members, but he or she is a judge and not a social worker.

At each team meeting, for all three of the PSC programs we studied, meeting notes (i.e., field notes) were taken and distributed to all team members. The following observations regarding distinctive types of team members and backstage activities are based on an analysis of three years' of field notes. The analysis applies to the forensic diversion and reentry PSC programs only, as the notes from the Title 33 program for sex offenders are not included here.

A Competitive Prosecutor

The elected prosecutor attends reentry team meetings but not the court sessions. He delegates responsibility for the forensic diversion PSC to a deputy prosecuting attorney. The prosecutor is a dedicated and competitive member of the team. Although he works, in his words, "to protect public safety at all times," he often expresses his support of reentry and the other PSC programs. However, he wants all the court programs to be uniform, an impossibility when the participants, as groups, are qualitatively different from each other.

The prosecutor is sharp-witted and defers professionally to the judge. Nonetheless, he fights to win. If he and the judge disagree, for example, on accepting a new participant, the prosecutor will instantly exercise his veto power. During meetings in the team meeting room, which is a jury room with a large table surrounded by a back row of seats, the prosecutor never sits at the table. Instead, he comes prepared with paper files on each participant and sits in the row of seats behind the table. During the years we observed him as a team member, he never disputed the treatments or sanctions ordered by the judge. He reserves his competitiveness for battles over admission to the program.

A Cooperative Public Defender

The public defender is often absent from team meetings, whether for the forensic diversion or the reentry court program. For approximately one year, she experimented with assigning various part-time defenders to the different programs, eventually deciding that she should monitor defendants in all programs. She alone represents her office in all the PSC programs. She understands clearly the unique missions of each PSC, while she works to ensure that defense is uniformly guaranteed in all the programs.

The public defender attends team meetings sporadically; yet, she is among the most cooperative of the team members. Almost the opposite side of the coin compared to the prosecutor, she is more likely to attend a court session than a meeting. She tends to walk into the courtroom, look around, check to see if anyone participating in a PSC is cuffed (which, at the beginning of the court session, implies that the participant spent the week in jail for a program violation), and talk with the participant. If a new participant is starting the program or if an expulsion hearing is scheduled, she meets with the defendant or the offender to facilitate the entry process and to defend the rights of participants coming into a PSC and those leaving one nonvoluntarily.

When she attends team meetings, she argues forcefully to admit a public-defense client as a participant and readily acknowledges that PSC programs are the "best thing" that some of her clients can experience.

Law Enforcement: Differences in Style

Two law-enforcement officers are represented on the teams. One is a deputy county sheriff, and the other is a city police captain. The deputy sheriff is responsible for monitoring (in a records management system) all participants' police contacts. He is supposed to report police contacts each Monday, but he does not. The team tends to learn about a traffic accident or the police stopping a participant from the probation officer assigned to the team.

The deputy sheriff's immediate supervisor is the jail commander. Before the judge enters the jury room for team meetings, the deputy sheriff tends to lean on the jury table, with his hands stretched out in front of him, and make crude remarks about the "scum" and the "poison" in the jail. The use of expletives is common. Before every team meeting, he talks about how the court programs are a waste of time and the judges who run them are misusing their authority. As the judge enters the room, his posture straightens, and he smiles and responds to questions as if he supports the PSC programs. He misses as many meetings as possible, and when he does attend one, he announces his resentment at being compelled to attend (these comments are never made with the judge present). He is a true nine-to-five worker and will never pretend to be interested in the job after he goes off shift.

His team responsibilities include interviewing participants before they are moved up a phase in a program. He always returns a positive, yet nonspecific, response. When the judge asks for something unusual, however, he will go out of his way to fulfill his duty. In July 2007, for example, he checked out the foreclosure status of a participant's home.

The city police captain, unlike the deputy sheriff, expresses strong approval of the forensic diversion and reentry PSCs. When the reentry court program was initiated, however, he claimed that returning prison inmates made him "throw up on his shoes." He asked if he could have veto power over admitting a participant. Although he was reassured that he had veto power, he never exercised it. Instead, he became a tremendous reentry and forensic diversion advocate. He is the officer who gives out his cell phone number and business card to participants he interviews for phase moves. When he reports on interviews, he gives specifics: he discloses where he interviewed the participant and tells the team the themes he discussed, the potential problems he saw, and what he thinks the team should do. We posit that his participation in a police department that endorses community policing explains his dedication to the reentry participants (Ford 2007; Moon and Zager 2007).

Probation Officers: A Change of Pace

Each PSC is served by a unique probation officer. The probation office works totally in house (i.e., it sees all probationers in the office and does no fieldwork). In forensic diversion, the chief probation officer attends meetings to summarize information from the presentence report when asked. He is otherwise likely to stay silent at meetings, unless a change to the program is proposed, which he resists strongly. He distributes e-mails to the team to express his opposition and states at team meetings that his officers will not be able to adjust to the change proposed. When the Addiction Severity Index was proposed for forensic diversion, his resistance, which included joining forces with the social worker, caused the team to drop the matter.

The probation officer assigned to reentry court is the most experienced member of the team. She was there for the first reentry meeting and attends all staffing meetings and court sessions. The reentry PSC has brought in many changes, ranging from the assessment tools used to the services and programs it provides participants. On her own, this probation officer keeps records to show who has been considered for admission to the program, when each participant started the program, what his or her violations are, and when each participant graduates or is expelled. She has more institutional memory of reentry than any team member other than the judge. On many occasions, she talks about how "interesting" reentry court work is. Contrary to taking a social worker's role, she is quick to point out criminal thinking and to advise the judge to impose punishments. She is also one of the two persons, claims the judge, who he can trust to give him up-to-date and accurate information (the other is a member of the drug task force team who is a "silent partner" in the reentry enterprise).

Social Workers

More than any other type of team member, the social workers assigned to the PSCs resist the programs and their role on the teams. This is the case for social workers in both the reentry and forensic diversion courts. The social worker on the reentry court team pretends to disclose information about the participants, but she is known for disclosing erroneous information or making it up on the spot. She also fails to report relevant information to the team, such as a participant harassing her coworkers. (The information was sent to the presiding judge by a police officer who answered a complaint.)

The social worker in the reentry court is responsible for telling the team which participants are behind in their payments to the provider, but she tends to wait, on average, for eight weeks before disclosing a participant's delinquency. Because paying for treatment is a program regulation, this sets the participant up to face stiff consequences or expulsion. If such a response is proposed, the social worker objects on the premise that the mental-health agency will lose all the money it is owed by the participant returned to prison. The catch-22 position brought to the reentry court team continuously causes frustration for the judge, the other team members, and the participants.

The social worker assigned to forensic diversion left the position on the court team after two years. She could not and would not develop case plans based on the Level of Services Inventory domains. She stated a strong preference for staying in the office to meet with participants, as well as a dislike for working with the program's mentally ill participants (i.e., in the program designed for persons with co-occurring mental-health and drug-addiction problems). When the Addiction Severity Index was proposed to the team as an additional testing instrument, the social worker, with the chief probation officer, called for "an educational meeting" of the team to protest its adoption. When the forensic diversion social worker left the team, her position remained vacant. Case management was transferred entirely to community corrections.

Not all Team Members Deliver

A small number of team members on both the reentry and the forensic diversion PSC teams attend meetings and nod politely when the judge asks them to do something. These members do not deliver what they promise and never attend court sessions. As a consequence, they are not familiar with participants' needs or demeanors. One team member who falls into this category is assigned to reentry to help participants prepare for the GED exam and to direct participants to job-skills classes. He does nothing. When queried, he may claim to have been too busy the previous week or that his employer is thinking about changing a particular program.

Another example of a social actor who falls into this category on the forensic diversion team is a faith-based representative. He attends team meetings but offers no advice to the team or information on or for the participants. What he does do is complain about the twelve-step-meeting attendance requirement on the premise that an explicitly religious program (his) would help. He remains on the team because he causes no harm to participants.

THE PROBLEM SOLVING COURTROOM WORK GROUP

Perhaps most important to the ongoing success or survival of any problem solving court program is the judge-prosecutor-defender work group. On both the forensic diversion and the reentry court teams, it is apparent that these are first-rate partnerships of legal and social actors who share a common mission. Maneuvers and strategies played out backstage by the work group can be tense: will they agree to take in this new participant? The interactions include humor largely based on long-term professional relationships, respect, and familiarity. If the judge teases the defender for how she worked out a "sweetheart deal" with the prosecutor, the team feels as if it is brought into the criminal justice process. When the prosecutor teases the judge for being approximately thirty seconds late for a meeting, the team lets the usual authoritative barrier between "the judge" and the "layperson" break down. All told, the backstage banter and action provide a sense of camaraderie, bringing most team members together to prepare the problem solving court programs for addressing participants' needs. It is simply not "business as usual"—not even business as usual for the courtroom work group. The backstage work of the problem solving court is clearly a new form of delivering criminal justice, anchored by the rule of law and by a PSC work group.

Our three-year observational study of problem solving court work groups supports what other researchers have found and what other social scientists contend (Maruna and LeBel 2003; Ward and Brown 2004). Shared values and purposes among team members, especially an appreciation for human needs and strengths and a commitment to rehabilitation and change, are necessary to recruit the best social and legal actors to create a work group that will deliver the necessary services and programs participants need to succeed and thrive as contributing members of society. Cooperation from all team members is difficult to achieve and should not be assumed. In putting together a good PSC program, it takes time to recruit and build a smoothly functioning team. This starts with a memorandum of understanding between an organization and the PSC that articulates what an agency will provide. We would be remiss to ignore the financial strain that a PSC program can put on a public or non-profit agency or service provider. While the PSC is focused on doing everything possible for each unique participant, an agency or organization may be challenged to provide the services that participants cannot afford. Ironically, if participants had all the resources to pay providers, they would be much less likely to be involved in criminal court programs. Thus, it is imperative for the PSC programs themselves to pursue the funds necessary to help support the social service and educational agencies that work with the problem solving courts and their participants.

11

Front-Stage Performances

*Jeralyn Long Faris, JoAnn Miller,
and the Hon. Donald C. Johnson*

THE STAGE

Shakespeare's stage was simple; some would call it austere. Language, dialogue, and actors and audiences transformed the plain space into a battle scene or a room where lovers would reunite. Passionate pleas or clever tricks to guarantee justice and mercy brought actor and audience together emotionally to regret a decision, anticipate marriage or death, or cheer or complain.

The traditional U.S. courthouse tends not to be like Shakespeare's stage but, rather, elaborate in design. Its exterior and interior are typically adorned with symbols of the most important U.S. values—liberty and justice—with large columns, statues, flags, and portraits. However, the courtroom's function is similar to Shakespeare's stage, as it becomes a space where social actors perform to, and sometimes with, audiences. In the problem solving court, the audience is a blend of the state's authority, the helping professions, friends, family members, and sponsors. Some audience members are seated in the gallery, while others get (jury) box seats due to their commitment to, or involvement with, the PSC process. The lead actors are attorneys, case managers, and participants.

The social actors in a PSC give impromptu performances and return to the same stage each week to enact another scene. As observers and researchers, we are members of the audience; yet, as analysts we work to make sense of what performances mean for the social actors. The challenge in this chapter is to understand the participant's reality, as it is presented and understood by them, and how it is performed for the audience. To meet this challenge, we feature two reentry PSC participants, Audrey and Dan, both young parents, who struggle to succeed in reentry, with their families, and in their communities.

INSTITUTIONAL ETHNOGRAPHY

We move, from the backstage to the front-stage action, by using an institutional ethnographic approach. We use this method to analyze the effects of the PSC's organization and rules on all the social actors in the PSC: the participants, the judge, the agents of criminal justice, and the social service providers.

Researchers use institutional ethnography (IE) to see or understand the everyday world of the other and to conceptualize or explain how things happen the way they do. Dorothy Smith states, "The central project [of IE] is one of inquiry which begins with the issues and problems of people's lives and develops inquiry from the standpoint of their experiences in . . . everyday living" (2006, 18). The subject of study can be anyone, the painter or the priest, the potter or the prison inmate.

The "anyone" in the reentry problem solving court includes all of the participants, the judge, members of the reentry team, and a number of observers, some of whom are the participants' family members, twelve-step sponsors, employers, or friends. In this chapter, we investigate "our" practices, as researchers, which requires a substantial dose of self-overhearing, or self-reflection. Earlier chapters told the stories of participants' based exclusively on what "they" disclosed in the public courtroom.

Here, we take an IE approach to explore and describe the social organization of the everyday experiences of one particular young mother, a reentry court participant named Audrey, and one particular father, a reentry court participant named Dan. We chose to focus on them rather than other participants because they share some family circumstance yet not others. Both have children, and both have alcoholic mothers. Audrey is a single mother of one child, and she is an only child.[1] Dan is the father of two children and lives with his ex-wife and children. He is in marital therapy and preparing to remarry. Both Audrey and Dan violated minor program regulations numerous times, yet continue to make progress in the reentry court as measured by their Level of Service Inventory (LSI) and Addiction Severity Index (ASI) scores and lack of police contacts. Finally, they both devote hours of volunteer time on weekends to the city's Shelter Plus Care program, a federal- and state-funded program to provide permanent housing assistance to the chronically homeless disabled by serious mental illness, drug addiction, or HIV/AIDS. Audrey and Dan were selected to represent the city's volunteers for the

Shelter Plus Care program at its annual Good News Day held at city hall and covered by the local and state media.

We analyze how Dan's and Audrey's actions and the judge's and reentry team members' reactions to them are framed. For this analysis we use their courtroom dialogues and their written essays.

When Audrey and Dan were released from prison and became participants in reentry, they entered a unique network, or system, of blended organizations governed by legal processes constituting what institutional ethnographers call "a system of ruling." Reentry court is linked to other ruling systems, particularly community corrections and a community mental-health provider. Most of the activities related to Audrey and Dan are textually mediated or affected by the case reports and test scores referenced by reentry team members and the judge when they interact with Audrey and Dan. Texts, which are documents of any type, are "essential to the objectification of organizations and institutions and to how they exist as such" (Smith 2006, 160). They are important devices used to connect and coordinate people's activities. The scope of the institutional ethnographic method is expanded beyond the observational limits of courtroom and personal interactions. Texts used by the reentry court team are focal points of the inquiry because they are primary instruments of the implementation and action that takes place in the reentry PSC.

The social organization of the reentry PSC scene is not wholly contained in the public courtroom setting. Rather, this blended organization is constructed by social relations outside of the setting that are partially visible within it (Smith 1987). The institution is not a singular form of an organization but a functional complex. In this case, a reentry PSC is located within a general-jurisdiction state court, in which several forms of organization are interwoven. Foremost among these are the bureaucratic forms of organization that make actions accountable in terms of abstract, generalized categories (Grahame 1998). The reentry court case manager creates a textual account of the participants' activities in ways that express the functions of the reentry court.

Primary texts that, using IE terms, "objectify" Audrey and Dan are the weekly individual case reports prepared by the community-corrections case manager. These reports are used to direct and connect the working activities of the reentry PSC and the team. The texts are compiled by the case manager, updated weekly, duplicated, and distributed to the team members via e-mail and in printed form at the weekly team meetings. These documents are used to present an "objectified reality" of all the participants by naming, defining, and standardizing the "terms" used to know, understand, and evaluate the reentry PSC environment.

For example, the weekly case reports for each individual show a history of the LSI and ASI scores to provide ratings on a participant's level of risk and his or her needs in many domains of life. Through the use of terms like "legal problems" and "accommodations," an individual participant's activities appear in an objectified form so that he or she is defined in terms of the expectations and procedures of the reentry court team. If Audrey has a high "legal problems" score, the team asks specific questions: What are her problems? Does she need counsel to represent her? Does the Division of Family and Social Services need to be contacted? If Dan scores high on "accommodations," the team wants to know, Does he need better housing? Can both of his children have the privacy they need at their ages?

Smith (2001) explains that the texts provide "an order of fact-icity" so that divergent views on how to interpret the facts no longer appear. Audrey's and Dan's personal and nuanced realities are placed into a regulatory text that team members can use. These texts, however, do not stand alone. Rather, they are embedded in the courses of action taken by the reentry court team and the conversations that occur publicly in the courtroom.

AUDREY'S ENTRANCE

Audrey served prison time (twice) for dealing cocaine and gave birth to her daughter while incarcerated. Audrey's alcohol and drug risk levels did not decrease during her first three months in the reentry PSC. During a reentry court session, the judge asked, "Audrey, are you an addict?" She answered, "I was. I used to be," to which the judge responded, "Now Audrey, you can't turn a pickle into a cucumber. Have you ever heard of that?" After Audrey paused, nodded, and then looked at the judge, he added, "Once an addict, always an addict. Now let me ask again. Audrey, are you an addict." This time, Audrey simply said, "Yes, your honor, I am an addict."

STRUGGLES AND STANDPOINTS

The stated purpose of reentry court is to increase public safety by facilitating the transformation of "felons" into "productive members of society" or "citizens" within the community. Inevitably, struggles or various forms of resistance arise, sometimes on the part of the reentry court team and sometimes on the part of the participants. The team may perceive a participant as not making progress because there is no decrease in his or her risk of reoffending when the participant is tested six months or nine months into the program. There is concern that the participant may not be developing the skills, attitudes, or behaviors required to succeed in the community.

Audrey's and Dan's perspectives on their everyday experiences are revealed in their written and oral narratives as they interact with the judge and reentry PSC team. Researchers use the institutional ethnography method of taking the standpoint of the reentry participants to avoid reproducing the objectified discourse of social organizations (Smith 1987). It enables the researcher to begin the analysis while recognizing that all the team members and participants in the reentry PSC are working to achieve the same goals. However, there is also an awareness that the relations among those in reentry court are organized from somewhere else (i.e., from the statutory language that regulates reentry courts, from what the community mental-health organization requires, and so forth). We need to know how this blended organization called the reentry court is put together, how we talk about it, and how the texts purporting to describe it are a part of the process.

To understand Dan's and Audrey's perspectives in reentry, we analyze the everyday talk and texts (the case manager's weekly reports and the essays that participants write) and the conversations observed and recorded in the public courtroom.

AUDREY AND HER LAUNDRY

Audrey's situation, in many ways, represents what women in the reentry PSC experience (Alleyne 2006; Arditti and Few 2006). Most of the women in the program are younger than their male counterparts, and they return home from prison seeking custody of their children. Most are unprepared for the labor market, because they have only experienced either interrupted or underground (e.g., drug dealing or prostitution) employment. A female participant with a high school diploma is the exception. Most of the women in this reentry PSC dropped out of school due to a pregnancy or the escalation of a drug habit.

Audrey is young. She has been a chronic polysubstance abuser since the age of twelve and has faced serious legal trouble for approximately seven years. During her initial incarceration, she lost custody of her infant son, and he was adopted. During her most recent period of incarceration, Audrey gave birth to a daughter, who was placed in the guardianship of the maternal grandmother (Audrey's alcoholic mother and her only family member).

Two months after her daughter was born, Audrey was released from prison, placed in the county's community-corrections facility, and admitted to the reentry PSC. She had known a member of the reentry court team, and they met in the rotunda of the courthouse. Audrey was very excited to be out of prison. She said that she was unaware of how she got out (her sentence was modified after her attorney petitioned the court for modification) or what the program was all about, although she had signed the PSC participation agreement (see appendix B) and the public defender had walked her through each and every rule and procedure. This encounter revealed she was naïve, somewhat immature, and in need of a mentor to get through the reentry court. The person she first met as the jail minister became that person.

The judge was firm with Audrey in her first court appearance. She needed to find a job, and he was not yet interested in learning what her problems and preferences were. She returned the second week, beaming, and reported to the judge that she had obtained a job at a fast-food restaurant. She also now eagerly told how she was aware of the requirements of the program. However, the case manager's weekly report documented that a surveillance officer had seen Audrey talking "out back" before one of the required daily Alcoholics or Narcotics Anonymous meetings, causing her to be three minutes late for the meeting. Thus, while in court, expecting praise for getting her first-ever job, she instead received a consequence, eight hours of work crew, for being late and was assigned to write a one-page essay on what it means to be punctual.

During the third week, the judge queried the mental-health counselor about Audrey during the team meeting. The counselor reported that Audrey had a "bad attitude." No specific examples, no clarification, and no elaboration followed. When asked by the judge what that meant, the counselor said, "You know, she's not enthusiastic like the rest of them. She whines and complains. She seems pretty immature. I don't think she likes this program. I don't have a lot of confidence in her."

In court, the judge addressed the issue. With his hands crossed on his bench, he said to Audrey,

> People at [the community mental-health center] report that you are whining, complaining about the program. We can't have that. It's bad for everyone in the program. What do you have to say? [Following a minute of silence, he spoke again.] Okay, I'm sending you back to the jail for a week. I don't want to talk to you about anything else today. I'll see you next Monday. Keep a journal of what you are learning every day.

The judge instructed the bailiff standing the back of the courtroom to put the cuffs on. Audrey began to tear up as her hands were cuffed and her feet shackled. The judge addressed her again and said, "You are not engaged in the program, Audrey. You need to get engaged. Talk to your sponsor. Talk to your case manager."

Audrey cried and was seated in a back corner of the courtroom. Her emotional response seemed reasonable, but Audrey later disclosed that she was "an emotional basket case." The following week's court session was cancelled because the case manager had not met with the participants or prepared weekly case reports. As a result, Audrey remained in jail for a second week. The jail minister met with her and offered encouragement, and she noted her personal concerns about Audrey's fragility to both Audrey and the judge.

When the judge called her name the next (fifth) week, Audrey shuffled to the front of the courtroom in her jail blues, still handcuffed and shackled. The judge stated,

> You're young and green, but that won't be permanent. You're immature, and that's not all that bad. You expressed bad attitudes about the program. I find those things out, you know. A little birdie told me. That's criminal thinking for you to be complaining. I don't want you to go back to prison, but that's where you're headed unless you engage in this program and turn things around.

Audrey volunteered to read her assigned one-page essay, and, in the courtroom, she also admitted to the judge that he made her nervous. When he replied, "That's my job," she laughed nervously and quipped, "You're doing a good job of it!" She then read the essay, humbly apologizing for "complaining and being impatient and immature." Audrey acknowledged that before being placed in jail, she had "a lack of commitment or seriousness for the program"; she now realized that she wanted "to be a part of the program, accomplish something, and one day complete the program." Furthermore, Audrey hinted that she perceived the judge to be a type of father image for her, having imposed a jail sanction, when she read, "Without this bit of personal reflection, and I had been free just living life, if I did not get ordered back to jail, these attitudes and behaviors could have eventually led me back out to using which could have resulted in either death or prison."

The judge responded, "Let's give Audrey a hand. Thank you, Audrey. You did a very good job with that essay." Audrey blushed as most of the people in the courtroom applauded.

Tension emerged, however, when the team recognized Audrey's succeeding required that she conform to the mental-health counselor's perception of a "good attitude," a criterion the team had heard the same woman comment on often, generally leaving her pronouncements vague at best. Audrey could not engage in personal conversations that would cause her to be late to meetings, and she needed to meet the judge's and the team's expectations for "being engaged in the program," which also, from Audrey's perspective, were somewhat unclear.

When the judge states that he "finds these things out," as he did to Audrey, he reveals to her that others are telling him their perceptions of her "whining and complaining." Her weekly case reports are supposed to indicate the accounts of the mental-health counselor (though they rarely do) and the surveillance officer. Documents are placed in Audrey's file, and the texts serve to establish future expectations. A focus on the actual activities of the reentry court team reveals that they do what E. Pence (2001) calls "processing interchanges." The team is not simply processing paper documents. They are focusing on the ways that practitioners, the mental-health worker and the case manager, act on Audrey's situation and then process it through a sequence of practices. They go over the numbers reported on the case reports and take them as indisputable facts. Power relations are revealed as practitioners and court officials manage this young woman's case. The judge (who is a judge and not a therapist) turns to a police captain to see if he agrees with the assessment that Audrey "is a bit immature." "Yes, sir, I think she is." Curiously, the police captain, substituting for a colleague, had never met Audrey.

This example illustrates the relationships that characterize the reentry front-stage performances that are directed by the backstage, or team meeting, activities. The members engage in a process of documentary interpretation, the production of factual accounts, and commitments to specific goals for the participant to achieve. The judge has no option but to take the counselor's statements (she has a "bad attitude") at face value.

The judge's documentary interpretation of Audrey's behaviors and interactions (i.e., she is "not engaged in the program") is a necessary condition for presenting both a coherent factual account to Audrey and giving her a jail sanction with instructions to "keep a journal" of what she is learning and thinking about while incarcerated. The judge offered encouragement as he announced she was being sent to jail by stating that he did not want her "to go back to prison." He clearly directed Audrey in her presentation of a humble, public apology to all the members of the court, providing opportunity for her declaration of a strong commitment to the program and demonstration that she is "learning" what the reentry court expects of her. Finally, the factual account, as presented in the case report, gives the reader (the team members) no other option than to identify with the counselor and the police captain as competent professionals. The judge, the reentry court team members, and Audrey's fellow participants are expected to accept that she is "immature" and treat her accordingly.

Six months later, Audrey fully understood that she needed help and guidance to obtain permanent employment. She went through five fast-food restaurant jobs in six months. The judge ordered her to quit one job when she reported witnessing drug use in the work environment, but she had been released by other employers for such behaviors as not making sufficient eye contact with customers and leaving work early after having an altercation with another waitress. Audrey's unstable employment record is characteristic of her bipolar disorder diagnosis, recorded on her weekly case reports but not mentioned for six months. The mental-health counselor was aware of her documented diagnosis but did not act on it. It is, however, a partial explanation of her adolescent, or immature, behavior and her pattern of giving up when relationship challenges arise.

The following dialogue highlights the judge's discussion of Audrey's work and family situation.

> JUDGE: Someone on the team will help you get another job. How do you feel?
>> AUDREY: I need help. I'm alone.
> JUDGE: Rely on the team. Have you always felt that way? Alone?
>> AUDREY: I've many times felt like the world was out to get me.
> JUDGE: Do you feel like I'm out to get you?
>> AUDREY: [With a big smile] Not today!
> JUDGE: How do you feel about the program?
>> AUDREY: I feel more confident now . . . not so alone.
> JUDGE: How does your family feel about you being in this program?
>> AUDREY: They have mixed feelings. They don't understand about all this extra stuff I have to do. They would rather see me take the easy route. [Audrey did not disclose that "family" was an alcoholic mother and no others.]

The judge then talked with her about the importance of thinking for herself, counseling that if her family was not supportive in appropriate ways, she needed to "stand up" to them. The judge continued his instructions:

> Audrey, your family might not see it, but you're doing the right thing. I remember my father. . . . He was angry that I wanted to go to college and told me that I needed to go out and get one of the high-paying factory jobs. He never approved of my going to college. But if you're doing the right thing, it's okay. You'll make it. You really have no other choice.

This directive clearly reveals the judge's expectation that there is "no other choice" for Audrey but to succeed. She is a single mother in need of a steady income. This fatherlike position that the judge took with Audrey continued through several of their weekly courtroom interactions. He reiterated Audrey's lack of family support and her need to assume responsibility for her life and her daughter's well-being. Audrey admitted in the courtroom that she was "not used to being a grown-up," and when the judge once asked her what it means to be an adult, Audrey said, "It means making consistent and making good decisions, putting my child first, living life, and not being crazy."

With each passing week, as Audrey lived through her struggles with jobs, family, and the rules of the court, she self-evaluated her past "crazy" life and learned strategies for making responsible choices. Verbal messages from the judge and team are sometimes empathizing and caring; at other times, they are scolding. Whatever approach is taken at any given weekly court session, the stated and unwavering goal is to assist Audrey in developing new ways of thinking and living. Each week in court, Audrey faces the challenge of filtering in the helpful comments and filtering out what she perceives to be the negative comments that refer more to her past behaviors than to strategies for doing well in the reentry court program.

We examined the expectations communicated to Audrey front stage as she began the program. She expressed them in an essay she read in court.

> I was asked to do a "one-pager" on what I think it will take for me to be a productive member of society. Your Honor, I'm going to be perfectly honest with you. I would absolutely love to be able to go home and be with my daughter and be an awesome mom and everything be great, but I feel that is unrealistic at this time. I feel it would be best for me to re-lay the foundation of recovery and go back to the basics of NA, maintain employment and get a better job and become stable and gain some sense of balance in my life.

Audrey expressed a desire to be realistic and become "stable" with "a sense of balance." The essay reflects that she is trying to internalize a definition of herself that corresponds to the definition of "a productive member of society" that the reentry court team members will adhere to. Six weeks later, Audrey read another assigned essay. She was asked to explain the greatest challenges she anticipated with her newly acquired private apartment. She read the following text in court:

> I've only had independent living for about a month or so prior to my incarceration. One of my biggest challenges will probably be laundry. I'm always busy so that might be time-consuming. Beyond that, I can't think of anything but I'm always open to suggestions. When it comes to people coming over to my place who are not authorized to be there, if that situation was to come up, I would immediately tell the person or persons that I can't be around anyone who is not approved by my program and I would immediately tell them to leave. Then I would call [the case manager] immediately and let him know the situation. If the person, for some reason would not leave, I would probably have to call the police. Beyond that, I'm not sure the steps reentry would want me to take.

Audrey's essay reveals an uncertainty about the team's expectations of her, and though she can articulate what she would anticipate her actions to be, she says that she is "open to suggestions" and wants the reentry court team's expectations clarified in terms of what steps she should take when different situations arise. An institutional ethnographer, Alison Griffith, points out,

> The "ex-prisoner" is in a relatively powerless position at the point of release when their reentry is being organized by others. At this point, they will, of

course, try to appear as model citizens, repentant, ready to take on all the responsibilities on the "outside." But they are not pawns. They are strategically coordinating their future possibilities (as they see them) with what they think the team wants to hear as well as with what they think they can do. Some are good at managing this intersection and others are not. (Personal correspondence, October 19, 2008)

In order to learn how to manage the team's expectations, Audrey reaches out in the text of her essay, seeking direction that can aid her in managing the intersection of her and the team's expectations.

Three weeks following the interaction reported above, Audrey was sanctioned with sixteen hours of road crew for "missing a meeting." Although a missed meeting is the factual violation recorded in the weekly case report, we also found that the text (i.e., the case report) does not reveal the situation accurately. Audrey was ten minutes late to a group-therapy session at the mental-health facility and was therefore denied entry by the counselor (the same person who had pronounced her as having a "bad attitude").[2] One week after the sanction was imposed, Audrey was surprised in court when the judge's initial comment to her was, "So, you went home to see your mother on your laundry pass." (She was on home detention and was granted a three-hour pass to do her laundry. The case manager reported that she was "out of bounds" from her home detention.)

Audrey looked puzzled and replied, "No, I had a pass to do my laundry and went to Mom's to do it."

The judge then looked at the case manager and asked, "Did she violate or not? Check it out. We need to know what we're doing here." The case manager responded definitively, "My report says she did violate. She was out of bounds." The judge affirmed the case manager's authority by telling Audrey, "He says you did not have permission to visit your mother. You've got to get things right." She acquiesced with a quiet "okay." The judge said, "I am sending you back to work release, and we'll look at this issue again in a week. Talk to the [community-corrections case manager]. Talk to him to see what he needs you to do."

Field notes from the court session indicate our surprise over how calmly Audrey took the latest sanction, but she immediately began to talk to the community-corrections officer, attempting to obtain an explanation from him for what she did not understand to be a program violation. It is important to note that the text of the weekly case report simply states that Audrey was sent to work release for being "out of bounds on home detention." Again, we see how activities that occur in the processing of Audrey's case are textually mediated. The mental-health counselor denied her access to a meeting when she was late, but the text records show that she missed a meeting. The case manager, who received information from the home-detention surveillance officer, declared Audrey "out of bounds" without ever talking to her in order to understand her perspective. Audrey had never been told that she must do her laundry at a commercial laundry mat. She was simply told that she had a laundry pass. She interpreted the pass to indicate that she could do her laundry wherever she chose to use washers and dryers. She chose to use her mother's laundry machines for the dual purpose of seeing her child and saving money.

For a couple of months, the reentry court process went smoothly for Audrey, with her case reports being positive and the weekly court conversations with the judge marked by such comments as "I'm seeing a change in you. . . . I like what I'm seeing. You're working, taking parenting classes, great at keeping your apartment clean." The judge activates the texts that are gathered in concert—from the surveillance officer who drops by to check her apartment (she earned an excellent rating on the cleanliness of her apartment) and the case manager who checks on her employment and attendance at parenting classes and other required meetings. This activation process, the heart of the front-stage performances in reentry, gives the judge the opportunity to use the text and to coordinate activities to get tasks accomplished (Wright 2003).

The reentry PSC in this particular city connects to a U.S. Department of Justice Weed and Seed initiative that works to weed out crime and plant the seeds of prevention. Audrey and other reentry participants have benefited from Weed and Seed and related programs by receiving housing assistance, and they reciprocate by volunteering to help the homeless in the community move into apartments provided through a state housing grant. The Weed and Seed coordinator and his assistant work with Audrey and other volunteers in the reentry problem solving court. Reports are posted on a website accessed by the judge and members of the reentry team. Summaries of the reports are sometimes publicized in the local media. A front-page article in the local paper described Audrey as one "who has been able to turn her life around in a way she never imagined possible" through participation in reentry (Voravong 2008). The public texts (newspaper accounts) are referenced and used by the judge and team members at court sessions to congratulate and praise participants for their volunteer work and their perseverance in reentry.

DAN AND FAMILY MATTERS

Dan's circumstances parallel Audrey's in many ways, and he can be viewed as a typical example of the male reentry court participants (Cooke 2005; Department of Justice and Office of Programs 2008). He was convicted of burglary, operating a vehicle while intoxicated, possession of a controlled substance, and theft. He had served a little over four years of a twelve-year (do six) sentence when he was released from prison and began the reentry problem solving court program. Prior to his conviction, Dan had a good factory job for eight years, and during that time he came into contact with drug abusers and dealers, eventually becoming a serious abuser. His wife divorced him and provided all the care work and income to support their children during Dan's incarceration.

Dan, as of August 2008, had been a participant in the reentry PSC for fourteen months. He had a full-time job and was living with his ex-wife and their children in rent-assisted housing. He and his ex-wife were seeing a marriage counselor regularly, hoping to remarry. As with Audrey, we can analyze Dan's case by investigating how reentry PSC documents and texts are used to transform him. Program expectations and demands are juxtaposed with the narratives and observations of courtroom interactions.

Dan was placed in work release at community corrections and expected to fulfill the requirements of Community Transition Week; the case manager kept a record of his compliance. The initial requirements are strenuous, personally challenging, and time-consuming. Most importantly for Dan, during the first week he was also searching for a job without transportation because the bus routes are not available from the community-corrections facility. The case manager's record of Dan's compliance with these requirements became part of the texts referenced by the judge and the reentry team.

After three weeks, Dan explained to the judge in court that he had started a job at a small manufacturing firm. He had trouble finding an employer who would work around the demands of court appearances, meetings, and case manager check-ins, but this employer had called work release in search of employees. Fortunately, Dan's brother was available to provide transportation, allowing Dan to land the job. In his conversation with the judge that day, Dan was asked about his relationships with his brother, wife, and children.

DAN: He [his brother] is real big in my recovery. In the past, I had a lot of problems with drugs, and he was always the one there smacking me in the face, "Look what you're doing," you know? He came to me and said, "You need to come stay with me," so I can get my kids 'cause my kids fit right in there with his kids.

JUDGE: Where are your children now?

DAN: They live with my ex-wife.

JUDGE: Are you visiting your children?

DAN: Not yet. She's kind of mad at me still, but when I get my own place, I can see them.

JUDGE: Okay. How does she get along with your brother?

DAN: She don't really get along with anybody.

The judge then laughed, said he didn't need to go into "all the details," and instructed Dan to find a home group and twelve-step sponsor. Dan referenced another participant sitting in the gallery who had helped him with rides to meetings, calling him "a godsend." The judge asked him if he was fulfilling the requirement to get his driver's license. Dan reported that he had obtained his license but needed to save to buy a vehicle. In the meantime, he said, "that's a real humbling experience for me to have to ride a bike, but I'm doing it." The judge assured him by saying, "You'll work it out. Everybody does."

The conversation that day ended with the judge asking Dan how he felt about the program.

> DAN: So far, I mean, it's hard. It's a lot of stuff, but I mean . . . I'm not complaining.
> JUDGE: It's supposed to be hard.
> DAN: I knew it was gonna be.
> JUDGE: Keep up the good work. Keep struggling. It's okay.

In this early courtroom interaction between Dan and the judge, we can see important elements. Dan was required to fulfill the reentry court requirement of beginning the process of (re)establishing social connections with his family, a new employer, and his fellow participants in reentry. Having completed assessments, he knew that the judge and the team had "the results," but he did not know those scores. On this particular day, the judge discussed issues with Dan related to several distinctive risk areas important to Dan's overall high risk of reoffending. For example, his high score on the family and marital needs (3/4) and his high companion score (4/4) indicated that upon release from prison, his needs in these interpersonal areas put him at high risk for recidivism. The team could see in the weekly case report that Dan had the goals of rebuilding trust with his ex-wife and children, reclaiming the role of parent in his family, and developing relationships with nonusing friends so as to have a strong support system in place. The judge held him accountable to these goals, and Dan showed initial steps to reduce his risk scores and come into compliance with the reentry court's expectations.

Clearly, Dan's brother provided strong social support; yet, Dan was still required at times to experience the humiliation of riding a bicycle. Dan received encouragement from the judge when he told him, "You'll work it out. Everybody does." However, several sanctions would come in the course of Dan's "working it out."

Within three weeks of initiating reentry, Dan had been five minutes late for one of his daily check-ins with the case manager and missed another check-in altogether. He was given eight hours of road crew for each violation. After missing a third check-in, Dan was placed in work release and told to write an essay on the importance of showing up on time. During the front-stage court session, Dan explained that he had discussed his struggles and forgetfulness with a doctor at the mental-health clinic. He then stated,

> Since I recognize my forgetfulness today as a problem I must always be aware and not get too busy doing good things that I neglect to do what is right. I just hope that the judge and my peers understand that I do take my recovery very seriously and that my being in recovery is all a big change to me, and all addicts struggle with change, but at least today, I can understand that these struggles can make the weak places strong. Since I've been released from DOC [the Department of Correction] I've progressed a lot more than I thought I would. I'm going to continue working my program and try to not put as much on my plate and take the tools I've been taught and apply them one day at a time.

Dan's public statement sounds two noteworthy themes. First, he overtly references "good things" that he might "choose" to do being trumped by the requirement to "do what is right." The judge followed up on Dan's tardiness and found out that he had missed one check-in because of family commitments. At the time, he was just beginning his efforts to reestablish his relationship with his family. His ex-wife's working hours meant that the children needed transportation at a particular time, and in his efforts to help, he forgot a check-in. The official record, the text, only shows that Dan failed to comply. The weekly report defines Dan without regard for his taking responsibility for his family. The judge explained that being on time is "the right thing to do," and Dan quickly saw his need to comply with that definition of "it"—meeting check-in requirements on time.

A second theme in Dan's statement concerns the hardships imposed by the program that "can make the weak places strong." His identity as an addict in recovery is a central focus of the reentry PSC, and he points to the progress that he believes he has made as well as his commitment to "work the program." Dan clearly agrees to "take the tools" he has been taught and "apply them one day at a time."

What are those "tools," and how is he required to apply them? The structures set up by the judge and the team members become the tools. Daily check-ins are a major part of that structure, but Dan allowed family commitments to take priority. In order to help Dan learn not to forget his responsibilities to the program, the judge and the team placed him in work release.

Dan acknowledged that his "weakness" (forgetfulness) was "strengthened" by the hardship of losing his freedom. Dan also understood that his attempt to uphold his family commitments cost him a week in work release. The weekly case report simply shows that he "failed to check in."

One week later, Dan failed to check in again, and the mental-health counselor reported that Dan might be suffering from "postacute withdrawal," creating stress through commitment to his family, which aggravated the memory loss. The judge required that he check in twice a day, giving Dan a sanction that served to maintain the judge's commitment to the reentry court's goal. Dan began using the alarm on his cell phone, the mother of another participant called him with reminders, and he was able to adjust his schedule at work so that check-ins could occur before rather than after his shift. The combination of these efforts enabled Dan to conquer his problem with check-ins. However, Dan was late for curfew at his halfway house residence the following week, and when the incident was discussed with the judge, he explained that there had been confusion about the time requirement. He had been with his family and expressed frustration at being "stuck" in the first phase of the reentry court program for over six months. With growing family responsibilities, he was struggling with the rules. No excuses are allowed, however, and the textual record of the case manager's report reads, "Curfew violation, dishonesty about whereabouts." The sanction given for this offense was a delay in Dan's move to independent housing.

The punishment was compounded when a visiting judge was in the reentry courtroom the following week. The visitor wanted to know why Dan was still in Phase 1 and stated that he saw "significant problems" due to "blame shifting and lack of responsibility." The visitor then asked, "Are you sabotaging your own program?" Dan answered succinctly that he was still in Phase 1 because of his late check-ins, and although he briefly attempted to defend himself, he quickly took full responsibility and stated, "I'm bad at making excuses." When the judge asked for an explanation, Dan told him about his work to reunite with his family. The judge remarked,

> Do you know how many times I've heard this story? Everybody coming in to my court tells me that they are going to reunite. And you know how many do? [Holding his thumb and index finger together to signify a zero] None. That's right. Not a single one. Everyone wants to reunite, but I tell them to focus on their real problems.

This court exchange is a good example of a judge's documentary interpretation. The texts of the weekly reports are critical, and the judge takes them at face value, knowing little or nothing about the background of Dan's case. He interprets Dan's problems as "significant," and his use of the word "sabotage" indicates his perception that Dan is on a potentially self-destructive path. The word choice moves the dialogue toward suppression of Dan's response, giving him no ability to offer a defense. Rather, he is objectified, represented as an irresponsible, problematic, and self-destructive man. Like all others, he is doomed to fail in reuniting with his wife and children.

Interestingly, Dan took the six-month LSI assessment two weeks before this interaction, and his overall score had dropped to about half the risk level recorded on his initial assessment (from high to low/moderate). Only the psychological score on the ASI had increased, indicating the stress level that the mental-health counselor had noted but not acted on. The visiting judge did not notice the change in scores and may not even have been aware of their significance. He was basing his approach to Dan on the case manager's weekly report with its laundry list of violations and sanctions.[3]

The team used the LSI and ASI scores to gauge Dan's progress, and at the time of his last and final violation two weeks later, the light sanction imposed was an essay. Dan had failed to call the surveillance officer about an overnight stay with his family, but by this time, the presiding judge of the reentry PSC and the team knew that Dan was nearing the time of reunification with his ex-wife and children. Two of the team members who had personal contact with Dan reiterated the value of his family's wanting Dan to live with them. A counselor who had worked with Dan in the Dad's Make a Difference program gave the judge a very positive report of Dan's progress, and all of these reports together helped Dan to advance to Phase 2 of the reentry PSC program. Nine months following Dan's string of program violations, he was preparing to graduate from reentry. Dan and his wife and children were living together and planning to save for their first home.

ENACTING TEXTS

Texts are enacted differently in the various situational contexts of Dan's case, but the documents, or scripts, are essential to the objectification of Dan and the organization of the reentry PSC. They are important devices used to connect and coordinate the activities into an organization of ruling relations. In ongoing relationships, some social actors have more power to make some things happen than others. The judge, the case manager, and the mental-health counselor have more power than other members of the team, and the team has more power than the participants. But all the social actors, on the front stage, have social-interactional power, and all are circumscribed by the texts that coordinate different individual events as "the same" as other events. The weekly conversations between the judge(s) and participants like Audrey and Dan have different implications, but they all follow a textual script, written backstage at team meetings.

In the case of the reentry PSC, organizational processes shape the activities and produce similarities of experience for the participants who graduate from the program. Observing the reentry process through the lens of institutional ethnographic methods opens the analytic aperture, shifting focus away from the individual actors in the reentry court and "toward the coordination of their doings observed while doing them" (Diamond 2006). From the insider's position, we watched as texts were activated, and we observed how case files for Audrey and Dan were both products of and used by team members to account for coordinating several institutional functions, especially the work of a judge, a case manager, a mental-health counselor, and other social service providers. Our goal here was to produce an account useful for anyone who wants to grasp what people do routinely when "doing reentry court."

12

Finale

WAYWARD PURITANS: A CLASSIC TALE

Let us begin our conclusion by examining Kai Erikson's reflection on his study of deviance in *Wayward Puritans* (1966). In 2005, his classic was published yet again, this time with an afterword in which Erikson examines a claim he made in the 1966 volume:

> If the police should somehow learn to contain most of the crimes . . . and if at the same time medical science should discover a cure for most of the mental disorders . . . it is still improbable that the existing [social] control machinery [the mental hospitals] would go unused. (2005, 226)

He concludes, forty years later, that he was wrong. The old, foreboding mental hospitals have been closed, and society's commitment has shifted toward treating the mentally ill within the community.

Although nowadays the large mental hospitals are closed, psychiatric units in medical hospitals remain open, albeit with a dramatic shortage of psychiatrists. While there is no cure for mental illness, new pharmaceuticals effectively control symptoms of illness. Although many of the old hospitals are empty, many mentally ill persons, especially those who are poor or who drifted into poverty on account of their condition, are institutionalized by state prison systems or wander homeless in our cities.

Problem solving courts are blended social organizations or institutions that take mentally ill convicted offenders, returning prison inmates, and drug- or alcohol-addicted members of the community into the courts instead of prison or mental hospitals. The PSC provides a new layer of social control within the community, becoming the mechanism that maintains socially acceptable levels of crime and deviance for the community. The authority of the court implies that the participant who violates program regulations and deviates from the normative order of the PSC faces jail or prison. The court, as an institution, blends with corrections to maintain the normative order of the community.

The problem solving court,[1] regardless of variation in vision or mission statements, maintains three important functions. First, it facilitates the transformation of a negative master status into a pro-social one. While in a PSC program, participants advance from one phase of the program to the next and eventually graduate. The graduation ceremony is a ritual and a moment of celebration. To use the cliché, graduation is commencement, or the beginning of a life-building project that PSC graduates are equipped to handle as they continue adding new roles and their attendant expectations and responsibilities, new layers of identity, and new social statuses that will eventually shroud the negative master status—the "felon," "mentally ill," or "addict" status—that brought them to the attention of the police and eventually the problem solving court.

Second, the problem solving court provides the material resources, treatment, and services that transform a social actor from an outsider and a *threat to* the community into an insider, or a *member of* the community. Housing and income are the key symbols of a community's values, and they are the materials that alter the resource base for the PSC participant. Housing comes in the form of tenant-based rental assistance and facilitates asset building. A PSC participant can build assets only with income that exceeds living expenses. The level of income necessary to accumulate assets is achieved through assisted housing and an employment program within the PSC that builds human capital (through education and job training) and provides work opportunities through cooperative partnerships with the communities' major employers. The material resources or tangible support that participants receive are linked to a three-part social-control process. The PSC judge facilitates change as he or she monitors progress, community corrections screens for alcohol or drug abuse, and "plainclothes" surveillance officers visit the participant at work and at home.

Third, the problem solving court communicates a strong public-safety message to the community. The message functions to show PSC participants and other community residents what the boundaries are for acceptable or normative behavior. In PSC sessions, the judge reminds participants, "You need to become a contributing member of society," which gives them reintegrative opportunities within the community; however, he imposes consequences, including jail time, for rule violations in order to recognize deviance and clearly draw the boundary for acceptable social interactions. The problem solving court that encourages participants to take on the community's identity reinforces the boundaries that give the community its own cultural identity.

We borrow Émile Durkheim's and Erikson's conceptualizations of boundary work to look within a different type of community—a community of judges. Consider this bold proposition: a problem solving court judge is a deviant.

The judiciary willingly maintains a limited number of such deviants and goes so far as to proclaim in speeches to state legislatures and other influence brokers that problem solving courts represent our best hope for controlling the community's most pressing social problems. These proclamations are a double-edged sword. They identify the deviants—the PSC judges. The judges, in turn, are not able to alter the reality that PSC work "does not count" when their workloads or caseloads are measured. Thus, PSC work at best remains unrewarded. Proclamations regarding the success of the PSC movement allow the judiciary to sing praise for the problem solving court while holding the sword of punishment over the deviant's head. Once the PSC judges are identified, the other judges in a state or federal court system can gather together and reaffirm their collective identity: "Real judges" do not perform PSC work. "Real judges" read cases and rule on the law.

The boundary maintenance work applies to criminal justice agencies as well as social service agencies. Representatives from these agencies are assigned to problem solving courts and deliver the services needed for the PSC program and its participants to succeed; yet, their own agencies and organizations, which depend somewhat on PSC programs for clients and revenue, do not consider their work for the PSC as legitimate work. The "chosen one" (i.e., the representative from the agency) displays behaviors at the PSC team meetings intended to show others that they are indeed the "deviants." They feign embarrassment, acting as if they must have done something wrong (as a police officer, as a jail worker, as a social worker) to have been selected to represent their agency.

THE TRAGEDY, THE COMEDY, AND THE FARCE

Our study of problem solving courts focused on identifying the factors that account for the success or failure of three programs. The reentry court is a wonderful success, as measured by outcome data,[2] by observing how participants and graduates find places for themselves and their families within their communities, and by the ways in which the community welcomes persons who "come home for good."[3] Some readers may be offended by our claim that it represents the comedy in our analysis of a trio of problem solving courts. We do indeed acknowledge that life for everyone, especially the PSC participants, is a struggle. Ned read his essay in reentry court on October 1, 2007.

> Jeff Foxworthy uses redneck jokes all the time in his comedy routine. The reason I like it is because it makes me laugh. It makes me laugh because I can relate to it. For example, I grew up in the country, so I can really identify with the joke about finding a car when you mow your lawn. When we first moved out to [the country] we were mowing some trails and came across a pile of junk. Surprise! Old refrigerators and tractor parts. Lots of junk! So why is it important that we laugh, that we have humor in our lives? For one thing, it can take a serious situation and make it comical. I might be really stressed about moving into my apartment this Friday. It's scary, but I look at it as an adventure. I don't have much furniture, so I could go to some abandoned apartments and get some free stuff. That makes me laugh. Another thing about laughter is that it is really good for your health. I don't remember the numbers but I know if you laugh really hard you burn lots of calories.

Tragically, the forensic diversion PSC, unlike reentry, struggles to maintain its existence. Participants experience the futility of working to maintain program regulations for the purpose of avoiding state prison. One-half fail and are sentenced to a term of incarceration. Ironically, forensic diversion is the only PSC that receives Department of Correction money to finance its program. In our observation it cannot, however, provide the material and support services that the participants and the program need to succeed. No matter what the presiding judge offered or did to bridge the gap between criminal justice and mental-health services, providers pushed back and resisted. Workers, representing distinct agencies, refused to let go of what they mistakenly took to be the boundary of their professional identity. "It's confidential" sums up the resistance by social workers, and "It's criminal thinking" sums up the resistance by criminal justice workers. As a result, participants suffer, no attempts are made to develop personal strengths or integration within the community, and the program itself faces threats to its own survival. This tragedy demonstrates the dire need for a collective identity to emerge across occupations that can promote the purpose of the problem solving court.

Our farce is the Title 33 program for sex offenders returning from prison. Criminal justice and mental-health workers assigned the ultimate outsider status to "the" sex offender—as though there is only one type—in spite of ample research literature and financial sponsorship to guide program and policy development in protecting the general population and effectively responding to ex-offenders within the community (Birgden 2007; Edwards and Hensley 2001; Petrunik 2002). Sex offenders, regardless of their offenses, are symbolically the devil in this and most communities within the United States nowadays. In a parallel to Salem's witch hunts, community leaders and their followers worked to drive out the Title 33 problem solving court. In practice, county community and criminal justice leaders clearly identified the boundary for acceptable problem solving courts, and the Title 33 program fell outside the boundary.

IT CANNOT BE A ONE-MAN SHOW

The failure of the Title 33 program ostensibly suggests that problem solving courts will inevitably face problems as they attempt to "go to scale"(Berman and Feinblatt 2005). However, going to scale does not mean that a PSC must be established to tackle each and every serious community problem. We contend that problem solving courts should be used carefully and sparingly. That is our advice to policy makers and lawmakers. The general population must become comfortable with a problem solving court to support its implementation.

Going to scale can mean that the practices of the PSC should be transferred to the conventional courtroom to settle the everyday disputes processed by civil and criminal courts. It is within the rule of law for the criminal court judge to ask the convicted offender about his family and support system before he imposes a sentence. It is within the rule of law for the sentencing judge to mandate drug-abuse treatment within the sentencing order. Not every judge has the ability or the inclination to face the challenges of the problem solving court. Nonetheless, each individual judge bears the ethical responsibility to rule on matters of law and to be members of the community they serve. We can think of no reasonable explanation or justification for any trial court judge to do otherwise.

Appendix A

Biographical Sketches

Twenty-nine reentry, forensic diversion, and Title 33 problem solving court participants tell their stories, front stage, in the various chapters of this volume. Fourteen are white men, ten are white women, and five are black men. Their biographic information is current as of January 2009. One person, Janise, was not admitted to reentry though she was interviewed by the team.

1. Audrey, a reentry court participant, is a twenty-two-year-old white mother of two. She lost her first child to adoption during her first period of incarceration and is struggling to reunite with her second child. She was incarcerated for a B-level felony drug offense. For years she has been diagnosed as suffering from bipolar disorder, type II. As she was preparing to exit prison, she was taken off all medications. She currently resides in rent-assisted housing.

2. Albert is a reentry court graduate and the noncustodial father of one nine-year-old son. He is a white, thirty-nine-year-old man, incarcerated for an A-level felony offense. When he was released from prison, his parents immediately helped him buy a small apartment building. The purchase was to help him stay busy and give him a small amount of money coming in on a regular basis. Albert had trouble with his tenants and needed to have two evicted. He works full-time, on the night shift, cleaning a hog plant in a neighboring county. He drives other participants to work on a regular basis. His demeanor is quiet and shy. In court, he tends to stroke his long beard while talking, never raising his eyes.

3. Beth was the first forensic diversion problem solving court graduate. When she was arrested for cocaine dealing, she was working as an exotic dancer. Beth entered the program at age twenty-five, a never-married

white woman. She earned the GED while in forensic diversion. Beth faced several years in prison but only spent time in the county jail while waiting to enter the forensic diversion program. She completed the program in eighteen months, followed by eighteen month's probation. She is now married and runs a small business, caring for pets and cleaning homes.

4. Bob is a reentry court participant who, for more than one year, refused to leave work release. He feared he would return to his old ways and his old friends. Bob is a black man in his mid-forties and has never been married. He wants to be an entrepreneur and plans to open an ice-cream stand. He sells motor scooters that require no driving license in the state. Thus, he can sell transportation to those who have permanently lost their driver's license on account of multiple driving violations, such as driving under the influence on a suspended license. Bob had a tendency to explain every problem he faced in terms of what others had done to him. Once confronted with that tendency, he made a deliberate effort to change. Often he would remind the judge how he, Bob, was responsible for being late, for not cleaning his apartment, and so forth.

5. Billy was eventually expelled from reentry court. For nine months he did well, advancing across the phases. However, he never managed to leave transitional housing. He was caught, on a surveillance tape, engaged in sexual intercourse with a case manager at transitional housing. He is a white man, currently thirty-five years old, and was orphaned at twelve when one parent died in a car accident and the other committed suicide. He came into reentry from state prison, where he served time for dealing cocaine. His criminal history includes auto theft, shoplifting, dealing methamphetamine (Class B felony), forgery, and armed robbery. He is a local high school graduate. He came out of prison married with one child, but he and his wife soon divorced. When he was expelled for program violations, not new crimes, he returned to prison.

6. Charles is a twenty-three-year-old, white, never-married reentry court graduate who had been an "A" university student until he began using drugs on a daily basis. He had very supportive parents who often attended the court sessions. His mother died during his program participation. Charles is a community spokesperson for the reentry court, called on often to tell his story. He received a full tuition scholarship at a community college to complete his associate's degree and will be returning to the university full-time during the fall 2009 semester.

7. Caroline is a white woman in her mid-twenties. She has had one child, born addicted to cocaine, who was adopted out. She was expelled from reentry for program violations and failing to make any measurable progress for more than six months. Caroline dropped out of high school and has not yet earned the GED. Her parents attempt to be supportive, but the social workers would call them "enablers."

8. Carter is a reentry graduate who was incarcerated for twelve years. A white, single man, he returned home to his girlfriend. He earned a bachelor's degree in prison and wants to start a food catering business with his girlfriend. During his participation in reentry, his program violations all centered on his girlfriend. She was found with alcohol in the house, and she reportedly asked him to check the car one night while he was on home detention, setting off the out-of-bounds signal at community corrections.

9. Dan, a reentry participant, is the father of three children and readily talks about the struggles his mother has with alcohol. His conviction offenses included drug crimes and burglary. Dan lives in rent-assisted housing and is expected to graduate from the program in the next few months.

10. Donna was expelled from the forensic diversion problem solving court after one year of making good progress. She is a white, divorced woman who had medical (including hepatitis C) and psychological problems that made work difficult. She officially "relapsed" and tested positive for cocaine. At her expulsion hearing, she admitted that she was selling cocaine to a fellow participant.

11. Fabian is a graduate of reentry. He is a twenty-nine-year-old, quiet black man with an extensive criminal history, including theft, numerous possession and dealing convictions, and resisting arrest while smoking crack cocaine. He was expelled from school in the eleventh grade for fighting. His only work history prior to reentry was working as a garbage collector at $8 an hour. He is the father of two children. He is now employed full-time at a meat-processing plant and pays regular child support.

12. Haley is a forensic diversion graduate in her late twenties who has one child. She has never been married, and she had never worked for a paycheck until she returned from prison. Haley was convicted on B-level felony drug charges but struggled with alcohol as much as with drugs. She often volunteered and made friends readily while in the program. She relapsed once, buying and using nonprescribed Klonopin.

13. Holly is a reentry court graduate who is currently twenty-four years old. She is white, has never married, and is the mother of one child.

Her father was granted guardianship of the child and demanded back child support from Holly when she was released. He would not let Holly see her toddler-aged son until she gave him a plan to pay him for caring for the child. Her mother is a well-known prostitute in town who would trick out Holly to increase her income. She forced Holly to live in the crawl space of her home. Holly twice attempted suicide.

14. Janise was approached to enter the reentry court program. She was scheduled for release from state prison within three months and was therefore not able to participate. She is a white, thirty-five-year-old woman who has given birth to four children and has never been married. Her youngest child was born in prison and has been adopted. Janise's mother cares for her three daughters but would not agree to bring the youngest child, a boy, into the household. The boy was named but Janise does not refer to his name because his adoptive parents changed it.

15. Joanie is a reentry court graduate who is now forty-one years old. She is a white woman, remarried to the man who divorced her on her way into prison. They have a child who lived out of state during the time Joanie was in prison for dealing narcotics at the A felony level. Joanie left high school after the tenth grade and worked off and on as a laborer. Now she is employed full-time as a supervisor at a car-manufacturing plant. On her own, with no advice from case managers or social workers, she decided to keep her child out of state, living with his paternal grandmother, until Joanie put her life back together. She reunited with her husband, and they brought their child home.

16. Jack is a reentry court graduate, now age forty-one, who was incarcerated for eight years before his sentence was modified. Prior to his arrest, he was a member of the Iron Workers, earning $21.50 per hour, plus benefits. He had earned his GED in the "Boys School" in 1983. He had been housed in the oldest prison in the state. He was convicted of many offenses, including dealing meth at the A felony level and running a meth lab in the presence of children.

17. Joe was expelled from the reentry court after he was arrested for driving while intoxicated on a moped in a neighboring county. He had nine prior convictions, most of them misdemeanors, all of them connected to alcohol abuse. Joe is thirty-eight, white, and the father of one child. Joe does not see his child or his ex-wife but worked hard to maintain his father's home. A generous and well-to-do social worker in town gave Joe money to avoid foreclosure on his home. She also hired him full-time to work on her farm.

18. Kathleen is a reentry court graduate, white, now age twenty-five and the mother of two children. Prior to incarceration she was a certified nursing assistant. Her first child was five when Kathleen was released from prison. While in reentry she became pregnant again. Kathleen is articulate and smart (though she has not completed high school or the GED) and wants to work in the helping professions. She and her sister are the children of a professor, divorced from his wife, who expresses concerns over the social embarrassment Kathleen causes the family.

19. Kyle, a reentry court participant, is a forty-eight-year-old black man. He has never married and has no children. He was in business with his father for many years, conning well-to-do business men in Ohio and Illinois. When his father settled down in Illinois, Kyle set up shop in Indiana, where he was arrested and convicted for defrauding a financial institution.

20. Kurt is a black man who was expelled from reentry for program violations. He reports that he has been homeless or in prison most of his life due to his cocaine and alcohol problems. He was employed by the same woman who helped Joe and, as a consequence, never developed the independence necessary to succeed.

21. Kipp is a black man who is a reentry graduate. He is thirty-two years old, married, and the father of two children. During the time he was in the program, he took in his brother's two children, which put stress on his marriage. Kipp took responsibility for placing his nephew in school and making sure he was doing well. Kipp was laid off from a manufacturing firm that paid well. He is currently unemployed and lives with his family in an apartment sponsored by a HUD Section VIII voucher. His criminal history begins in 1996 with a conviction for cocaine possession (out of state) and ends in 2002 with multiple A-level felony convictions for dealing cocaine.

22. Len, an older white man (in his fifties) who never married, participated in the Title 33 problem solving court for sex offenders. He had been convicted of rape in three states prior to his conviction (for rape) and prison sentence in this state. He returned from prison with severe breathing and circulatory problems. He lived in solitude, and the case manager often reported that he would sit on the end of his bed for hours at a time. He had no family and no friends in town. When asked about his family, he claimed he had no one. In one court session, he began talking with the judge about how he hated women because his mother had abused him. She molested him and later forced him to have intercourse with her. Only now, decades later, could he come to terms with what happened to him.

23. Mike is a reentry court graduate who was jailed for public intoxication after he completed reentry. He is forty-seven and white and has never been married. His criminal history includes robbery, theft, driving on a suspended license, operating a motor vehicle while intoxicated, public intoxication, and criminal trespassing. He is the youngest of five children and earned his GED in 1978. He admits to having severe substance-abuse problems since age fifteen. His live-in girlfriend often came to court with him. Mike has a short fuse and often got into trouble at work and during leisure activities on account of his uncontrollable anger, which too often resulted in fistfights. After he completed reentry, he obtained a hardship license to drive to work. He went to a bar, passed out, and was admitted to the hospital. His blood-alcohol level tested 0.32, and he attempted battery on two police officers who were called to the hospital. As a result, he was jailed.

24. Morgan is a reentry graduate with a degree in political science (earned during his fifteen years in prison). He is also a military academy graduate. He was sentenced to forty-two years in prison (in 1992) for drug-dealing and weapons convictions. He is white, has never been married, and was arrested for selling drugs while he was a college student in the southern part of the state. He lives with his elder and frail parents in a luxury housing development. Most notably, he is a talker. If someone asks, "How are you?" that person should be prepared for a half-hour talk about how he really is. When he was sentenced, he said, "May God be with me!"

25. Marlon is a tall, young (in his early thirties), Eastern European immigrant who claims to have worked with his family in a "crime family." He was once married and had a child who died (causes unknown). He attempted suicide twice. He was expelled from reentry after reportedly harassing two social workers at the community mental health center.

26. Ned, a white man, was sentenced to prison at age twenty-two and returned to the reentry court at age thirty-four. He is one of seven children. While in prison, to prepare him to exit the system, he was taken off the psychotropic medications that controlled his extreme mood swings. He is now a reentry court graduate, known for his sense of humor. His favorite comedian is Jeff Foxworthy. As he started reentry, he was belligerent and had a great deal of difficulty with day-to-day living. Once he was diagnosed with bipolar type II disease and treated, he settled into his very pleasant and helpful way of dealing with the demands of everyday life.

27. Rick was expelled from the forensic diversion problem solving court. He is a white man, married, with no children. He served three years

in prison for drug dealing and several terms of incarceration at the county jail for minor drug or alcohol offenses. A model jail inmate, he was known as a great worker but never conquered his drug problems. While in forensic diversion, he overdosed on a cocktail of drugs, including meth, and nearly died. Weeks later, he was released from the hospital and appeared in court with a portable oxygen unit. He was friends with another forensic diversion participant who, at age twenty-two, died from a drug overdose.

28. Randy was incarcerated for two A-level felony drug-dealing convictions. He is a bright and well-spoken, young (twenty-six years old), white, never-married man who finds endless excuses not to work. He remains in the reentry court program, promising to begin college in the fall. He began the program claiming that his religion prohibited his participation in twelve-step programs.

29. Susan was expelled from reentry two weeks after she began the program. She is a forty-six-year-old white woman whose entire family resides in the county jail. She was in work release when she began reentry and thought she would benefit from housing. Susan wanted the housing but she refused to participate in any required program.

Appendix B

Reentry Court Participation Agreement

_____ County Reentry Court Program

Participation Agreement

date _____

_____ County Reentry Court Program

Superior Court I

Participant's Name (Print):

ID:

PARTICIPATION AGREEMENT

This Participation Agreement is an agreement by and between the Participant _____ and the _____ County Reentry Court Program. The Presiding Judge of the Program shall sign the Agreement on behalf of the Program.

This Participation Agreement will take effect at the time that it is executed by you and the Presiding Judge and will continue in effect for so long as you are a participant in the Reentry Court Program and, if you successfully complete the Program, for so long as you are on probation or parole after your active participation in the Reentry Court Program has been completed.

Program Requirements

1. You must be placed in the Reentry Court Program (RCP) by the Presiding Judge. Successful completion of the RCP is required for you to complete successfully parole, probation, or the community corrections portion of your sentence.
2. If you fail to complete the Reentry Court Program, or any phase of it, you will be scheduled for an expulsion hearing. If you are expelled from the RCP you will be returned to the Indiana Department of Correction. You will be ordered to serve out the entire sentence that you have left to serve. That is, you will serve the balance of your prison time; and you will serve in prison any time that you would have served on probation, or at _____ County Community Corrections that was either a condition of probation or an executed sentence.
3. You shall execute a waiver of extradition and surrender all passports, which will be held by Community Corrections.
4. You shall execute the RCP forms titled "Policy Concerning Drugs and Alcohol" and "Waiver and Consent to Search."
5. You shall execute all requested consents, authorizations and releases for information and records and waive any right of confidentiality in such information and records. You shall authorize the Presiding Judge, the Reentry Court Team and its staff, treatment providers and your attorney to obtain, receive, provide to others associated with the program and discuss all information and records regarding you, your history and your performance in order to evaluate your progress. Such information and records may be discussed in open court.
6. Neither the Presiding Judge, Reentry Court Team, its staff, nor the County of Tippecanoe, its personnel, employees, staff and agents is liable for any medical expenses, problems or injuries that you incur while at your place of employment while you are a participant in the Reentry Court Program or as a result of your participation in the Reentry Court Program.
7. You will be interviewed to determine the types and the levels of services that you need. The interviews will take at least two hours. The interviews will be repeated at three to six month intervals while you are in the RCP Program.
8. You must sign a Case Plan which is an individual plan for services and treatment. You must participate in the services and treatment specified by the Case Plan. You must meet the goals and objectives of the Case Plan.

9. The Presiding Judge and the Reentry Court Team will authorize your Case Plan and you shall follow the requirements set out for you. The requirements may be modified from time to time at the discretion of the Presiding Judge and the Reentry Court Team.

10. You must submit to additional risk assessment, mental heath assessments and substance abuse assessment as deemed appropriate. You may be required to participate in additional treatment and rehabilitative programs. Community Corrections programs such as work release, house arrest and work crew may be required. Transitional housing, residential treatment and rehabilitation placements may be required.

11. When you leave work release or a rehabilitation placement, you will be placed on home detention in Reentry Housing. Your housing placement will require the installation of a telephone line for home detention.

12. When you are allowed to live independently in private housing, the Presiding Judge and the Reentry Court Team must approve of the place that you reside and the person or persons with whom you reside. The person(s) with whom you reside must sign a waiver consenting to his/her/their being tested for drug and alcohol use if requested to do so. You may not change your place of residence without the consent of the Presiding Judge and the Reentry Court Team. You will be subject to unannounced home, work, and school visits by the Reentry Court Program staff at any time.

13. Other than spouses, you may not live with a romantic partner without the consent of the Presiding Judge and the Reentry Court Team. Generally, for the consent to be given, you must have lived independently for a minimum of three to six months. Independent living means living for three to six continuous months at the same location, having an income to meet basic living expenses, and showing evidence of pro-social relationships and activities and the avoidance of relapse or drug-seeking behaviors.

14. Your program will last between twelve and twenty-one months. If you complete the program you will be required to appear in court on a monthly basis for approximately one year.

15. Your program may be divided into four phases. Graduation from one phase to the next phase will not be automatic. The Presiding Judge and the Reentry Court Team will decide on your progression through the phases based upon your motivation, attitude, maturity and completion of program goals. Unless otherwise provided by the Presiding Judge and the Reentry Court Team, your Program will probably consist of these four phases:

Phase 1

Goal: Engage in the Rehabilitative Process

Length: Approximately 90 days

- Complete LS/CMI and ASI interviews to determine services and programs
- Meet with Community Corrections Case Manager and agree to services and treatment on your Case Plan
- Begin treatment and services within one week
- Complete Community Transition Week
- Begin job search
- Treatment services are based on: alcohol and substance abuse needs, education and employment services, financial needs and services, residential needs, leisure and recreation needs, companions, emotional and personal needs, and services to develop pro-social attitudes and orientations
- Report to the _____ County Community Corrections Case Manager daily
- Meet with Reentry Court Program (RCP) Manager at least weekly to report progress in treatment and services
- Attend 12-Step Meetings daily
- Have a Sponsor and a Home Group
- Urine Drug Screen randomly but at least once per week
- Breath Testing daily
- Judicial Supervision every week, generally on Mondays
    A family member or a close friend must accompany you to court at least once a month
    Your 12-Step Sponsor must accompany you to court at least once a month or send a report to the RCP Manager at least once a month
- Complete Worksheets to indicate how you have committed to the rehabilitative process
- Prior to completing Phase 1, complete LS/CMI and ASI interviews
- Complete a phase move interview with Law Enforcement based on Phase 1 goal
- Pay one-fourth of program fee

If you are on home detention or day reporting during Phase 1, you must comply with:

- Random Page Call-ins
- Home and workplace visits
- 9:00 PM Curfew

Phase 2

Goal: Gain the Tools for a Constructive Lifestyle

Length: 90–180 days

- Meet with Community Corrections Case Manager and Reentry Court Program Manager and agree to services and treatment on your Phase 2 Case Plan
- Attend treatment, services, and classes indicated by your Phase 2 Case Plan
- Report to the _____ County Community Corrections Case Manager daily
- Meet with Reentry Court Program (RCP) Manager weekly to report progress in treatment and services
- Attend 12-Step Meetings daily
- Have a Sponsor and a Home Group
- Urine Drug Screen randomly but at least once per week
- Breath Testing daily
- Show progress toward completing GED if relevant
- Obtain valid driver's license or photo identification
- Complete WorkKeys Assessment
- Improve employment if advised by Case Manager
- Judicial Supervision every week, generally on Mondays
    A family member or a close friend must accompany you to court at least once a month
    Your 12-Step Sponsor must accompany you to court at least once a month or send a report to the RCP Manager at least once a month
- Complete Worksheets to indicate how you have engaged in educational and employment services that will help you achieve Phase 2 Goals
- Prior to completing Phase 2, complete LS/CMI and ASI interviews
- Complete a phase move interview with Law Enforcement based on Phase 2 Goals
- Pay one-fourth of program fee

If you are on home detention or day reporting during Phase 2, you must comply with:

- Random Page Call-ins
- Home and workplace visits
- 10:00 PM Curfew

Phase 3

Goal: Commit to a Law-Abiding Lifestyle

Length: 90–180 days

- Meet with Community Corrections Case Manager and Reentry Court Program Manager and agree to services and treatment on your Phase 3 Case Plan
- Develop Relapse and Recidivism Plan with Program Manager
- Attend Relapse Prevention Classes if required by Case Plan
- Attend treatment and services indicated by Phase 3 Case Plan
- Report to the _____ County Community Corrections Case Manager five times a week on a schedule determined by the Case Manager
- Meet with Reentry Court Program (RCP) Manager weekly to report progress in treatment and services
- Attend 12-Step Meetings daily
- Have a Sponsor and a Home Group
- Urine Drug Screen randomly but at least once per week
- Breath Testing randomly
- Show progress at work
- Identify community volunteer opportunities
- Complete Worksheet to indicate crime avoidance strategies
- Judicial Supervision every other week, generally on Mondays
    A family member or a close friend must accompany you to court at least once a month
    Your 12-Step Sponsor must accompany you to court at least once a month or send a report to the RCP Manager at least once a month
- Complete Worksheets to indicate how you have achieved Phase 3 Goals
- Prior to completing Phase 3, complete LS/CMI and ASI interviews
- Complete a phase move interview with Law Enforcement based on Phase 3 Goals

If you are on home detention or day reporting during Phase 3, you must comply with:

- Random Page Call-ins
- Home and workplace visits
- 10:00 PM Curfew

Phase 4

Goal: Establish or Restore Your Rightful Place in Society

Length: 90–180 days

- Meet with Community Corrections Case Manager and Reentry Court Program Manager and agree to services and treatment on your Phase 4 Case Plan
- Attend treatment, classes, and services indicated by your Phase 4 Case Plan
- Report to the _____ County Community Corrections Case Manager three times a week on a schedule determined by the Case Manager
- Meet with Reentry Court Program (RCP) Manager biweekly to report progress in treatment and services
- Report biweekly on community volunteer activities
- Report biweekly on education, work, and family activities
- Develop plan for long-term, independent, crime-free, and drug- and alcohol-free living
- Attend 12-Step Meetings daily
- Have a Sponsor and a Home Group
- Urine Drug Screen randomly
- Breath Testing randomly
- Judicial Supervision every other week, generally on Mondays
    A family member or a close friend must accompany you to court at least once every two months
    Your 12-Step Sponsor must accompany you to court at least once every two months or send a report to the RCP Manager at least once every two months
- Complete Worksheets to indicate how you have worked toward restoring your rightful place in society
- Prior to completing Phase 4, complete LS/CMI and ASI interviews
- Complete an interview with Law Enforcement based on Phase 4 Goals
- Pay final one-fourth of program fee

If you are on home detention or day reporting during Phase 4, you must comply with:

- Random Pager Call-ins
- Home and workplace visits
- 10:00 PM Curfew
- Pay all fees for services, treatments, and classes provided by the Reentry Court Program

General Rules and Regulations

1. You shall report to the Presiding Judge and Reentry Court Team for status hearings as ordered and shall engage in discussions with the Presiding Judge, Team and Program staff regarding your progress in the Reentry Court Program.
2. You will be required to successfully participate in and complete cognitive-based programs, including "Thinking for a Change."
3. You will be required to complete drug or alcohol addiction treatment programs, such as the Matrix Model Program, and participate in social support groups.
4. You shall attend, actively participate in, and complete all evaluations and recommended treatment required by the Presiding Judge and the Reentry Court Team. You shall agree to enroll in and complete all courses and programs recommended by the Presiding Judge and the Reentry Court Team.
5. You will report in a timely manner for all appointments, therapy and counseling sessions, daily reporting requirements, court appearances, work and all other required meetings.
6. You will not purchase, possess, or use any prescription or over-the-counter products that appear on the list of prohibited products that is given to you by a Reentry Court Case Manager.
7. For daily reporting, you shall report in person to the Community Corrections Building at the times set by your Case Manager.
8. You shall submit to breath or blood test for alcohol or drug use at the request of the Reentry Court Program staff or any law enforcement officer.
   - You must submit a urine sample for testing whenever requested by Reentry Court Program staff. If you fail to give a sample within two hours, it will be considered a positive result. A test result returned from the lab will be considered positive. Refusal to submit a sample will be considered a positive result. If you fail a urinalysis, and a confirmation test is necessary, you will pay the additional $25.00 lab confirmation fee.
9. You must submit to a Breathalyzer whenever requested by Reentry Court Program staff. You shall not ingest or take anything into your mouth containing alcohol while on the Reentry Court Program, e.g., mouth wash, cough medicine, any foods containing alcohol.
10. You shall not use any controlled substances or illegal drugs. If you are under a doctor's care while on the program, you must tell the doctor you are in the program and not allowed to have any narcotic drugs. You will have one and only one primary doctor. You may

see another doctor only if you are referred by your primary doctor and receive the consent of your Case Manager. You shall report all doctor's appointments, hospital visits and clinic visits to your Case Manager. You must provide a valid copy of a prescription as soon as it is received. You must get approval from your Case Manager prior to filling any prescription. Without the consent of the Presiding Judge, your Case Manager will not give you permission to use or fill a prescription for any drug listed on the forbidden medication list. You must properly take the medications that are prescribed by your doctor and that are approved by the Presiding Judge and the Reentry Court Team.

11. You must have a current telephone number within _____ County, unless otherwise specifically allowed by the Program.

12. Any requests for trips outside of _____ County or county of residence must be made to the Case Manager. The Case Manager, the Presiding Judge and the Reentry Court Team must approve the request.

13. You shall obey all laws and shall not commit any criminal offenses. You shall notify your Case Manager immediately if arrested or questioned by Law Enforcement.

14. If you are requested to do so, you will give a full statement about your participation in and knowledge of unlawful use and dealing in controlled substances. If you are requested to do so, you shall submit to a polygraph examination to demonstrate that the information that you gave is accurate. If the polygraph examination concludes that you have been deceptive in the statement that you gave, you may be removed from the Reentry Court Program.

15. You are required to pay a $200.00 fee to the treatment service provider that will deliver the drug-treatment program. An additional $6.00 per day will be assessed for daily reporting cost. These fees are to be paid with a money order. Falling behind in your fees may result in sanctions and/or termination from the program. You will pay for all drug testing except for the baseline test. Probable cause testing is $25.00 and all other testing is $15.00.

16. You are required to pay the fees necessary to complete the treatment programs, services, and classes required by the Reentry Court Program. You are expected to ask the Program Manager how to qualify for Food Stamps, Medicaid, and/or the Hoosier Assurance Plan.

17. You must seek and maintain employment after your initial intensive treatment is completed. If you change your employment, you must notify your Case Manager within twenty-four hours. You will perform community service if unemployed and will register with the Indiana

Workforce Development Employment Service. A minimum of 5 employment applications must be submitted daily.

18. Once you complete the Four Phases of the Reentry Court Program you will attend and participate in monthly court sessions for approximately one year. The Presiding Judge may order a drug screen.

19. You will follow all orders and directions given to you by the Presiding Judge and the Reentry Court Team.

20. You will not possess any handgun, rifle, shotgun, switchblade, or any other type of firearm or deadly weapon, as defined by IC 35-41-1-8. You will turn over to the court any and all gun permits that have been issued to you.

21. You will be dressed appropriately when reporting for treatment, Court or to see your Case Manager and the Reentry Court Program Manager. You shall not wear shorts shorter than fingertip length, no tank tops, no halters, no sagging pants, and no clothes with obscenity, or with beer, alcohol, or drug advertisement printed on it. Shoes and shirts must be worn in the building. If you are not dressed appropriately, you will not be allowed to check in for daily reporting or participate in meetings or sessions until you are dressed appropriately.

22. You will not verbally or physically abuse the reporting staff, treatment provider staff, or any referral staff members.

23. You will be required to carry a pager while on the program which will be provided by the Program. You will pay $5.00 a month in advance for the pager service. If you lose or damage your pager, you will immediately inform the Community Corrections Case Manager. You will be responsible for paying the $25.00 replacement cost for the pager, and you are also responsible for replacement of the batteries when necessary.

24. You are to carry the pager issued to you 24 hours a day. If paged with the number 9999, you have two hours to report *in person* to Community Corrections. If you fail to report within eight hours a sanction will be imposed. If any other number appears on the pager screen, you are to call that number within 20 minutes. The only people who have your pager number are your Judge and the staff.

25. You will permit the Reentry Court Program personnel or any law enforcement officer to enter, visit and search your place of residence at any time without notice. Police narcotics dogs may be used in searches. All persons in your company whether at home or in the community shall be fully identified. You shall also permit the Reentry Court Program personnel to visit your places of work and school without notice. You may not associate with anyone who is currently on parole, probation, awaiting sentencing or is currently incarcerated.

26. The Presiding Judge and the Reentry Court Team will be informed of your risk assessment interviews, your case plans, and your attendance in treatment and counseling programs and classes. Treatment providers will submit progress reports, based on risk assessments (LS/CMI and ASI) to the Treatment and Reentry Court Teams. The Presiding Judge and the Reentry Court Team will be informed of the results of your urinalysis tests and your progression in the Reentry Court Program. You will authorize program personnel and/or treatment providers to provide all relevant information to the Presiding Judge, the Reentry Court Team, the staff and your attorney for the purpose of evaluating your progress in the Program.

27. You will not serve as a confidential informant for any law enforcement agency while you are a participant in the Reentry Court Program.

28. You will be interviewed prior to any Reentry Court Program phase move and prior to Graduation from the Reentry Court Program. The interviews are based on the goals of the Reentry Court Program phases.

29. You shall not operate any motor vehicle without permission of the Reentry Court Program staff. You shall have a valid driver's license, proper vehicle registration and insurance as required by Indiana law before you may drive.

30. You will meet these additional requirements:
    a. _____
    b. _____
    c. _____
    d. _____

Sanctions and Modification of Program

1. Violation of the requirements and rules may result in Presiding Judge's modifying your program and imposing sanctions that may include, but are not limited to:
    a. Geographic area restrictions
    b. Increased drug testing
    c. Educational programs
    d. Additional Court appearances
    e. Additional treatment or services
    f. Community service hours
    g. Road Crew
    h. Curfews
    i. Jail

  j. Home Detention

  k. Residential Work Release

  l. Increased Day Reporting

  m. Removal from the Reentry Court Program

2. You shall comply with sanctions that are imposed.

3. You must pay the fee of any program used as a sanction.

4. If you are found to be under the influence of, in possession of or having ingested a controlled substance or illegal drug without permission of the Program or contrary to law, sanctions will be imposed, including jail. The Presiding Judge may increase the sanction upon your next court appearance. Further you may be removed from the program after a hearing before the Presiding Judge.

5. Sanctions for having a positive drug screen or being in possession of materials to be used to alter, disguise, conceal or falsify a drug screen shall include your being required to serve jail time. The Presiding Judge may increase the sanction upon your next court appearance. Further you may be removed from the program after a hearing before the Presiding Judge.

6. Any positive Breathalyzer results will be considered positive for alcohol consumption. There will be sanctions for a positive Breathalyzer, including jail. The Presiding Judge may increase the sanction upon your next court appearance. Further you may be removed from the program after a hearing before the Presiding Judge.

7. If you do not report for daily check-in, treatment appointments, or any other activity assigned to you by your Case Manager, you may be dismissed from the Program and you will be charged with the crime of escape under Indiana Code 35-44-3.5.

8. You will be removed from the Program if arrested or convicted for a new criminal offense.

9. Evidence regarding any Reentry Court violation will be admissible in court and will be used against you in any violation proceedings and other prosecutions.

10. In the event you fail to make satisfactory progress in the Program for a period of time up to six (6) months or longer, at the discretion of the team, you may be removed from the Program.

11. You shall not have any contact or communication (written or verbal) with any person outside of 12-step meetings, counseling meetings, employment, or church unless prior approval has been given by the Reentry Team or Presiding Judge. If you would like to have approval, you must first submit the person's full name, date of birth, and social security number to the Case Manager. You must wait for the decision

to be made by the Reentry Team before any contact takes place. Any contact or communication with an unapproved person will be considered a violation.

12. You shall pay a program fee of $200. One-fourth ($50) of the program fee is due at the completion of each phase. The Case Manager will collect the fee, payable in full within 12 months of entering the program.

I have read the above Participation Agreement and agree to comply with and be bound by its terms and conditions.

Dated this _____ day of _____ 200_.

_____

Participant's Signature

_____

Program Manager's Signature

_____

Presiding Judge Signature

_____

Appendix C

Waiver Forms

_____ County Superior Court I Reentry Court Program

Case Number: _____

Form: Waiver and Consent to Search 1

Date _____

WAIVER AND CONSENT TO SEARCH

I have been advised of my rights under the Fourth Amendment to the U.S. Constitution and Article 1 § 11 of the Indiana Constitution, which are set out below, and understand those rights.

I hereby waive my right to object under the Fourth Amendment to the U.S. Constitution and Article 1 § 11 of the Indiana Constitution to searches of my person, residence, place of business, papers and effects and any place over which I have custody or control regardless of whether I share that custody or control with other persons, when conducted by representatives of the Reentry Court Program, members of the Reentry Court Team, Community Corrections staff, Probation Officers, treatment providers engaged in treatment with me through the Reentry Court Program, and police officers, irrespective of whether the search is supported by a warrant or reasonable and probable cause.

I hereby consent to search of my person, residence, place of business, papers and effects and any place over which I have custody or control regardless of whether I share that custody or control with other persons, when conducted by representatives of the Reentry Court Program, members of the Reentry Court Team, Community Corrections staff, Probation Officers, treatment providers engaged in treatment with me through the Reentry Court Program, and police officers, at any time, without prior notice, and irrespective of whether there is a warrant or reasonable and probable cause to search.

This Waiver and Consent shall take effect upon my acceptance to the Reentry Court Program and continue in effect for so long as I am a participant in the Reentry Court Program.

The constitutional provisions read:

1. U.S. Constitution Amendment IV:
   The right of the people to be secure in their persons, houses, papers and effects, against unreasonable searches and seizures, shall not be violated and no warrants shall issue, but upon probable cause, supported by Oath or affirmation and particularly describing the place to be searched and the persons or things to be seized.
2. Indiana Constitution Article 1 § 11:
   The right of the people to be secure in their persons, houses, papers, and effects, against unreasonable search or seizure, shall not be violated; and no warrant shall issue, but upon probable cause, supported by oath or affirmation, and particularly describing the place to be searched, and the person or thing to be seized.

I voluntarily sign this Waiver and Consent without threats, promises or coercion of any kind. I fully understand the meaning of this Waiver and Consent.

Participant's Signature: _____ Date: _____

Printed:

Witness's Signature: _____

_____ County Superior Court I Reentry Court Program

Form: Alcohol and Drugs Policy 1

Date _____

Participant's Name (Print): _____

Case Number: _____

POLICY CONCERNING DRUGS AND ALCOHOL

CAUTION: The following document is legally binding. Read and understand it before signing.

Participation in the _____ County Superior Court I Reentry Court Program is voluntary. Those who apply must understand that they do so of their own free will. Additionally, those who apply must understand that the program has a

zero tolerance of alcohol and drugs

Therefore every applicant for the Reentry Court Program is required to sign the following document prior to being accepted into the program.

If admitted to the _____ County Superior Court I Reentry Court Program, I agree to the following terms:

If I test positive for, possess or consume

- **any illegal drug or controlled substance for which I do not have a valid prescription or which I have possessed or consumed in a manner that violates the rules of the Reentry Court Program, or**
- **alcohol,**

I will immediately be taken to jail for 72 hours without the right of a disciplinary hearing and the presiding judge may impose additional jail time as a sanction. Further I may be removed from the Program.

Further I agree to submit to urine drug screens, breath test or blood tests when requested by Reentry Court personnel, a law enforcement officer or the sentencing court.

By my signature, I acknowledge that I have read and understood all of the above, and agree to all disciplinary terms as stated.

Signature: _____ Date: _____

Witness: _____

Appendix D

Reentry Court Participant's Handbook

Superior Court I

Reentry Court Program

_____ County

REENTRY COURT PARTICIPANT'S HANDBOOK

Revised May 21, 2006

A. Welcome

Welcome to the _____ County Reentry Court Program. This Handbook is designed to answer your questions and provide information about the Reentry Court Program.

As a participant, you will be expected to follow the rules and instructions given by the Presiding Judge and comply with the Case Plan developed with you by the Case Manager and the Program Manager.

This Handbook tells you what is expected of you as a Reentry Court Program participant. We encourage you to share this information with your attorney, family, friends, employer, or anyone else affected by your participation in this program.

It is our goal that you are not returned to prison but instead become a productive member of society and enjoy the benefits that a crime-free and drug-free life has to offer.

B. Overview of the Program

The Reentry Court Program is a Superior Court I program. The Presiding Judge is advised by a Team, representing the Prosecutor's Office, Victim Assistance, the Public Defender, Parole, Community Corrections, the Home with Hope, Police Agencies, Probation, and a number of service providers. Representatives from many community agencies, such as LARA, WorkOne, Wabash Valley Hospital, New Directions, Cummins, and Family Services are on the team.

By working together, team members provide you a strong, consistent program geared toward supporting and helping you become a productive member of society.

Reentry Court involves frequent court appearances, random drug testing, drug-abuse treatment programs, 12-Step Meeting participation, Community Corrections case management, and family services. Reentry Court rewards successful participation and imposes sanctions for noncompliance.

Experts in the community advise the Reentry Court Team. Experts include Pharmacists, Physicians, Psychologists, Addiction Specialists, and Education and Employment Specialists.

Your program will have specific goals for you to achieve. If you achieve your goals and complete the program successfully, you will be required to appear in court on a monthly basis for approximately one year.

C. Confidentiality

As a participant of the Reentry Court Program, you will also be involved with Case Management and Health or Mental Health and Addiction Treatment Programs.

HIPAA laws require that your privacy be protected. In response to these regulations, you will be asked to sign Authorizations for Release of Information. The disclosure of information is for the purpose of maintaining communication about your progress in the Reentry Court Program.

D. Team Meetings and Progress Reports

Before each court appearance, the Judge will be given a progress report discussing your drug test results, attendance, participation and cooperation in the treatment program, employment, or other requirements that may have been imposed. Progress and problems may be discussed. If you are doing well, incentives may be considered. If you are not doing well, the Judge may consider sanctions in order to help you achieve your goals in the program.

E. Court Appearances

As a Reentry Court participant, you will be required to appear in Reentry Court, Superior Court I, on a regular basis. The number of times you must appear depends upon the phase of the program you are currently in. If you have questions about your court appearances you may contact your Case Manager or the Program Manager.

F. Phases of the Reentry Court Program

Reentry Court is a 12 to 18 month program divided into four phases. Each phase has a unique goal for you to accomplish. Phases vary in duration for each participant, depending on needs and how well an individual progresses through a phase.

If you complete the Program you will appear in Court once a month for one year. You will be asked to tell the Presiding Judge and the Program participants how you are doing.

A participant must successfully complete each phase before moving to the next phase. Graduation from one phase to the next is not automatic.

Requirements for the phases may change at the discretion of the Reentry Court Team.

Phase 1

Goal: Engage in the Rehabilitative Process

Length: Approximately 90 days, depending on your progress

- Complete LS/CMI and ASI interviews to determine services and programs
- Meet with Community Corrections Case Manager and agree to services and treatment on your Phase 1 Case Plan
- Begin treatment and services within one week
- Report to the _____ County Community Corrections Case Manager daily
- Meet with Reentry Court Program (RCP) Manager at least weekly to report progress in treatment and services
- Attend 12-Step Meetings daily
- Have a Sponsor and a Home Group
- Urine Drug Screen randomly but at least once per week
- Breathalyzer Testing daily
- Judicial Supervision every week, generally on Mondays

A family member or a close friend must accompany you to court at least once a month

Your 12-Step Sponsor must accompany you to court at least once a month or send a report to the RCP Manager at least once a month

- Complete Worksheets to indicate how you have committed to the rehabilitative process
- Prior to completing Phase 1, complete LS/CMI and ASI interviews
- Complete a phase move interview based on Phase 1 Goal

If you are on home detention or day reporting during Phase 1, you must comply with:

- Random Page Call-ins
- Home and workplace visits
- 9:00 PM Curfew

Phase 2

Goal: Gain the Tools for a Constructive Lifestyle

Length: 90–180 days, depending on your progress

- Meet with Community Corrections Case Manager and Reentry Court Program Manager and agree to services and treatment on your Phase 2 Case Plan
- Attend treatment, services, and classes indicated by your Phase 2 Case Plan
- Report to the _____ County Community Corrections Case Manager daily
- Meet with Reentry Court Program (RCP) Manager weekly to report progress in treatment and services
- Attend 12-Step Meetings daily
- Have a Sponsor and a Home Group
- Urine Drug Screen randomly but at least once per week
- Breathalyzer Testing daily
- Obtain valid driver's license or photo identification
- Show progress toward completing GED if relevant
- Complete WorkKeys Assessment
- Obtain employment
- Judicial Supervision every week, generally on Mondays

A family member or a close friend must accompany you to court at least once a month

Your 12-Step Sponsor must accompany you to court at least once a month or send a report to the RCP Manager at least once a month

- Complete Worksheets to indicate how you have engaged in educational and employment services that will help you achieve Phase 2 Goals
- Prior to completing Phase 2, complete LS/CMI and ASI interviews
- Complete a phase move interview based on Phase 2 Goal

If you are on home detention or day reporting during Phase 2, you must comply with:

- Random Page Call-ins
- Home and workplace visits
- 10:00 PM Curfew

Phase 3

Goal: Commit to a Law-Abiding Lifestyle

Length: 90–180 days, depending on your progress

- Meet with Community Corrections Case Manager and Reentry Court Program Manager and agree to services and treatment on your Phase 3 Case Plan
- Develop Relapse and Recidivism Plan with Program Manager
- Attend Relapse Prevention Classes if required by Case Plan
- Attend treatment and services indicated by Phase 3 Case Plan
- Report to the _____ County Community Corrections Case Manager five times a week on a schedule determined by the Case Manager
- Meet with Reentry Court Program (RCP) Manager weekly to report progress in treatment and services
- Attend 12-Step Meetings daily
- Have a Sponsor and a Home Group
- Urine Drug Screen randomly but at least once per week
- Breathalyzer Testing randomly
- Show progress at work
- Identify community volunteer opportunities
- Complete Worksheet to indicate crime avoidance strategies
- Judicial Supervision every other week, generally on Mondays

A family member or a close friend must accompany you to court at least once a month

Your 12-Step Sponsor must accompany you to court at least once a month or send a report to the RCP Manager at least once a month

- Complete Worksheets to indicate how you have achieved Phase 3 goals
- Prior to completing Phase 3, complete LS/CMI and ASI interviews
- Complete a phase move interview based on Phase 3 Goal

If you are on home detention or day reporting during Phase 3, you must comply with:

- Random Page Call-ins
- Home and workplace visits
- 10:00 PM Curfew

Phase 4

Goal: Establish or Restore Your Rightful Place in Society

Length: 90–180 days, depending on your progress

- Meet with Community Corrections Case Manager and Reentry Court Program Manager and agree to services and treatment on your Phase 4 Case Plan
- Attend treatment, classes, and services indicated by your Phase 4 Case Plan
- Report to the _____ County Community Corrections Case Manager three times a week on a schedule determined by the Case Manager
- Meet with Reentry Court Program (RCP) Manager biweekly to report progress in treatment and services
- Register to vote
- Learn about and discuss candidates running for office
- Report biweekly on community volunteer activities
- Report biweekly on education, work, and family activities
- Develop plan for long-term, independent, crime-free, and drug- and alcohol-free living
- Attend 12-Step Meetings daily
- Have a Sponsor and a Home Group
- Urine Drug Screen randomly
- Breathalyzer Testing randomly
- Judicial Supervision every other week, generally on Mondays

A family member or a close friend must accompany you to court at least once every two months

Your 12-Step Sponsor must accompany you to court at least once every two months or send a report to the RCP Manager at least once every two months

- Complete Worksheets to indicate how you have worked toward restoring your rightful place in society
- Prior to completing Phase 4, complete LS/CMI and ASI interviews
- Complete an interview based on Phase 4 Goal

If you are on home detention or day reporting during Phase 4, you must comply with:

- Random Pager Call-ins
- Home and workplace visits
- 10:00 PM Curfew
- Pay all fees for services, treatments, and classes provided by the Reentry Court Program

G. Incentives and Sanctions

Incentives and Sanctions have been developed as a means of teaching participants that their choices will affect their environment and to provide ways to encourage individuals to avoid all criminal activity and to remain free of alcohol and/or substance abuse and develop a productive lifestyle. Before applying sanctions, the Reentry Court Team will consider all the facts of the situation and the participant's history.

Both progress and noncompliance will be reported to the Reentry Court Team. This will affect a participant's progress through the phases.

What Will Prompt the Use of Incentives?

- Consistent and full participation with no missed appointments or tardiness
- Positive reports from Case Manager and Program Manager for 4 consecutive weeks
- Consistently clean drug screens
- Consistent payment of fees on time or on a regular basis
- Promotion or recognition at work
- Obtaining additional education or job skills
- Promotion to the next phase of the Reentry Court Program

Possible Incentives

- Encouragement and recognition from the Judge
- Ceremonies and certificates of progress including advancement to the next phase
- Gift certificates (Food, Shopping, Gas, Bowling)
- Taxi to Community Corrections
- Recovery books
- Extended curfews
- Free drug screen
- Overnight visits

What Will Prompt the Use of Sanctions?

- Dishonesty, deception, and other manipulative maneuvers.
- Refusing or failing to comply with program requirements.
- Missing any scheduled meetings, court appearances, urine tests, family sessions, curfew, or any other group, class or program.
- Refusing to cooperate with the Reentry Court Team at each level.
- Engaging in any illegal or unlawful harassment or intimidation of others.
- Violating any city, state or federal laws. Any arrest or contact with police must be reported to the Reentry Court Team within twenty-four (24) hours.
- Committing any acts of violence or threats of violence.
- The use or possession of any paraphernalia or drug except as prescribed by a licensed physician and approved by the Reentry Court Team.
- The use of any prescription or over-the-counter drug or other product that is forbidden by the Program
- The use or possession of any alcoholic beverage or drugs.
- Possession of a weapon of any form, including firearms or knives.
- Associating with anyone on probation, parole, having pending charges, having a warrant for their arrest, or using alcohol or drugs.

Possible Sanctions

- Reading assignments and reports
- Essays
- Thinking log—tracking your thoughts about your program throughout the week
- Additional 12-Step Meetings
- Earlier curfew
- Extra drug screens

- Community service
- Work release
- Road crew
- Incarceration
- Expulsion from the program

A participant's progress should be measured by his or her progress. The Reentry Court Team will strive to build on the positives and reinforce those behaviors by acknowledging the small successes that eventually lead to meeting larger goals.

A successful participant graduates from the Reentry Court Program. All participants attend the graduation ceremony and the graduate's family and friends are invited to attend. The Presiding Judge awards a graduation certificate. Graduates tell the Reentry Court Team, the Reentry Court participants, and their family members what they have accomplished within the program and what their future goals are.

H. Medications and Products to Avoid

The Superior Court I Reentry Court Program is an alcohol- and drug-free program. It has a zero tolerance policy. As a participant in the Reentry Court Program, you may not consume alcohol or proscribed products or pharmaceuticals.

Your Case Manger will give you a list of products to avoid. If you have questions about any product, you must contact your Case Manager.

As a participant, if you are under a doctor's care while on the program, you must tell the doctor you are in the Reentry Court Program.

You are to have only one primary care doctor. You are only to see another doctor if you are referred by your primary doctor or with the consent of the Presiding Judge and the Reentry Court Team.

You are required to report all doctor's appointments, hospital and clinic visits to your Case Manager.

No prescription medication will be allowed without prior approval from the Presiding Judge and the Reentry Court Team. You must provide a valid copy of any prescription as soon as you receive it from a physician, prior to taking any prescription.

You must also properly take medications that are prescribed by your doctor (see your Reentry Court Participation Agreement).

Consult your Case Manager if you have any questions about the alcohol and drug policies and procedures of the Reentry Court Program.

Notes

INTRODUCTION

1. This is a state that imposes a two-year term of parole for all released from state prison unless convicted of a sex offense, which results in a two-year, ten-year, or lifetime term of parole.

2. The grandmother was not interviewed. These statements were made during a court hearing.

3. The city is the recipient of a U.S. Department of Justice Weed and Seed grant that brings crime-intervention and crime-prevention programs to the downtown area for a five-year period. The reentry problem solving court provided the basis for the Weed and Seed application.

4. Three other jurisdictions or counties have problem solving courts in this state with a total of ninety-two counties.

5. The observational studies we report on took place in a general-jurisdiction state court that protects state and federal rights within the United States. In other nations, various constitutional and other rights apply to the trial or court hearings.

6. An exemplary use of the dramaturgical model is found in James Nolan's *Reinventing Justice: The American Drug Court Movement* (Princeton, NJ: Princeton University Press, 2001).

7. We do not present the quantitative analyses we conducted over the years to explain change in the risk to recidivate as a function of offender and program characteristics. At times, we reference multivariate analyses, but we saw no need to present statistically significant "findings" because the dialogues of participants, judges, and team members are more than sufficient to illustrate the principles and practices of the court programs.

8. Arguably, these documents can be used in other nations. We claim no familiarity, however, with the laws and legal processes that are amenable to PSCs. We

encourage readers to advise and update us in preparation for subsequent volumes on problem solving courts.

CHAPTER 1

1. William Shakespeare, *The Merchant of Venice*, ed. John Russell Brown (London: Arden Shakespeare, 1959), 111–12.

2. By care work, we mean the unpaid labor that family members engage in to nurture each other. Care work is not limited to parenting; yet, what parents do for their children is the exemplar of care work.

3. We take the Durkheimian position that crime is a property of society and not of the social actor or behavior. Crime is what society (i.e., the law) defines as constituting criminal acts.

4. We do not refer here to the utilitarian rational choice theory that underlies deterrence perspectives. Law and literature contributors tend to focus on the truly rational or reasonable decision that accounts for goals, means, and the emotions and perceptions of the decision maker and the person being judged.

CHAPTER 2

1. The punitive response to crime, race and gender bias, disproportionate sentencing for drug abusers, and the transinstitutionalization problem, whereby psychiatric "patients" and criminal "offender" are not distinguished clearly by law or punishment, persist as the most important problems associated with delivering fair and just punishments in the United States.

2. Researchers find that instrumental, or property, crimes are most amenable to deterrence, while the threat of punishment is not likely to deter personal-injury crimes. For decades, deterrence studies attempted to distinguish the effects of punishment severity, certainty, and celerity. Proponents claim that capital punishment can deter homicide, while opponents claim that it has a brutalization effect. Some argue that specific deterrence can "work" but that general deterrence is not measurable; others find gender and race differences.

3. Generally people, not organizations, are held responsible for criminal wrongdoing. There are, of course, exceptions. Some states permit a case involving an organization to be adjudicated in a criminal court. Indiana provided a dramatic example when the Ford Motor Company faced criminal charges for deliberately manufacturing the Pinto, known to be likely to catch on fire and cause personal injury upon rear-end collision. Exceptions notwithstanding, the requirement of mens rea for most offenses precludes an organization from being charged with a crime.

4. A comprehensive approach to health requires dental health, especially if the participant has not had adequate dental care or was a methamphetamine abuser.

5. Some call these types of practices "virtual imprisonment" because the offender, although in the community, has little autonomy or control over how the twenty-four-hour day is spent.

6. The initial and sociolegal response to Attica was to formulate harsher drug laws. That change was initiated by lawmakers. Thus, though ironic, this example poses no challenge to the claim that sociolegal movements represent changes initiated from within centers of power or legitimated social institutions.

7. His court claim was filed on February 22, 1973. He requested a judgment in the sum of $500,000.

8. Forensic diversion is designed to divert those with behavioral health problems who are arrested for felony-level drug offenses from state prison. Participants tend to be located within the local jail while awaiting a court date. Their attorneys, or the prosecuting attorney, recommend candidates for the forensic diversion problem solving court. Unlike the adult and juvenile drug courts that were implemented, forensic diversion looks for persons charged with felony A, B, or C offenses only. Those charged with felony D or misdemeanor crimes are likely to be referred to drug court.

CHAPTER 3

1. If one compares problem solving court participants to criminal court defendants, controlling for all relevant variables, the recidivism rate for PSC participants is lower; therefore, the outcome is superior, relative to that of the approaches used by traditional criminal courts.

2. State fact sheets are produced annually by the U.S. Drug Enforcement Administration in the series "DEA Briefs & Background." The information here is taken from the fact sheets.

3. The Indiana Department of Correction, for some reason unknown to us, has always had a singular, not plural, name. Perhaps at one point there was a single prison. Today, twenty-four prisons make up the Department of Correction.

4. Community Transition Program funds, prior to the establishment of the reentry court, were directed to a community corrections facility that took responsibility for monitoring newly released prisoners for up to 180 days with drug and alcohol tests, home detention or work release, and other programs.

5. Arguably, the Lafayette model is premised on selective-incapacitation principles, whereas the Fort Wayne model is premised on specific deterrence principles. Although Lafayette begins with selective incapacitation, once participants enroll in the reentry court program, a specific deterrence model is operationalized.

6. There are exceptions for special types of reentry court programs. For example, Tippecanoe County, Indiana, was awarded a three-year grant from the Department of Justice to implement a sex-offender-reentry problem solving court.

7. Nowadays, public psychiatric services are more often found in prisons than in the community, and since *One Flew over the Cuckoo's Nest*, it has been difficult for the population to believe that hospitals do not operate on social-control principles.

8. An excellent source on jurisprudence is Stephen Presser and Jamil Zainaldin's *Law and Jurisprudence in American History: Cases and Materials.* 4th ed. (St. Paul, MN: West Group, 2000).

CHAPTER 5

1. We do not address federal prison for two reasons: (1) the federal laws apply uniformly across the states and do not include reentry courts that are statutorily authorized, and (2) a very small percentage of criminal offenders sentenced by a federal court would be good candidates for a reentry court. No one held federal laws responsible for the surge in incarceration. It is state laws and state courts that fill state prisons to levels that greatly exceed their capacity. One example suffices: California's state prisons remain overcrowded to the point that the state moves inmates to other less-populated state prison systems.

2. Fabian successfully completed reentry and is now on unsupervised probation.

3. Others commit crimes, such as robberies, that include drug offenses.

CHAPTER 6

*We thank Jeralyn Long Faris for the interview that she conducted with "Kyle," most of which appears in this chapter.

1. Her presentence report indicated that she was jailed while awaiting sentencing because, when she appeared in court for a plea hearing, knowing herself to be pregnant, she tested positive for cocaine. Her baby was born after she was sentenced, in state prison. Holly's father was granted guardianship of the child.

2. Holly had twice attempted suicide and had been diagnosed with general anxiety disorder. Once she began reentry court, she was interviewed by a psychiatrist and prescribed Lexapro.

CHAPTER 7

1. Actually, she had not completed high school or the GED. Many team members, including the mental health counselor, argued that she clearly demonstrated an antisocial personality and was not likely to complete a reentry program without considerable therapy beforehand. Her clinical assessment indicated she showed "characteristics supportive of an anti-personality disorder." Further, the team argued that her parents were enablers and socially embarrassed by Caroline's incarceration and the birth of her child. They were anything but supportive of her participation in a program that required public court appearances.

2. The two additional PSC programs not studied here are a drug court and a juvenile drug court. While interesting in their own ways, they were designed as compliance

courts and not problem solving courts. The drug courts are designed to respond to misdemeanants and not convicted felons.

3. The version of the instrument used is the Level of Services Inventory, Revised (LSI R). We refer to it as the LSI because the Canadian firm that sells the instrument has a full complement of instruments—useful for juveniles, those incarcerated, those under correctional supervision in the community, and so forth.

4. A tenth and static dimension measures criminal history.

5. An anonymous reviewer points out that the focus on surveillance is a likely explanation for the program's inability to succeed within the community. If surveillance and monitoring are the foci, the team members may develop the attitude that "nothing can be done." It is the case that negative comments about the program and its participants were commonly heard during team meetings.

CHAPTER 8

1. The ten key components are as follows: (1) drug courts integrate treatment services with justice system case processing, (2) a nonadversarial approach is used to promote public safety and protect due process rights, (3) participants are identified early and quickly placed in drug courts, (4) drug courts provide access to a continuum of services and programs, (5) abstinence is monitored by frequent drug and alcohol testing, (6) a coordinated strategy governs court responses to compliance/noncompliance, (7) ongoing and frequent judicial interaction with participants is necessary, (8) measuring program effectiveness is important, (9) continuing interdisciplinary education is essential, and (10) partnerships among drug courts, nonprofit and public agencies, and community-based organizations is necessary to enhance drug court effectiveness. Bureau of Justice Assistance, "Defining Drug Courts: The Key Components," in *Drug Court Resources Series*, 1997, 2004.

2. Needless to say, prediction or actuarial devices for identifying those to incapacitate selectively generate false negatives and false positives. While incarcerating the wrong offenders and failing to incarcerate those who should be incarcerated are serious and potentially life-threatening problems, using actuarial devices to select the best candidates for a problem solving court may result in false positives and negatives. They are, however, far less consequential when the decisions made are about persons within the community and not in prison.

3. We compared a matched sample to a sample of successful reentry court participants (in 2007) with data provided by the police department. Within one year following release from prison, 56 percent had negative police contacts, generally resulting in arrest. On average, each person arrested was responsible for nearly three crimes within that year.

4. The term *criminal justice system* is used to summarize all the agencies that respond to crime. Many empirical studies, published over many decades, have shown convincingly that criminal justice is anything but a "system" of interrelated parts. Autonomous agencies, for example, a local law firm that handles criminal defense and the state prison for women, do not tend to work together on a shared mission.

Many authors refer to the "criminal justice process" to summarize more accurately how persons charged with crimes are handled by the separate and distinct criminal justice agencies. This distinction is important to recognize because it is the PSCs that bring otherwise adversarial groups to the table in attempts to resolve problems.

5. Kurt eventually relapsed and was returned to prison.

6. Caroline was deceitful. She gave birth to a cocaine-addicted baby who was adopted. Her use of the drug began before the baby was born.

CHAPTER 9

1. Rehabilitation, in the 1960s and 1970s, was difficult to achieve through prison programs and in jurisdictions with an indeterminate sentencing practice for two central reasons. First, it was difficult or impossible to tell if a person "on the inside" would stay rehabilitated "on the outside" when he or she returned to familiar places and familiar people. Second, those states that insisted on rehabilitation were insisting on a total transformation of the person. Such transformations take a protracted period relative to what the taxpayer is willing to spend on incarceration. Transformation can better be achieved in the community, which is one of the key criminal law and criminal justice lessons of the twenty-first century.

2. Will and Paul were participants in the reentry court program. Will did indeed return to prison, and Paul continues, in 2009, to work and volunteer in his community. Conversations with Paul do not focus on his past. They tend to focus on what he can do next.

CHAPTER 10

1. James Nolan's extraordinary and exemplary *Reinventing Justice* provides the model for our work. His work focused on first-generation drug courts.

2. At an expulsion hearing, the same judge reverts to the traditional judicial role. It is only during team meetings and PSC sessions that the role is reversed.

CHAPTER 11

1. Audrey gave birth to two children. Her first, a son, was born while she was incarcerated for the first time. She gave him up for adoption. Her second child, a girl, was born during her second term of imprisonment. In both cases she was convicted of drug-dealing offenses.

2. The counselor should have exercised an ethical duty. The counselor neither liked nor got along with Audrey yet did nothing to have Audrey assigned to another counselor.

3. A focus on Dan's strengths would have shown the progress he was making toward family reunification. Relying too heavily on "violations" or "lack of progress"

undermines Dan's work to reintegrate within his community and to reunite with his family.

CHAPTER 12

1. Here, we do not refer to compliance courts or the drug courts for minor offenses. We refer only to the comprehensive problem solving court, defined in the introduction and in subsequent chapters.

2. On a monthly basis, the program evaluator provides reports to the county's courts that summarize the number of participants in a program, their progress, and the number of violations or expulsion hearings held. Once a year, the program evaluator gives a presentation to the Department of Correction. The presentation includes an analysis of success or failure as a function of criminal history, family composition, and the number of program violations.

3. The city, at least twice a year, invites participants to public events and publicly acknowledges contributions made to the city's well-being by PSC participants.

References

Abramowitz, M. Z. 2005. Prisons and the human rights of persons with mental disorders. *Current Opinion in Psychiatry* 18: 525–29.

Adams, K., and J. Ferrandino. 2008. Managing mentally ill inmates in prisons. *Criminal Justice and Behavior* 35: 913–27.

Alan, Ryan. 2003. The legal theory of no legal theory. *New York Times Book Review*. September 14, 20.

Alemi, F., M. Haack, and S. Nemes. 2004. Statistical definition of relapse: Case of family drug court. *Addictive Behaviors* 29: 685–98.

Alexander, C. M. S. 2005. Shakespeare, law, and marriage. *Modern Language Review* 100: 482–84.

Alleyne, V. 2006. Locked up means locked out: Women, addiction and incarceration. *Women & Therapy* 29: 181–94.

Alter, A. L., J. Kernochan, and J. M. Darley. 2007. Transgression wrongfulness outweighs its harmfulness as a determinant of sentence severity. *Law and Human Behavior* 31: 319–35.

Andrews, D. A., and Craig Dowden. 2007. The risk-need-responsivity model of assessment and human service in prevention and corrections: Crime prevention jurisprudence. *Canadian Journal of Criminology and Criminal Justice* 49: 439–64.

Anker, Elizabeth S. 2008. Human rights, social justice, and J. M. Coetzee's *Disgrace*. *Modern Fiction Studies* 54: 233–67.

Anon. 2003. Symposium—empirical legal realism: A new social scientific assessment of law and human behavior. *Northwestern University Law Review* 97: 1075–76.

———. 2005a. Good courts: The case for problem solving justice. *Future Survey* 27: 23.

———. 2005b. NACDL report: Truth in sentencing? The Gonzales cases. *Federal Sentencing Reporter* 17: 327–34.

———. 2005c. Re-entry issues take center stage with release of report, legislation. *Mental Health Weekly* 15: 1–4.

————. 2008. Imprisoning communities: How mass incarceration makes disadvantaged neighborhoods worse. *Harvard Law Review* 121: 940–1040.

Arboleda-Florez, J. 1999. Mental illness in jails and prisons. *Current Opinion in Psychiatry* 12: 677–82.

Arditti, Joyce A., and April L. Few. 2006. Mothers' reentry into family life following incarceration. *Criminal Justice Policy Review* 17: 103–23.

Arkfeld, L. C. 2007. Ethics for the problem solving court judge: The new ABA model code. *Justice System Journal* 28: 317–23.

Armstrong, G. S., and M. L. Griffin. 2007. The effect of local life circumstances on victimization of drug-involved women. *Justice Quarterly* 24: 80–105.

Arneson, Richard. 2007. Shame, stigma, and disgust in the decent society. *Journal of Ethics* 11: 31–63.

Arnold, E. M., J. C. Stewart, and C. A. McNeece. 2001. Enhancing services for offenders: The impact on treatment completion. *Journal of Psychoactive Drugs* 33: 255–62.

Arvanites, T. M., and M. A. Asher. 1998. State and country incarceration rates: The direct and indirect effects of race and inequality. *American Journal of Economics and Sociology* 57: 207–21.

Attica, New York State Special Commission on. 1972. *Attica: The Official Report of the New York State Special Commission on Attica.* New York: Bantam Book.

Auberlen, E. 2003. Shakespeare in the Restoration: Puritan austerity and its cure in Davenant's adaptation of *Measure for Measure. Zeitschrift fur Anglistik und Amerikanistik* 51: 437–51.

Auerhahn, K. 1999. Selective incapacitation and the problem of prediction. *Criminology* 37: 703–34.

————. 2004. California's incarcerated drug offender population, yesterday, today, and tomorrow: Evaluating the War on Drugs and Proposition 36. *Journal of Drug Issues* 34: 95–120.

August, G. J., M. L. Bloomquist, S. S. Lee, G. M. Realmuto, and J. M. Hektner. 2006. Can evidence-based prevention programs be sustained in community practice settings? The Early Risers' advanced-stage effectiveness trial. *Prevention Science* 7: 151–65.

Austin, James. 2001. Prisoner reentry: Current trends, practices, and issues. *Crime & Delinquency* 47: 314.

Aviram, A. 2006. The placebo effect of law: Law's role in manipulating perceptions. *George Washington Law Review* 75: 54–104.

Banks, D., and D. C. Gottfredson. 2003. The effects of drug treatment and supervision on time to rearrest among drug treatment court participants. *Journal of Drug Issues* 33: 385–412.

————. 2004. Participation in drug treatment court and time to rearrest. *Justice Quarterly* 21: 637–58.

Barker, V. 2007. The prison and the gallows: The politics of mass incarceration in America. *Punishment & Society: International Journal of Penology* 9: 426–29.

Barkow, Rachel E., and Kathleen M. O'Neill. 2006. Delegating punitive power: The political economy of sentencing commission and guideline formation. *Texas Law Review* 84: 1973–2022.

Barmash, P. 2004. The narrative quandary: Cases of law in literature. *Vetus Testamentum* 54: 1–16.

Barnett, C., and F. C. Mencken. 2002. Social disorganization theory and the contextual nature of crime in nonmetropolitan counties. *Rural Sociology* 67: 372–93.

Baron, Jane B. 1999. Law, literature, and the problems of interdisciplinarity. *Yale Law Journal* 108: 1059.

Barrett, B. F. D. 1999. Environmentalism in periods of rapid societal transformation: The legacy of the industrial revolution in the United Kingdom and the Meiji Restoration in Japan. *Sustainable Development* 7: 178–90.

Barton, T. D. 1999. Therapeutic jurisprudence, preventive law, and creative problem solving—an essay on harnessing emotion and human connection. *Psychology, Public Policy, and Law* 5: 921–43.

Basile, V. D. 2005. Getting serious about corrections. *Federal Probation* 69: 29ff.

Bauman, Z. 2000. Social issues of law and order. *British Journal of Criminology* 40: 205–21.

Baxter, L. A. 1990. Dialectical contradictions in relationship development. *Journal of Social and Personal Relationships* 7: 69–88.

——. 1992. Forms and functions of intimate play in personal relationships. *Human Communication Research* 18: 336–63.

Baxter, L. A., and B. M. Montgomery. 1996. *Relating: Dialogues and Dialectics.* New York: Guilford Press.

——. 1997. Rethinking communication in personal relationships from a dialectical perspective. In *Handbook of Personal Relationships: Theory, Research and Interventions*, edited by S. Duck, 325–50. 2nd ed. West Sussex, UK: John Wiley & Sons.

——. 1998. A guide to dialectical approaches to studying personal relationships. In *Dialectical Approaches to Studying Personal Relationships*, edited by B. M. Montgomery and L. A. Baxter, 1–17. Mahwah, NJ: Lawrence Erlbaum Associates.

Belenko, S. 2002. The challenges of conducting research in drug treatment court settings. *Substance Use & Misuse* 37: 1635–64.

Bell, R. H. 2001. The anatomy of folly in Shakespeare's Henriad. *Humor: International Journal of Humor Research* 14: 181–201.

Benedikt, Fischer. 2003. "Doing good with a vengeance": A critical assessment of the practices, effects and implications of drug treatment courts in North America. *Criminal Justice: International Journal of Policy & Practice* 3: 227.

Bennett, Christopher. 2004. The limits of mercy. *Ratio* 17: 1–11.

Bennett, Jamie. 2008. They hug hoodies, don't they? Responsibility, irresponsibility and responsibilisation in conservative crime policy. *Howard Journal of Criminal Justice* 47: 451–69.

Berman, Greg. 2004. Redefining criminal courts: Problem solving and the meaning of justice. *American Criminal Law Review* 41: 1313.

Berman, Greg, and John Feinblatt. 2001. Problem solving courts: A brief primer. *Law & Policy* 23.

——. 2003. Problem solving justice: A quiet revolution. *Judicature* 86: 182.

——. 2005. *Good Courts: The Case for Problem Solving Justice.* New York: New Press.

Berman, Greg, and Eric Lane. 2000. What is a traditional judge anyway? Problem solving in the state courts. *Judicature* 84: 78.

Bernard, Thomas J., and R. Richard Ritti. 1991. The Philadelphia birth cohort and selective incapacitation. *Journal of Research in Crime and Delinquency* 28: 33–54.

Bernburg, J. G., M. D. Krohn, and C. J. Rivera. 2006. Official labeling, criminal embeddedness, and subsequent delinquency—a longitudinal test of labeling theory. *Journal of Research in Crime and Delinquency* 43: 67–88.

Birgden, A. 2002. Therapeutic jurisprudence and good lives: A rehabilitation framework for corrections. *Australian Psychologist* 37: 180–86.

——. 2004. Therapeutic jurisprudence and responsivity: Finding the will and the way in offender rehabilitation. *Psychology, Crime & Law* 10: 283–95.

——. 2007. Serious Sex Offenders Monitoring Act 2005 (*vic*): A therapeutic jurisprudence analysis. *Psychiatry Psychology and Law* 14: 78–94.

Birgden, A., and T. Ward. 2003. Pragmatic psychology through a therapeutic jurisprudence lens—psycholegal soft spots in the criminal justice system. *Psychology, Public Policy, and Law* 9: 334–60.

Bjerk, D. 2005. Making the crime fit the penalty: The role of prosecutorial discretion under mandatory minimum sentencing. *Journal of Law & Economics* 48: 591–625.

Boezeman, Edwin J., and Naomi Ellemers. 2008. Pride and respect in volunteers' organizational commitment. *European Journal of Social Psychology* 38: 159–72.

Bonnet, F. 2006. From an economic analysis of crime to the new Anglo-Saxon criminologies? The theoretical underpinnings of contemporary penal policy. *Déviance et Société* 30: 137–54.

Bouffard, J., and F. Taxman. 2004. Looking inside the black box of drug court treatment services using direct observations. *Journal of Drug Issues* 34: 195–218.

Bouffard, J. A., and S. Smith. 2005. Programmatic, counselor, and client-level comparison of rural versus urban drug court treatment. *Substance Use & Misuse* 40: 321–42.

Bourgois, P. 2003. Crack and the political economy of social suffering. *Addiction Research & Theory* 11: 31–37.

Bourgois, P., A. Martinez, A. Kral, B. R. Edlin, J. Schonberg, and D. Ciccarone. 2006. Reinterpreting ethnic patterns among white and African American men who inject heroin: A social science of medicine approach. *PLoS Medicine* 3: 1805–15.

Bozza, John A. 2007. Benevolent behavior modification: Understanding the nature and limitations of problem solving courts. *Widener Law Journal* 17: 97–143.

Braude, Lisa, and Carl Alaimo. 2007. A large court system tackles a huge problem. *Behavioral Healthcare* 27: 41.

Bredemeier, Harry Charles, and Jackson Toby. 1960. *Social Problems in America: Costs and Casualties in an Acquisitive Society.* New York: Wiley.

Broner, N., D. W. Mayrl, and G. Landsberg. 2005. Outcomes of mandated and nonmandated New York City jail diversion for offenders with alcohol, drug, and mental disorders. *Prison Journal* 85: 18–49.

Brownfield, David, Ann Marie Sorenson, and Kevin M. Thompson. 2001. Gang membership, race, and social class: A test of the group hazard and master status hypotheses. *Deviant Behavior* 22: 73–89.

Bruegge, A. V. 2006. Eternal bonds, true contracts: Law and nature in Shakespeare's problem plays. *Sixteenth Century Journal* 37: 274–75.

Brunsden, A. 2006. Hepatitis C in prisons: Evolving toward decency through adequate medical care and public health reform. *UCLA Law Review* 54: 465–507.

Buchanan, J., and L. Young. 2000. The War on Drugs—a war on drug users? *Drugs: Education Prevention and Policy* 7: 409–22.

Burdon, W. M., and C. A. Gallagher. 2002. Coercion and sex offenders—controlling sex-offending behavior through incapacitation and treatment. *Criminal Justice and Behavior* 29: 87–109.

Burdon, William M., John M. Roll, Michael L. Prendergast, and Richard A. Rawson. 2001. Drug courts and contingency management. *Journal of Drug Issues* 31: 73–90.

Bureau of Justice Assistance. 1997, 2004. Defining drug courts: The key components. In *Drug Court Resources Series.* Washington, DC: U.S. Department of Justice.

Burton, Mandy. 2006. Judicial monitoring of compliance: Introducing "problem solving" approaches to domestic violence courts in England and Wales. *International Journal of Law, Policy and the Family* 20: 366.

Bushway, Shawn D. 2006. The problem of prisoner (re)entry. *Contemporary Sociology Journal of Reviews* 35: 562–65.

Bushway, Shawn, Robert Brame, and Raymond Paternoster. 1999. Assessing stability and change in criminal offending: A comparison of random effects, semiparametric, and fixed effects modeling strategies. *Journal of Quantitative Criminology* 15: 23–61.

Bushway, Shawn D., and David McDowall. 2006. Here we go again: Can we learn anything from aggregate-level studies of policy interventions? *Criminology & Public Policy* 5: 461–70.

Bushway, Shawn D., and Anne Morrison Piehl. 2007. The inextricable link between age and criminal history in sentencing. *Crime & Delinquency* 53: 156–83.

Butler, T., G. Andrews, S. Allnutt, C. Sakashita, N. E. Smith, and J. Basson. 2006. Mental disorders in Australian prisoners: A comparison with a community sample. *Australian and New Zealand Journal of Psychiatry* 40: 272–76.

Butzin, C. A., C. A. Saum, and F. R. Scarpitti. 2002. Factors associated with completion of a drug treatment court diversion program. *Substance Use & Misuse* 37: 1615–33.

Campbell, H. 2005. Drug trafficking stories: Everyday forms of narco-folklore on the U.S.-Mexico border. *International Journal of Drug Policy* 16: 326–33.

Carrington, P. J. 2001. Population aging and crime in Canada, 2000–2041. *Canadian Journal of Criminology and Criminal Justice [Revue Canadienne de Criminologie]* 43: 331–56.

Casciano, Rebecca. 2007. Political and civic participation among disadvantaged urban mothers: The role of neighborhood poverty. *Social Science Quarterly* 88: 1124–51.

Casey, P., and D. B. Rottman. 2000. Therapeutic jurisprudence in the courts. *Behavioral Sciences & the Law* 18: 445–57.

Castillo, Larisa T. 2008. Natural authority in Charles Dickens's *Martin Chuzzlewit* and the Copyright Act of 1842. *Nineteenth-Century Literature* 62: 435–64.

Cates, J. A., D. A. Dian, and G. W. Schnepf. 2003. Use of protection motivation theory to assess fear of crime in rural areas. *Psychology, Crime & Law* 9: 225–36.

Caulkins, J. P. 2001. How large should the strike zone be in "three strikes and you're out" sentencing laws? *Journal of Quantitative Criminology* 17: 227–46.

Cavallaro, R. 2004. *Pride and Prejudice* and proof: Quotidian fact-finding and rules of evidence. *Hastings Law Journal* 55: 697–735.

Chadee, D., and J. Ditton. 2003. Are older people most afraid of crime? Revisiting Ferraro and LaGrange in Trinidad. *British Journal of Criminology* 43: 417–33.

Chandler, R. K., R. H. Peters, G. Field, and D. Juliano-Bult. 2004. Challenges in implementing evidence-based treatment practices for co-occurring disorders in the criminal justice system. *Behavioral Sciences & the Law* 22: 431–48.

Chen, Elsa Y. 2008. Impacts of "three strikes and you're out" on crime trends in California and throughout the United States. *Journal of Contemporary Criminal Justice* 24: 345–70.

Chinlund, Stephen. 2004. Calming the storm. *Journal of Religion & Health* 43: 7–10.

Chiricos, T., R. McEntire, and M. Gertz. 2001. Perceived racial and ethnic composition of neighborhood and perceived risk of crime. *Social Problems* 48: 322–40.

Cho, Richard. 2005. Instead of more jails, consider alternatives. *New York Times*, February 13, 2005. Letter to the editor.

Chunn, D. E., and S. A. M. Gavigan. 2004. Welfare law, welfare fraud, and the moral regulation of the "never deserving" poor. *Social & Legal Studies* 13: 219–43.

Citti, P. 2004. Prisons at the end of the century: Prisons to laugh, prisons to die—on Maurice Barres' "Enemy of the Law." *Romantisme* 34: 53–69.

Clark, R. E., S. K. Ricketts, and G. J. McHugo. 1999. Legal system involvement and costs for persons in treatment for severe mental illness and substance use disorders. *Psychiatric Services* 50: 641–47.

Clear, T. R. 2005. Imprisoning America: The social effects of mass incarceration. *American Journal of Sociology* 111: 923–25.

Cloyes, K. G. 2007. Prisoners signify: A political discourse analysis of mental illness in a prison control unit. *Nursing Inquiry* 14: 202–11.

Cohen, F. 2008. Penal isolation—beyond the seriously mentally ill. *Criminal Justice and Behavior* 35: 1017–47.

Cohen, S., L. G. Underwood, and B. H. Gottlieb. 2000. *Social Support Measurement and Intervention: A Guide for Health and Social Scientists.* New York: Oxford University Press.

Comfort, M. L. 2003. In the tube at San Quentin—the secondary prisonization of women visiting inmates. *Journal of Contemporary Ethnography* 32: 77–107.

Cooke, C. L. 2005. Going home: Formerly incarcerated African American men return to families and communities. *Journal of Family Nursing* 11: 388–404.

Cooper, C. S. 2002. Juvenile drug treatment courts in the United States: Initial lessons learned and issues being addressed. *Substance Use & Misuse* 37: 1689–722.

———. 2003. Drug courts: Current issues and future perspectives. *Substance Use & Misuse* 38: 1671–711.

———. 2007. Drug courts—just the beginning: Getting other areas of public policy in sync. *Substance Use & Misuse* 42: 243–56.

Corrado, R. R., I. M. Cohen, W. Glackman, and C. Odgers. 2003. Serious and violent young offenders' decisions to recidivate: An assessment of five sentencing models. *Crime & Delinquency* 49: 179–200.

Corva, D. 2008. Neoliberal globalization and the War on Drugs: Transnationalizing illiberal governance in the Americas. *Political Geography* 27: 176–93.

Courtwright, D. T. 2004. The Controlled Substances Act: How a big tent reform became a punitive drug law. *Drug and Alcohol Dependence* 76: 9–15.

Craddock, S. G., J. L. Rounds-Bryant, P. M. Flynn, and R. L. Hubbard. 1997. Characteristics and pretreatment behaviors of clients entering drug abuse treatment: 1969 to 1993. *American Journal of Drug and Alcohol Abuse* 23: 43–59.

Crane, G. D. 1997. The path of law and literature (recent publications by Richard A. Posner, Martha C. Nussbaum, and Wai Chee Dimock). *American Literary History* 9: 758–75.

Crisp, Roger. 2008. Compassion and beyond. *Ethical Theory & Moral Practice* 11: 233–46.

Cross, W. E. 2003. Tracing the historical origins of youth delinquency and violence: Myths and realities about black culture. *Journal of Social Issues* 59: 67–82.

Cusick, L., and J. Kimber. 2007. Public perceptions of public drug use in four UK urban sites. *International Journal of Drug Policy* 18: 10–17.

Cyrus, Tata. 2007. Sentencing as craftwork and the binary epistemologies of the discretionary decision process. *Social & Legal Studies* 16: 425.

Dagan, Hanoch. 2007. The realist conception of law. *University of Toronto Law Journal* 57: 607–60.

Dalessio, S. J., and L. Stolzenberg. 1995. Unemployment and the incarceration of pretrial defendants. *American Sociological Review* 60: 350–59.

Darjee, R., J. Crichton, and L. Thomson. 2000. Crime and Punishment (Scotland) Act 1997: A survey of psychiatrists' views concerning the Scottish "hybrid order." *Journal of Forensic Psychiatry* 11: 608–20.

Decoursey, M. 2003. The logic of inequality: Caliban's baseness in *The Tempest. Cahiers Élisabéthains* 64: 43–51.

DeLone, G. J. 2008. Public housing and the fear of crime. *Journal of Criminal Justice* 36: 115–25.

DeMatteo, D. S., D. B. Marlowe, and D. S. Festinger. 2006. Secondary prevention services for clients who are low risk in drug court: A conceptual model. *Crime & Delinquency* 52: 114–34.

Department of Justice, U.S., and Office of Justice Programs. 2008. Reentry. www.reentry.gov//learn.htm. (retrieved July 5, 2009).

Diamond, P. M., E. W. Wang, C. E. Holzer, C. Thomas, and D. A. Cruser. 2001. The prevalence of mental illness in prison. *Administration and Policy in Mental Health* 29: 21–40.

Diamond, T. 2006. Where did you get the fur coat, Fern? In *Institutional Ethnography as Practice*, edited by D. Smith, 45–64. Lanham, MD: Rowman & Littlefield.

Diederich, B. R. 1999. Risking retroactive punishment: Modifications of the supervised release statute and the ex post facto prohibition. *Columbia Law Review* 99: 1551–83.

Doob, A. N., and J. B. Sprott. 2006. Punishing youth crime in Canada—the blind men and the elephant. *Punishment & Society: International Journal of Penology* 8: 223–33.

Dorf, M. C. 2003. Legal indeterminacy and institutional design. *New York University Law Review* 78: 875–981.

Dorf, Michael C., and Jeffrey A. Fagan. 2003. Problem solving courts: From innovation to institutionalization. *American Criminal Law Review* 40: 1501.

Draine, J., N. Wolff, J. E. Jacoby, S. Hartwell, and C. Duclos. 2005. Understanding community re-entry of former prisoners with mental illness: A conceptual model to guide new research. *Behavioral Sciences & the Law* 23: 689–707.

Ducci, M. E. 2000. Territories, yearnings, and fears: Social and spatial effects of urban expansion. *Eure: Revista Latinoamericana de Estudios Urbano Regionales* 26: 5–24.

Dvoskin, J. A., and E. M. Spiers. 2004. On the role of correctional officers in prison mental health. *Psychiatric Quarterly* 75: 41–59.

Earthrowl, M., and R. N. McCully. 2002. Screening new inmates in a female prison. *Journal of Forensic Psychiatry* 13: 428–39.

Earthrowl, M., J. O'Grady, and L. Birmingham. 2003. Providing treatment to prisoners with mental disorders: Development of a policy—selective literature review and expert consultation exercise. *British Journal of Psychiatry* 182: 299–302.

Eaton, Leslie, and Leslie Kaufman. 2005. Judges turn therapist in problem solving court. *New York Times*, April 26, A1, B7.

Edwards, W., and C. Hensley. 2001. Contextualizing sex offender management legislation and policy: Evaluating the problem of latent consequences in community notification laws. *International Journal of Offender Therapy and Comparative Criminology* 45: 83–101.

Engen, R. L., and S. Steen. 2000. The power to punish: Discretion and sentencing reform in the War on Drugs. *American Journal of Sociology* 105: 1357–95.

Erikson, Kai T. 1966. *Wayward Puritans: A Study in the Sociology of Deviance*. New York: John Wiley & Sons.

———. 2005. *Wayward Puritans: A Study in the Sociology of Diviance*, rev. ed. Boston: Allyn & Bacon.

Eschholz, S., T. Chiricos, and M. Gertz. 2003. Television and fear of crime: Program types, audience traits, and the mediating effect of perceived neighborhood racial composition. *Social Problems* 50: 395–415.

Eskridge, Chris W. 2005. The state of the field of criminology. *Journal of Contemporary Criminal Justice* 21: 296–308.

Evans, D., and G. A. Tyson. 2001. Crime seriousness and sentencing: Primary perceptual processes in a random sample. *Australian Journal of Psychology* 53: 11–12.

Evans, Donald G. 2005. The case for inmate reentry. *Corrections Today* 67: 28–29.

Farber, D. A. 2001. Toward a new legal realism. *University of Chicago Law Review* 68: 279–303.

Farole, D. J., Jr., N. Puffett, M. Rempel, and F. Byrne. 2005. Applying the problem solving model outside of problem solving courts. *Judicature* 89, no. 1 (July–August): 40.

Feather, N. T., and J. Souter. 2002. Reactions to mandatory sentences in relation to the ethnic identity and criminal history of the offender. *Law and Human Behavior* 26: 417–38.

Feld, B. C. 2001. Race, youth violence, and the changing jurisprudence of waiver. *Behavioral Sciences & the Law* 19: 3–22.

Ferrall, Bard R. 2004. Criminal law and criminology. *Journal of Criminal Law & Criminology* 94: 497–501.

Fierke, K. M. 2004. Whereof we can speak, thereof we must not be silent: Trauma, political solipsism and war. *Review of International Studies* 30: 471–91.

Fisler, C. 2005. Building trust and managing risk—a look at a felony mental health court. *Psychology, Public Policy, and Law* 11: 587–604.

Ford, J. K. 2007. Building capability throughout a change effort: Leading the transformation of a police agency to community policing. *American Journal of Community Psychology* 39: 321–34.

Fortier, M. 2004. Elizabethan literature and the law of fraudulent conveyance: Sidney, Spenser, and Shakespeare. *Renaissance Quarterly* 57: 1513–14.

Foucault, Michel. 1975. *Discipline and Punish: The Birth of Prison*. New York: Vintage Books.

Fox, J. A., and A. R. Piquero. 2003. Deadly demographics: Population characteristics and forecasting homicide trends. *Crime & Delinquency* 49: 339–59.

Frable, Deborrah E. S. 1993. Being and feeling unique: Statistical deviance and psychological marginality. *Journal of Personality* 61: 85–110.

Frable, Deborrah E. S., Tamela Blackstone, and Carol Scherbaum. 1990. Marginal and mindful: Deviants in social interactions. *Journal of Personality & Social Psychology* 59: 140–49.

Franklin, T. W., C. A. Franklin, and T. C. Pratt. 2006. Examining the empirical relationship between prison crowding and inmate misconduct: A meta-analysis of conflicting research results. *Journal of Criminal Justice* 34: 401–12.

Frase, R. S. 2005. Sentencing guidelines in Minnesota, 1978–2003. *Crime and Justice: A Review of Research* 32: 131–219.

Freedman, E. 2002. A strange pair (law and literature). *Europe: Revue Littéraire Mensuelle* 80: 3–6.

Freeman, K. 2003. Health and well-being outcomes for drug-dependent offenders on the NSW drug court programme. *Drug and Alcohol Review* 22: 409–16.

Freudenberg, N. 2001. Jails, prisons, and the health of urban populations: A review of the impact of the correctional system on community health. *Journal of Urban Health: Bulletin of the New York Academy of Medicine* 78: 214–35.

Friedler, E. Z. 2000. Essay: Shakespeare's contribution to the teaching of comparative law—some reflections on *The Merchant of Venice. Louisiana Law Review* 60: 1087–102.

Friedman, Lawrence M. 1993. *Crime and Punishment in American History.* New York: Basic Books.

———. 2002. *American Law in the 20th Century.* New Haven, CT: Yale University Press.

Friedmann, P. D., F. S. Taxman, and C. E. Henderson. 2007. Evidence-based treatment practices for drug-involved adults in the criminal justice system. *Journal of Substance Abuse Treatment* 32: 267–77.

Frison, D. 2000. Law and laws in *The Merchant of Venice* (William Shakespeare). *Cahiers Élisabéthains* 61: 49–60.

Fulton Hora, Peggy. 2002. A dozen years of drug treatment courts: Uncovering our theoretical foundation and the construction of a mainstream paradigm. *Substance Use & Misuse* 37: 1469.

———. 2004. Trading one drug for another? What drug treatment court professionals need to learn about opioid replacement therapy. *Journal of Maintenance in the Addictions* 2: 71–76.

Galanter, M. 1974. Why the "haves" come out ahead: Speculations on the limits of social legal change. *Law & Society Review* 9: 95–160.

Galloway, A. L., and L. A. Drapela. 2006. Are effective drug courts an urban phenomenon? Considering their impact on recidivism among a nonmetropolitan adult sample in Washington State. *International Journal of Offender Therapy and Comparative Criminology* 50: 280–93.

Galster, G., K. Pettit, A. Santiago, and P. Tatian. 2002. The impact of supportive housing on neighborhood crime rates. *Journal of Urban Affairs* 24: 289–315.

Garland, Diana R., Dennis M. Myers, and Terry A. Wolfer. 2008. Social work with religious volunteers: Activating and sustaining community involvement. *Social Work* 53: 255–65.

Garrity, T. F., M. L. Hiller, M. Staton, J. M. Webster, and C. G. Leukefeld. 2002. Factors predicting illness and health services use among male Kentucky prisoners with a history of drug abuse. *Prison Journal* 82: 295–313.

Gelles, Richard J. 1993. Constraints against family violence: How well do they work? *American Behavioral Scientist* 36: 575–86.

Goldkamp, J. S., M. D. White, and J. B. Robinson. 2001. Do drug courts work? Getting inside the drug court black box. *Journal of Drug Issues* 31: 27–72.

Goldstein, Daniel M. 2005. Flexible justice. *Critique of Anthropology* 25: 389–411.

Gondolf, E. W. 2000. Mandatory court review and batterer program compliance. *Journal of Interpersonal Violence* 15: 428–37.

Goodwin, Doris Kearns. 1987. *The Fitzgeralds and the Kennedys: An American Saga*. New York: Simon and Schuster.

Goren, P. 2003. Race, sophistication, and white opinion on government spending. *Political Behavior* 25: 201–20.

Gormsen, Lia. 2007. Ensuring offender success from entry to reentry. *Corrections Today* 69: 18.

Gottfredson, D. C., and M. L. Exum. 2002. The Baltimore City drug treatment court: One-year results from a randomized study. *Journal of Research in Crime and Delinquency* 39: 337–56.

Gottfredson, D. C., B. W. Kearley, and S. D. Bushway. 2008. Substance use, drug treatment, and crime: An examination of intra-individual variation in a drug court population. *Journal of Drug Issues* 38: 601–30.

Gottschalk, M. 2008. Hiding in plain sight: American politics and the carceral state. *Annual Review of Political Science* 11: 235–60.

Grahame, P. 1998. Ethnography, institutions, and the problematic of the everyday world. *Human Studies* 21: 347–60.

Gravier, B. 2004. The psychiatrist, the judge and the sentence. *Annales Médico-psychologiques* 162: 676–81.

Griset, P. L. 2002. New sentencing laws follow old patterns: A Florida case study. *Journal of Criminal Justice* 30: 287–301.

Grudzinskas, A. J., J. C. Clayfield, K. Roy-Bujnowski, W. H. Fisher, and M. H. Richardson. 2005. Integrating the criminal justice system into mental health service delivery: The Worcester diversion experience. *Behavioral Sciences & the Law* 23: 277–93.

Hadfield, G. K. 2005. Feminism, fairness, and welfare: An invitation to feminist law and economics. *Annual Review of Law and Social Science* 1: 285–306.

Hafemeister, T. L. 1999. Law in a therapeutic key: Developments in therapeutic jurisprudence. *Behavioral Sciences & the Law* 17: 673–82.

Haldane, John. 2008. Recognising humanity. *Journal of Applied Philosophy* 25: 301–13.

Hamm, M. S. 1998. Descent into madness: An inmate's experience of the New Mexico state prison riot. *Contemporary Sociology: A Journal of Reviews* 27: 412–13.

Hammett, Theodore M., Cheryl Roberts, and Sofia Kennedy. 2001. Health-related issues in prisoner reentry. *Crime & Delinquency* 47: 390.

Hanafin, Patrick, Adam Geary, and Joseph Brooker. 2004. Introduction: On writing: law and literature. *Journal of Law and Society* 31: 1–2.

Harrison, L. D., and F. R. Scarpitti. 2002. Introduction: Progress and issues in drug treatment courts. *Substance Use & Misuse* 37: 1441–67.

Hart, J. 2005. Eternal bonds, true contracts: Law and nature in Shakespeare's problem plays. *Renaissance Quarterly* 58: 1043–45.

Hartford, K., R. Carey, and J. Mendonca. 2006. Pre-arrest diversion of people with mental illness: Literature review and international survey. *Behavioral Sciences & the Law* 24: 845–56.

———. 2007. Pretrial court diversion of people with mental illness. *Journal of Behavioral Health Services & Research* 34: 198–205.

Hartley, Carolyn Copps. 2003. A therapeutic jurisprudence approach to the trial process in domestic violence felony trials. *Violence against Women* 9: 410.

Hartwell, S. 2003. Short-term outcomes for offenders with mental illness released from incarceration. *International Journal of Offender Therapy and Comparative Criminology* 47: 145–58.

Harty, M. A., J. Tighe, M. Leese, J. Parrott, and G. Thornicroft. 2003. Inverse care for mentally ill prisoners: Unmet needs in forensic mental health services. *Journal of Forensic Psychiatry & Psychology* 14: 600–614.

Heckert, D. A., and E. W. Gondolf. 2000. The effect of perceptions of sanctions on batterer program outcomes. *Journal of Research in Crime and Delinquency* 37: 369–91.

Heflick, N. A. 2005. Sentenced to die: Last statements and dying on death row. *Omega: Journal of Death and Dying* 51: 323–36.

Heidari, E., C. Dickinson, R. Wilson, and J. Fiske. 2007. Oral health of remand prisoners in HMP Brixton, London. *British Dental Journal* 202.

Helland, E., and A. Tabarrok. 2007. Does three strikes deter? A nonparametric estimation. *Journal of Human Resources* 42: 309–30.

Henderson, C. E., F. S. Taxman, and D. W. Young. 2008. A Rasch model analysis of evidence-based treatment practices used in the criminal justice system. *Drug and Alcohol Dependence* 93: 163–75.

Herd, D. 2008. Changes in drug use prevalence in rap music songs, 1979–1997. *Addiction Research & Theory* 16: 167–80.

Herinckx, H. A., S. C. Swart, S. M. Ama, C. D. Dolezal, and S. King. 2005. Rearrest and linkage to mental health services among clients of the Clark County mental health court program. *Psychiatric Services* 56: 853–57.

Herzog, S. 2004. The effect of motive on public perceptions of the seriousness of murder in Israel. *British Journal of Criminology* 44: 771–82.

———. 2006. Battered women who kill—an empirical analysis of public perceptions of seriousness in Israel from a consensus theoretical perspective. *Homicide Studies* 10: 293–319.

Hiller, Dana V. 1982. Overweight as master status: A replication. *Journal of Psychology* 110: 107.

Hjalmarsson, R. 2008. Criminal justice involvement and high school completion. *Journal of Urban Economics* 63: 613–30.

Hochstetler, A. L., and N. Shover. 1997. Street crime, labor surplus, and criminal punishment, 1980–1990. *Social Problems* 44: 358–68.

Holmes, Oliver Wendell. 1881. *The Common Law*. Boston: Little, Brown, and Co.

Huffine, Carol L., and John A. Clausen. 1979. Madness and work: Short- and long-term effects of mental illness on occupational careers. *Social Forces* 57: 1049–62.

Hughes, E. C. 1945. Dilemmas and contradictions of status. *American Journal of Sociology* 50: 353–59.

Huspek, M. 2000. Oppositional codes: The case of the penitentiary of New Mexico riot. *Journal of Applied Communication Research* 28: 144–63.

Immarigeon, Russ. 2003. Parole, probation and prisoner reentry. *Federal Probation* 67: 73–74.

Ip, W. C., Y. K. Kwan, and L. L. Chiu. 2007. Modification and simplification of Thurstone scaling method and its demonstration with a crime seriousness assessment. *Social Indicators Research* 82: 433–42.

Izenman, A. J. 2003. Sentencing illicit drug traffickers: How do the courts handle random sampling issues? *International Statistical Review* 71: 535–56.

Jacobs, D., and S. L. Kent. 2007. The determinants of executions since 1951: How politics, protests, public opinion, and social divisions shape capital punishment. *Social Problems* 54: 297–318.

Jacobs, D., and R. Kleban. 2003. Political institutions, minorities, and punishment: A pooled cross-national analysis of imprisonment rates. *Social Forces* 82: 725–55.

Jacobs, D., Z. C. Qian, J. T. Carmichael, and S. L. Kent. 2007. Who survives on death row? An individual and contextual analysis. *American Sociological Review* 72: 610–32.

Jacobson, Michael. 2006. Reversing the punitive turn: The limits and promise of current research. *Criminology & Public Policy* 5: 277–84.

James, D. V. 2006. Court diversion in perspective. *Australian and New Zealand Journal of Psychiatry* 40: 529–38.

Jamieson, L., and P. J. Taylor. 2002. Mental disorder and perceived threat to the public: People who do not return to community living. *British Journal of Psychiatry* 181: 399–405.

Jessup, M. A., J. C. Humphreys, C. D. Brindis, and K. A. Lee. 2003. Extrinsic barriers to substance abuse treatment among pregnant drug dependent women. *Journal of Drug Issues* 33: 285–304.

Johnson, Spencer. 1998. *Who Moved My Cheese?* New York: Penguin Group.

Joosen, M., T. F. Garrity, M. Staton-Tindall, M. L. Hiller, C. G. Leukefeld, and J. M. Webster. 2005. Predictors of current depressive symptoms in a sample of drug court participants. *Substance Use & Misuse* 40: 1113–25.

Jordan-Zachery, J. S. 2008. A declaration of war: An analysis of how the invisibility of black women makes them targets of the War on Drugs. *Journal of Women, Politics & Policy* 29: 231–59.

Jurik, Nancy C. 2004. Imagining justice: Challenging the privatization of public life. *Social Problems* 51: 1–15.

Kanan, J. W., and M. V. Pruitt. 2002. Modeling fear of crime and perceived victimization risk: The (in)significance of neighborhood integration. *Sociological Inquiry* 72: 527–48.

Kariminia, A., M. G. Law, T. G. Butler, S. P. Corben, M. H. Levy, J. M. Kaldor, and L. Grant. 2007. Factors associated with mortality in a cohort of Australian prisoners. *European Journal of Epidemiology* 22: 417–28.

Kassebaum, G., and S. M. Chandler. 1994. Polydrug use and self-control among men and women in prisons. *Journal of Drug Education* 24: 333–50.

Kaye, Judith S. 1999. Making the case for hands-on courts. *Newsweek* 134: 13.

Kellogg, Frederic R. 2004. Holistic pragmatism and law: Morton White on Justice Oliver Wendell Holmes. *Transactions of the Charles S. Peirce Society* 40: 559–67.

Kelly, B. D. 2005. Structural violence and schizophrenia. *Social Science & Medicine* 61: 721–30.

Kelly, K. A. 2004. Working together to stop domestic violence: State-community partnerships and the changing meaning of public and private. *Journal of Sociology and Social Welfare* 31: 27–47.

Kennedy, Duncan. 2000. From the will theory to the principle of private autonomy: Lon Fuller's "Consideration and Form." *Columbia Law Review* 100: 94.

Kessler, D., and S. D. Levitt. 1997. Using sentence enhancements to distinguish between deterrence and incapacitation. In *Conference on Penalties—Public and Private.* Chicago, IL: University of Chicago Law School, 343–63.

King, R. D., M. Massoglia, and R. MacMillan. 2007. The context of marriage and crime: Gender, the propensity to marry, and offending in early adulthood. *Criminology* 45: 33–65.

Kleck, G., B. Sever, S. Li, and M. Gertz. 2005. The missing link in general deterrence research. *Criminology* 43: 623–59.

Knudsen, Katherine, Sarah Vorobjovs, and Elizabeth Gordon. 2008. An analysis of judicial pragmatism and feminine jurisprudence. Paper presented at the annual meeting of the Southern Political Science Association, Hotel Intercontinental, New Orleans, LA, January 9, 2008. Available at www.allacademic.com/meta/p212277_index.html.

Kokish, R., J. Levenson, and G. Blasingame. 2005. Post-conviction sex offender polygraph examination: Client-reported perceptions of utility and accuracy. *Sexual Abuse: A Journal of Research and Treatment* 17: 211–21.

Konrad, N. 2002. Prisons as new asylums. *Current Opinion in Psychiatry* 15: 583–87.

Korobkin, Laura H. 2007. Appropriating law in Harriet Beecher Stowe's *Dred. Nineteenth-Century Literature* 62: 380–406.

Kotter, John P. 1996. *Leading Change.* Cambridge, MA: Harvard Business School Press.

Krebs, C. P., C. H. Lindquist, W. Koetse, and P. K. Lattimore. 2007. Assessing the long-term impact of drug court participation on recidivism with generalized estimating equations. *Drug and Alcohol Dependence* 91: 57–68.

Krecke, E. 2003. Economic analysis and legal pragmatism. *International Review of Law and Economics* 23: 421–37.

Kruttschnitt, C. 2006. Downsizing prisons: How to reduce crime and end mass incarceration. *Law & Society Review* 40: 740–42.

Kruttschnitt, C., and R. Gartner. 2003. Women's imprisonment. *Crime and Justice: A Review of Research* 30: 1–81.

Kruttschnitt, C., R. Gartner, and J. Hussemann. 2008. Female violent offenders: Moral panics or more serious offenders? *Australian and New Zealand Journal of Criminology* 41: 9–35.

Kubrin, C. E., and E. A. Stewart. 2006. Predicting who reoffends: The neglected role of neighborhood context in recidivism studies. *Criminology* 44: 165–97.

Kupers, T. A. 2008. What to do with the survivors? Coping with the long-term effects of isolated confinement. *Criminal Justice and Behavior* 35: 1005–16.

Kurlychek, Megan C., Robert Brame, and Shawn D. Bushway. 2006. Scarlet letters and recidivism: Does an old criminal record predict future offending? *Criminology & Public Policy* 5: 483–504.

Kushel, M. B., J. A. Hahn, J. L. Evans, D. R. Bangsberg, and A. R. Moss. 2005. Revolving doors: Imprisonment among the homeless and marginally housed population. *American Journal of Public Health* 95: 1747–52.

Kwan, Y. K., L. L. Chiu, W. C. Ip, and P. Kwan. 2002. Perceived crime seriousness—consensus and disparity. *Journal of Criminal Justice* 30: 623–32.

La Fond, J. Q., and B. J. Winick. 2003. Sex offender reentry courts—a cost effective proposal for managing sex offender risk in the community. *Sexually Coercive Behavior: Understanding and Management* 989: 300–323.

La Prairie, C., L. Gliksman, P. G. Erickson, R. Wall, and B. Newton-Taylor. 2002. Drug treatment courts—a viable option for Canada? Sentencing issues and preliminary findings from the Toronto court. *Substance Use & Misuse* 37: 1529–66.

Ladipo, D. 2001. The rise of America's prison-industrial complex. *New Left Review* 7: 109–19.

Lamb, H. R., and L. E. Weinberger. 1998. Persons with severe mental illness in jails and prisons: A review. *Psychiatric Services* 49: 483–92.

———. 2005. The shift of psychiatric inpatient care from hospitals to jails and prisons. *Journal of the American Academy of Psychiatry and the Law* 33: 529–34.

Lane, R. 1974. Crime and industrial revolution—British and American views. *Journal of Social History* 7: 287–303.

Lazare, D. 2007a. Marked: Race, crime, and finding work in an era of mass incarceration. *Nation* 285: 29–31.

———. 2007b. The prison and the gallows: The politics of mass incarceration in America. *Nation* 285: 29–31.

Lencioni, Patrick. 2002. *The Five Dysfunctions of a Team: A Leadership Fable.* San Francisco: Jossey-Bass.

Leukefeld, C., H. S. McDonald, M. Staton, and A. Mateyoke-Scrivner. 2004. Employment, employment-related problems, and drug use at drug court entry. *Substance Use & Misuse* 39: 2559–79.

Leukefeld, C., J. M. Webster, M. Staton-Tindall, and J. Duvall. 2007. Employment and work among drug court clients: 12-month outcomes. *Substance Use & Misuse* 42: 1109–26.

Levin, B. 2002. From slavery to hate crime laws: The emergence of race and status-based protection in American criminal law. *Journal of Social Issues* 58: 227–45.

Levinson, S. 2000. Return of legal realism. *Nation* 272: 8.

Levitt, S. D. 1999. The limited role of changing age structure in explaining aggregate crime rates. *Criminology* 37: 581–97.

Levitt, S. D., and T. J. Miles. 2006. Economic contributions to the understanding of crime. *Annual Review of Law and Social Science* 2: 147–64.

Lewis, C. F. 2000. Successfully treating aggression in mentally ill prison inmates. *Psychiatric Quarterly* 71: 331–43.

Light, Stephen C. 1995. The Attica litigation. *Crime, Law and Social Change* 23: 215–34.

Lindloff, T. R., and B. C. Taylor. 2002. *Qualitative Communication Research Methods*. 2nd ed. Thousand Oaks, CA: Sage.

Lindquist, C. H., C. P. Krebs, and P. K. Lattimore. 2006. Sanctions and rewards in drug court programs: Implementation, perceived efficacy, and decision making. *Journal of Drug Issues* 36: 119–45.

Liptak, Adam. 2002. Next on the syllabus, *Romeo v. Juliet*. *New York Times*, October 30, 11.

Listwan, S. J., J. L. Sundt, A. M. Holsinger, and E. J. Latessa. 2003. The effect of drug court programming on recidivism: The Cincinnati experience. *Crime & Delinquency* 49: 389–411.

Loue, S. 2005. Redefining the emotional and psychological abuse and maltreatment of children—legal implications. *Journal of Legal Medicine* 26: 311–37.

Lovell, D. 2008. Patterns of disturbed behavior in a supermax population. *Criminal Justice and Behavior* 35: 985–1004.

Lovell, D., G. J. Gagliardi, and P. D. Peterson. 2002. Recidivism and use of services among persons with mental illness after release from prison. *Psychiatric Services* 53: 1290–96.

Lovell, D., and R. Jemelka. 1998. Coping with mental illness in prisons. *Family & Community Health* 21: 54–66.

Lovell, D., L. C. Johnson, and K. C. Cain. 2007. Recidivism of supermax prisoners in Washington State. *Crime & Delinquency* 53: 633–56.

Lurigio, A. J., A. Watson, D. J. Luchins, and P. Hanrahan. 2001. Therapeutic jurisprudence in action—specialized courts for the mentally ill. *Judicature* 84: 184–89.

Lynch, James P. 2006. Prisoner reentry: Beyond program evaluation. *Criminology & Public Policy* 5: 401–12.

Lyng, Stephen. 2004. Crime, edgework and corporeal transaction. *Theoretical Criminology* 8: 359–75.

Lyons, C. J. 2008. Individual perceptions and the social construction of hate crimes: A factorial survey. *Social Science Journal* 45: 107–31.

MacKay, L. 2001. Moral paupers: The poor men of St. Martin's, 1815–1819. *Histoire Sociale [Social History]* 34: 115–31.

Madden, Robert G., and Raymie H. Wayne. 2003. Social Work and the law: A therapeutic jurisprudence perspective. *Social Work* 48: 338–47.

Manza, J. 2007. The prisons and the gallows: The politics of mass incarceration in America. *American Journal of Sociology* 113: 899–901.

Manza, Jeff, and Christopher Uggen. 2006. *Locked Out: Felon Disenfranchisement and American Democracy*. New York: Oxford University Press.

Marbley, Aretha Faye, and Ralph Ferguson. 2005. Responding to prisoner reentry, recidivism, and incarceration of inmates of color. *Journal of Black Studies* 35: 633–49.

Markowitz, F. E. 2006. Psychiatric hospital capacity, homelessness, and crime and arrest rates. *Criminology* 44: 45–72.

Marlowe, D. B. 2006. Judicial supervision of drug-abusing offenders. *Journal of Psychoactive Drugs* 3: 323–31.

Marlowe, D. B., D. S. Festinger, P. A. Lee, K. L. Dugosh, and K. M. Benasutti. 2006. Matching judicial supervision to clients' risk status in drug court. *Crime & Delinquency* 52: 52–76.

Martin, S. E., C. D. Maxwell, H. R. White, and Y. Zhang. 2004. Trends in alcohol use, cocaine use, and crime: 1989–1998. *Journal of Drug Issues* 34: 333–59.

Martinez, Damian J. 2006. Informal helping mechanisms: Conceptual issues in family support of reentry of former prisoners. *Journal of Offender Rehabilitation* 44: 23–37.

Maruna, Shadd, and Thomas P. LeBel. 2003. Welcome home? Examining the "reentry court" concept from a strength-based perspective. *Western Criminology Review* 4: 91–107.

Maxwell, S. R. 2000. Sanction threats in court-ordered programs: Examining their effects on offenders mandated into drug treatment. *Crime & Delinquency* 46: 542–63.

Mayrack, B. R. 2008. The implications of *State ex rel. Thomas v. Schwarz* for Wisconsin sentencing policy after truth-in-sentencing II. *Wisconsin Law Review* 1: 181–223.

Maze, C. L., and S. A. Hannah. 2008. Perspectives on therapeutic jurisprudence in dependency court in cases involving battered mothers. *Juvenile and Family Court Journal* 59: 33–45.

McBride, Elizabeth C., Christy Visher, and Nancy La Vigne. 2005. Informing policy and practice: Prisoner reentry research at the Urban Institute. *Corrections Today* 67: 90–93.

McCall, P. L., K. F. Parker, and J. M. MacDonald. 2008. The dynamic relationship between homicide rates and social, economic, and political factors from 1970 to 2000. *Social Science Research* 37: 721–35.

McClure, Craig. 2004. Prisoner reentry programs: What are the common variables that predict implementation success among various delivery methods? Paper presented at the annual meeting of the Midwest Political Science Association, Palmer House Hilton, Chicago, Illinois, April 15, 2004. Available at www.allacademic.com/meta/p83875_index.html.

McGrath, R. J., G. F. Cumming, S. E. Hoke, and M. O. Bonn-Miller. 2007. Outcomes in a community sex offender treatment program: A comparison between polygraphed and matched non-polygraphed offenders. *Sexual Abuse: A Journal of Research and Treatment* 19: 381–93.

McGuire, J. 2002. Criminal sanctions versus psychologically-based interventions with offenders: A comparative empirical analysis. *Psychology, Crime & Law* 8: 183–208.

Mears, Daniel P., Caterina G. Roman, Ashley Wolff, and Janeen Buck. 2006. Faith-based efforts to improve prisoner reentry: Assessing the logic and evidence. *Journal of Criminal Justice* 34: 351–67.

Messina, N., W. Burdon, G. Hagopian, and M. Prendergast. 2004. One year return to custody rates among co-disordered offenders. *Behavioral Sciences & the Law* 22: 503–18.

Metraux, S. 2008. Examining relationships between receiving mental health services in the Pennsylvania prison system and time served. *Psychiatric Services* 59: 800–802.

Miceli, T. J., and K. Segerson. 2007. Punishing the innocent along with the guilty: The economics of individual versus group punishment. *Journal of Legal Studies* 36: 81–106.

Miles, T. J., and C. R. Sunstein. 2008. The new legal realism. *University of Chicago Law Review* 75: 831–51.

Miller, Eric J. 2007. The therapeutic effects of managerial reentry courts. *Federal Sentencing Reporter* 20: 127.

Miller, J. 2003. An arresting experiment—domestic violence victim experiences and perceptions. *Journal of Interpersonal Violence* 18: 695–716.

Miller, J. L., P. H. Rossi, and J. E. Simpson. 1986. Perceptions of justice—race and gender differences in judgments of appropriate prison sentences. *Law & Society Review* 20: 312–34.

———. 1991. Felony punishments—a factorial survey of perceived justice in criminal sentencing. *Journal of Criminal Law & Criminology* 82: 396–422.

Miller, JoAnn, and Dean D. Knudsen. 2007. *Family Abuse and Violence: A Social Problems Perspective.* Lanham, MD: Alta Mira Press.

Mirchandani, Rekha. 2005. What's so special about specialized courts? The state and social change in Salt Lake City's domestic violence court. *Law & Society Review* 39: 379–418.

Moon, B., and L. J. Zager. 2007. Police officers' attitudes toward citizen support—focus on individual, organizational and neighborhood characteristic factors. *Policing: An International Journal of Police Strategies & Management* 30: 484–97.

Morrison, Wayne. 2004. "Reflections with memories": Everyday photography capturing genocide. *Theoretical Criminology* 8: 341–58.

Moss, S. A. 2007. Students and workers and prisoners—oh, my! A cautionary note about excessive institutional tailoring of First Amendment doctrine. *UCLA Law Review* 54: 1635–79.

Mount, Barsha. 2007. The impact of motivations on judicial role conceptions and behavior. Paper presented at the annual meeting of the Midwest Political Science Association, Palmer House Hotel, Chicago, IL, April 12, 2007. Available at www.allacademic.com/meta/p196930_index.html.

Muir, G., and M. D. MacLeod. 2003. The demographic and spatial patterns of recorded rape in a large UK metropolitan area. *Psychology, Crime & Law* 9: 345–55.

Murdoch, L. D. 1998. Workhouse children: Infant and child paupers under the Worcestershire Poor Law, 1780–1871. *Victorian Studies* 41: 331–33.

Murray, B. A. 2003. "Transgressing nature's law": Representations of women and the adapted version of *The Tempest*, 1667 (Shakespeare). *Literature & History, Third Series* 12: 19–40.

Myton, T., T. Carnwath, and I. Crome. 2004. Health and psychosocial consequences associated with long-term prescription of dexamphetamine to amphetamine misusers in Wolverhampton, 1985–1998. *Drugs: Education Prevention and Policy* 11: 157–66.

Naser, Rebecca L., and Nancy G. La Vigne. 2006. Family support in the prisoner reentry process: Expectations and realities. *Journal of Offender Rehabilitation* 43: 93–106.

National Center for State Courts (NCSC). 2008. *A Unifying Framework for Court Performance Measurement—Final Report*. Arlington, VA: National Center for State Cours.

Needels, K., S. Jarnes-Burdurny, and J. Burghardt. 2005. Community case management for former jail inmates: Its impacts on rearrest, drug use, and HIV risk. *Journal of Urban Health: Bulletin of the New York Academy of Medicine* 82: 420–33.

Nolan, J. L., Jr. 2001. *Reinventing Justice: The American Drug Court Movement*. Princeton, NJ: Princeton University Press.

Nolan, J. L. 2002. Drug treatment courts and the disease paradigm. *Substance Use & Misuse* 37: 1723–50.

———. 2003. Redefining criminal courts: Problem solving and the meaning of justice. *American Criminal Law Review* 40: 1541–65.

Norrie, A. 2000. From critical to socio-legal studies: Three dialectics in search of a subject. *Social & Legal Studies* 9: 85–113.

Nussbaum, Martha. 1995. *Poetic Justice: The Literary Imagination and Public Life*. Boston: Beacon Press.

———. 2004. *Hiding from Humanity: Disgust, Shame, and the Law*. Princeton, NJ: Princeton University Press.

———. 2006. Law, literature, and empathy: Between withholding and reserving judgment—reply to Amnon Reichman. *Journal of Legal Education* 56: 320–29.

———. 2008. Hiding from humanity: Replies to Charlton, Haldane, Archard, and Brooks. *Journal of Applied Philosophy* 25: 335–49.

O'Connell, Daniel J., Tihomir N. Enev, Steven S. Martin, and James A. Inciardi. 2007. Working toward recovery: The interplay of past treatment and economic status in long-term outcomes for drug-involved offenders. *Substance Use & Misuse* 42: 1089–107.

O'Connor, F. W., D. Lovell, and L. Brown. 2002. Implementing residential treatment for prison inmates with mental illness. *Archives of Psychiatric Nursing* 16: 232–38.

O'Donnell, I. 2005. The virtual prison: Community custody and the evolution of imprisonment. *British Journal of Criminology* 45: 986–89.

Oh, J. H. 2005. Social disorganizations and crime rates in U.S. central cities: Toward an explanation of urban economic change. *Social Science Journal* 42: 569–82.

Ohnesorge, J. K. M. 2007. The rule of law. *Annual Review of Law and Social Science* 3: 99–114.

Oliver, P. E. 2008. Repression and crime control: Why social movement scholars should pay attention to mass incarceration as a form of repression. *Mobilization* 13: 1–24.

Osher, F., and H. J. Steadman. 2007. Adapting evidence-based practices for persons with mental illness involved with the criminal justice system. *Psychiatric Services* 58: 1472–78.

Osher, F., H. J. Steadman, and H. Barr. 2003. A best practice approach to community reentry from jails for inmates with co-occurring disorders: The APIC model. *Crime & Delinquency* 49: 79–96.

Pager, Devah. 2006. Evidence-based policy for successful prisoner reentry. *Criminology & Public Policy* 5, no. 3: 505–14.

Park, H. 2004. Shakespeare, law, and marriage. *Notes and Queries* 51: 439–40.

Pence, E. 2001. Safety for battered women in a textually mediated legal system. *Studies in Cults, Organizations, and Societies* 7: 199–299.

Perez-Carceles, M., C. Inigo, A. Luna, and E. Osuna. 2001. Mortality in maximum security psychiatric hospital patients. *Forensic Science International* 119: 279–83.

Perlin, M. L. 2003. Therapeutic jurisprudence and outpatient commitment law — Kendra's law as case study. *Psychology, Public Policy, and Law* 9: 183–208.

Persico, N. 2002. Racial profiling, fairness, and effectiveness of policing. *American Economic Review* 92: 1472–97.

Petersilia, Joan. 2001. Prisoner reentry: Public safety and reintegration challenges. *Prison Journal* 81: 360.

———. 2004. What works in prisoner reentry? Reviewing and questioning the evidence. *Federal Probation* 68: 4–8.

Petrucci, C. J. 2002. Apology in the criminal justice setting: Evidence for including apology as an additional component in the legal system. *Behavioral Sciences & the Law* 20: 337–62.

Petrunik, M. G. 2002. Managing unacceptable risk: Sex offenders, community response, and social policy in the United States and Canada. *International Journal of Offender Therapy and Comparative Criminology* 46: 483–511.

Pettit, B., and B. Western. 2004. Mass imprisonment and the life course: Race and class inequality in U.S. incarceration. *American Sociological Review* 69: 151–69.

Pettus, C. A., and M. Severson. 2006. Paving the way for effective reentry practice — the critical role and function of the boundary spanner. *Prison Journal* 86: 206–29.

Piquero, N. L., S. Carmichael, and A. R. Piquero. 2008. Assessing the perceived seriousness of white-collar and street crimes. *Crime & Delinquency* 54: 291–312.

Planty, Mike, Robert Bozick, and Michel Reginer. 2006. Helping because you have to or helping because you want to? Sustaining participation in service work from adolescence through young adulthood. *Youth & Society* 38: 177–202.

Plourde, C., and S. Brochu. 2002. Drugs in prison: A break in the pathway. *Substance Use & Misuse* 37: 47–63.

Pogorzelski, W., N. Wolff, K. Y. Pan, and C. L. Blitz. 2005. Behavioral health problems, ex-offender reentry policies, and the Second Chance Act. *American Journal of Public Health* 95: 1718–24.

Posner, R. A. 2000. Past-dependency, pragmatism, and critique of history in adjudication and legal scholarship. *University of Chicago Law Review* 67: 573–606.

———. 2004. Legal pragmatism defended. *University of Chicago Law Review* 71: 683–90.

———. 2006. A review of Steven Shavell's *Foundations of Economic Analysis of Law. Journal of Economic Literature* 44: 405–14.

Poythress, N. G., J. F. Edens, and M. M. Watkins. 2001. The relationship between psychopathic personality features and malingering symptoms of major mental illness. *Law and Human Behavior* 25: 567–82.

Pridemore, W. A. 2007. Change and stability in the characteristics of homicide victims, offenders and incidents during rapid social change. *British Journal of Criminology* 47: 331–45.

Prince, J. D. 2006. Incarceration and hospital care. *Journal of Nervous and Mental Disease* 194: 34–39.

Prouteau, Lionel, and François-Charles Wolff. 2006. Does volunteer work pay off in the labor market? *Journal of Socio-Economics* 35: 992–1013.

Purvin, Diane M. 2007. At the crossroads and in the crosshairs: Social welfare policy and low-income women's vulnerability to domestic violence. *Social Problems* 54: 188–210.

Raco, M. 2007. Securing sustainable communities—citizenship, safety and sustainability in the new urban planning. *European Urban and Regional Studies* 14: 305–20.

Redlich, A. D., H. J. Steadman, J. Monahan, P. C. Robbins, and J. Petrila. 2006. Patterns of practice in mental health courts: A national survey. *Law and Human Behavior* 30: 347–62.

Redlich, A. D., H. J. Steadman, P. C. Robbins, and J. W. Swanson. 2006. Use of the criminal justice system to leverage mental health treatment: Effects on treatment adherence and satisfaction. *Journal of the American Academy of Psychiatry and the Law* 34: 292–99.

Reisig, Michael D., William D. Bales, Carter Hay, and Wang Xia. 2007. The effect of racial inequality on black male recidivism. *Justice Quarterly* 24: 408–34.

Ren, L., J. S. S. Zhao, N. P. Lovrich, and M. J. Gaffney. 2006. Participation community crime prevention: Who volunteers for police work? *Policing: An International Journal of Police Strategies & Management* 29: 464–81.

Renneville, M. 2004. Psychiatry and prison: A parallel history. *Annales Médico-psychologiques* 162: 653–56.

Rhodes, L. A. 2000. Taxonomic anxieties: Axis I and axis II in prison. *Medical Anthropology Quarterly* 14: 346–73.

Rhodes, Tim, and Carla Treloar. 2008. The social production of hepatitis C risk among injecting drug users: A qualitative synthesis. *Addiction* 103: 1593–603.

Rich, J. D., L. Holmes, C. Salas, G. Macalino, D. Davis, J. Ryczek, and T. Flanigan. 2001. Successful linkage of medical care and community services for HIV-positive offenders being released from prison. *Journal of Urban Health: Bulletin of the New York Academy of Medicine* 78: 279–89.

Riches, V. C., T. R. Parmenter, M. Wiese, and R. J. Stancliffe. 2006. Intellectual disability and mental illness in the NSW criminal justice system. *International Journal of Law and Psychiatry* 29: 386–96.

Ritter, Nancy. 2006. No shortcuts to successful reentry: The failings of Project Greenlight. *Corrections Today* 68: 94–96.

Rivera, M. 2008. Healing families: An outcome evaluation of a community family court. *Juvenile and Family Court Journal* 59: 17–32.

Roberts, D. 2003. "As-rude-as-you-like-honest"—theatre criticism and the law. *New Theatre Quarterly* 19: 264–77.

Roberts, D. E. 2004. The social and moral cost of mass incarceration in African American communities. *Stanford Law Review* 56: 1271–305.

Roberts, J. V. 2003. Public opinion and mandatory sentencing—a review of international findings. *Criminal Justice and Behavior* 30: 483–508.

Rocque, M. 2008. Strain, coping mechanisms, and slavery: A general strain theory application. *Crime, Law and Social Change* 49: 245–69.

Rodriguez, N., and V. J. Webb. 2004. Multiple measures of juvenile drug court effectiveness: Results of a quasi-experimental design. *Crime & Delinquency* 50: 292–314.

Roh, S., and W. M. Oliver. 2005. Effects of community policing upon fear of crime—understanding the causal linkage. *Policing: An International Journal of Police Strategies & Management* 28: 670–83.

Room, R. 2005. Stigma, social inequality and alcohol and drug use. *Drug and Alcohol Review* 24: 143–55.

Rosen, E., and S. Venkatesh. 2007. Legal innovation and the control of gang behavior. *Annual Review of Law and Social Science* 3: 255–70.

Rossi, Peter, Richard A. Berk, and Kenneth Lenihan. 1980. *Money, Work, and Crime: The TARP Experiments.* New York: Academic Press.

Rotter, M., B. Way, M. Steinbacher, D. Sawyer, and H. Smith. 2002. Personality disorders in prison: Aren't they all antisocial? *Psychiatric Quarterly* 73: 337–49.

Rutherford, H., and P. J. Taylor. 2004. The transfer of women offenders with mental disorder from prison to hospital. *Journal of Forensic Psychiatry & Psychology* 15: 108–23.

Sabet, K. A. 2005. Making it happen: The case for compromise in the federal cocaine law debate. *Social Policy & Administration* 39: 181–91.

Sanderson, C. A., A. S. Zanna, and J. M. Darley. 2000. Making the punishment fit the crime and the criminal: Attributions of dangerousness as a mediator of liability. *Journal of Applied Social Psychology* 30: 1137–59.

Saxe, L., C. Kadushin, E. Tighe, A. A. Beveridge, D. Livert, A. Brodsky, and D. Rindskopf. 2006. Community-based prevention programs in the War on Drugs: Findings from the Fighting Back demonstration. *Journal of Drug Issues* 36: 263–93.

Schafer, J. A., B. M. Huebner, and T. S. Bynum. 2006. Fear of crime and criminal victimization: Gender-based contrasts. *Journal of Criminal Justice* 34: 285–301.

Schen, C. R. 2005. When mothers leave their children behind. *Harvard Review of Psychiatry* 13: 233–43.

Schmertmann, C. P., A. A. Amankwaa, and R. D. Long. 1998. Three strikes and you're out: Demographic analysis of mandatory prison sentencing. *Demography* 35: 445–63.

Schneider, A. K. 1999. The intersection of therapeutic jurisprudence, preventive law, and alternative dispute resolution. *Psychology, Public Policy, and Law* 5: 1084–102.

Schrantz, Dennis. 2007. Coordinating community development: The heart of the Michigan Prisoner Reentry Initiative. *Corrections Today* 69: 42–49.

Seal, D. W. 2005. HIV-related issues and concerns for imprisoned persons throughout the world. *Current Opinion in Psychiatry* 18: 530–35.

Seiter, R. P. 2002. Prisoner reentry and the role of parole officers. *Federal Probation* 66: 50–54.

Sellin, T., and M. E. Wolfgang. 1991. A psychosocial scaling of the seriousness of crime—a citation-classic commentary on the measurement of delinquency by Sellin, T. and Wolfgang, M. E. *Current Contents/Arts & Humanities* 8: 20–26.

Senior, J., A. J. Hayes, D. Pratt, S. D. Thomas, T. Fahy, M. Leese, A. Bowen, et al. 2007. The identification and management of suicide risk in local prisons. *Journal of Forensic Psychiatry & Psychology* 18: 368–80.

Shapiro, H. 2002. From Chaplin to Charlie—cocaine, Hollywood and the movies. *Drugs: Education Prevention and Policy* 9: 133–41.

Shearer, J., B. White, S. Gilmour, A. D. Wodak, and K. A. Dolan. 2006. Hair analysis underestimates heroin use in prisoners. *Drug and Alcohol Review* 25: 425–31.

Sheehy, Elizabeth. 2004. Advancing social inclusion: The implications for criminal law and policy. *Canadian Journal of Criminology and Criminal Justice* 46: 73–95.

Shepherd, J. M. 2002. Police, prosecutors, criminals, and determinate sentencing: The truth about truth-in-sentencing laws. *Journal of Law & Economics* 45: 509–34.

Sherman, L. W. 2000. Reducing incarceration rates: The promise of experimental criminology. *Crime & Delinquency* 46: 299–314.

Sherman, L. W., and R. Berk. 1984. The specific deterrent effects of arrest for domestic assault. *American Sociological Review* 49: 261–72.

Siennick, Sonja E. 2007. The timing and mechanisms of the offending-depression link. *Criminology* 45: 583–615.

Simpson, A. I. F., R. M. Jones, C. Evans, and B. McKenna. 2006. Outcome of patients rehabilitated through a New Zealand forensic psychiatry service: A 7.5 year retrospective study. *Behavioral Sciences & the Law* 24: 833–43.

Siobhan, Morrissey. 2004. Revising the rules. *ABA Journal* 90: 62.

Skeem, J. L., P. Emke-Francis, and J. E. Louden. 2006. Probation, mental health, and mandated treatment—a national survey. *Criminal Justice and Behavior* 33: 158–84.

Skinner, S. 2003. "A benevolent institution for the suppression of evil": Joseph Conrad's *The Secret Agent* and the limits of policing. *Journal of Law and Society* 30: 420–40.

Smith, D. 1987. *The Everyday World as Problematic: A Feminist Sociology.* Stony Stratford, Canada: Open University Press.

———. 2001. Texts and the ontology of organizations and institutions. *Studies in Cults, Organizations, and Societies* 7: 159–98.

———. 2006. Incorporating texts into enthographic practices. In *Institutional Ethnography as Practice*, edited by D. Smith, 65–88. Lanham, MD: Rowman & Littlefield.

Smith, D. J. 2005. Ethnic differences in intergenerational crime patterns. *Crime and Justice: A Review of Research* 32: 59–129.

Smith, H., D. A. Sawyer, and B. B. Way. 2002. Central New York Psychiatric Center: An approach to the treatment of co-occurring disorders in the New York State correctional mental health system. *Behavioral Sciences & the Law* 20: 523–34.

Sokol, B. J., and M. Sokol. 1999. Shakespeare and the English equity jurisdiction: *The Merchant of Venice* and the two texts of *King Lear*. *Review of English Studies* 50: 417–39.

Sorensen, J., and D. Stemen. 2002. The effect of state sentencing policies on incarceration rates. *Crime & Delinquency* 48: 456–75.

Spohn, Cassia, R. K. Piper, Thomas J. Martin, and Erika Davis Frenzel. 2001. Drug courts and recidivism: The results of an evaluation using two comparison groups and multiple indicators of recidivism. *Journal of Drug Issues* 31: 149–76.

Spunt, B. 2003. The current New York City heroin scene. *Substance Use & Misuse* 38: 1539–49.

Stafford, Christopher. 2006. Finding work: How to approach the intersection of prisoner reentry, employment, and recidivism. *Georgetown Journal on Poverty Law & Policy* 13: 261–81.

Stefan, S., and B. J. Winick. 2005. A dialogue on mental health courts. *Psychology, Public Policy, and Law* 11: 507–26.

Stevens, A., D. Berto, W. Heckmann, V. Kerschl, K. Oeuvray, M. Van Ooyen, E. Steffan, et al. 2005. Quasi-compulsory treatment of drug-dependent offenders: An international literature review. *Substance Use & Misuse* 40: 269–83.

Stiles, Beverly L., and Howard B. Kaplan. 1996. Stigma, deviance, and negative social sanctions. *Social Science Quarterly* 77: 685–96.

Stone, T. H., W. J. Winslade, and C. M. Klugman. 2000. Sex offenders, sentencing laws and pharmaceutical treatment: A prescription for failure. *Behavioral Sciences & the Law* 18: 83–110.

Strauss, A., and J. Corbin. 1990. *Basics of Qualitative Research: Grounded Theory Procedures and Techniques.* Newbury Park, CA: Sage.

Sullivan, C. J., K. McKendrick, S. Sacks, and S. Banks. 2007. Modified therapeutic community treatment for offenders with MICA disorders: Substance use outcomes. *American Journal of Drug and Alcohol Abuse* 33: 823–32.

Sullivan, M., and D. J. Solove. 2003. Law, pragmatism, and democracy. *Yale Law Journal* 113: 687–741.

Sutton, J. R. 2001. *Law/Society: Origins, Interactions, and Change.* Thousand Oaks, CA: Pine Forge Press.

Tauber, Jeffrey S. 2001. Therapeutic jurisprudence holds potential for drug offenders. *Alcoholism & Drug Abuse Weekly* 13: 5.

Taylor, R. B., and J. Covington. 1993. Community structural-change and fear of crime. *Social Problems* 40: 374–97.

Taylor, S. M., M. Galanter, H. Dermatis, N. Spivack, and S. Egelko. 1997. Dual-diagnosis patients in the modified therapeutic community: Does a criminal history hinder adjustment to treatment? *Journal of Addictive Diseases* 16: 31–38.

Tenorio, R., and N. Hernandez. 2005. State of social work research within the scope of mental health. *Salud Mental* 28: 18–32.

Terry, Carter. 2004. Red Hook experiment. *ABA Journal* 90: 36.

Thomas, J. C., and L. A. Sampson. 2005. High rates of incarceration as a social force associated with community rates of sexually transmitted infection. *Journal of Infectious Diseases* 191: S55–S60.

Tinto, E. K. 2001. The role of gender and relationship in reforming the Rockefeller drug laws. *New York University Law Review* 76: 906–44.

Toby, Jackson. 1964. *Contemporary Society: Social Process and Social Structure in Urban Industrial Societies.* New York: Wiley.

Toch, H. 2003. The contemporary relevance of early experiments with supermax reform. *Prison Journal* 83: 221–28.

———. 2008. Punitiveness as behavior management. *Criminal Justice and Behavior* 35: 388–97.

Travis, J. 2005. *They All Come Home: Facing the Challenges of Prisoner Reentry.* Washington, D.C.: Urban Institute Press.

Trevino, A. Javier. 2003. *Goffman's Legacy.* Lanham, MD: Rowman & Littlefield.

Tsai, B. 2000. The trend toward specialized domestic violence courts: Improvements on an effective innovation. *Fordham Law Review* 68: 1285–327.

Turner, Susan, Peter W. Greenwood, Terry Fain, and James R. Chiesa. 2006. An evaluation of the federal government's Violent Offender Incarceration and Truth-in-Sentencing incentive grants. *Prison Journal* 86: 364–85.

Turner, S., D. Longshore, S. Wenzel, E. Deschenes, P. Greenwood, T. Fain, A. Harrell, et al. 2002. A decade of drug treatment court research. *Substance Use & Misuse* 37: 1489–527.

Uchino, B. 2004. *Social Support and Physical Health.* New Haven, CT: Yale University Press.

Ulmer, J. T., and J. H. Kramer. 1998. The use and transformation of formal decision-making criteria: Sentencing guidelines, organizational contexts, and case processing strategies. *Social Problems* 45: 248–67.

Useem, B. 1985. Disorganization and the New Mexico prison riot of 1980. *American Sociological Review* 50: 677–88.

Useem, Bert, and Anne Morrison Piehl. 2008. *Prison State: The Challenge of Mass Incarceration.* New York: Cambridge University Press.

Visher, Christy A., and Jeremy Travis. 2003. Transitions from prison to community: Understanding individual pathways. *Annual Review of Sociology* 29: 89–113.

Vogel, B. L., and J. W. Meeker. 2001. Perceptions of crime seriousness in eight African American communities: The influence of individual, environmental, and crime-based factors. *Justice Quarterly* 18: 301–21.

Vogel, R. D. 2004. Silencing the cells—mass incarceration and legal repression in U.S. prisons. *Monthly Review: An Independent Socialist Magazine* 56: 37–43.

Voravong, S. 2008. Savings initiative "not a handout": Weed and seed program expands to help with college, housing. *Lafayette Journal and Courier,* A1, A6, 5/3/08.

Wacquant, L. 1998. The rise of the penal state in the United States. *Actes de la Recherche en Sciences Sociales* 124: 7–26.

———. 2002. From slavery to mass incarceration—rethinking the "race question" in the U.S. *New Left Review* 13: 41–60.

Walklate, S., and G. Mythen. 2008. How scared are we? *British Journal of Criminology* 48: 209–25.

Ward, D. A., M. C. Stafford, and L. N. Gray. 2001. Choice models of deterrence: Another look. *Journal of Applied Social Psychology* 31: 2292–300.

Ward, Tony, and Mark Brown. 2004. The good lives model and conceptual issues in offender rehabilitation. *Psychology, Crime & Law* 10: 243–57.

Ward, Tony, and Claire Stewart. 2003. Criminogenic needs and human needs: A theoretical model. *Psychology, Crime & Law* 9: 125–43.

Watson, A., P. Hanrahan, D. Luchins, and A. Lurigio. 2001. Mental health courts and the complex issue of mentally ill offenders. *Psychiatric Services* 52: 477–81.

Webster, C. M., and A. N. Doob. 2007. Punitive trends and stable imprisonment rates in Canada. *Crime, Punishment, and Politics in Comparative Perspective* 36: 297–369.

Webster, J. M., P. J. Rosen, J. Krietemeyer, A. Mateyoke-Scrivner, M. Staton-Tindall, and C. Leukefeld. 2006. Gender, mental health, and treatment motivation in a drug court setting. *Journal of Psychoactive Drugs* 38: 441–48.

Weiman, David F. 2007. Barriers to prisoners' reentry into the labor market and the social costs of recidivism. *Social Research* 74: 575–611.

Weisz, V., R. C. Lott, and N. D. Thai. 2002. A teen court evaluation with a therapeutic jurisprudence perspective. *Behavioral Sciences & the Law* 20: 381–92.

Weitzel, J. A., T. H. Nochajski, S. F. Coffey, and M. G. Farrell. 2007. Mental health among suburban drug court participants. *American Journal of Drug and Alcohol Abuse* 33: 475–81.

Wells, C. P. 2000. Why pragmatism works for me. *Southern California Law Review* 74: 347–59.

Wenzel, S. L., D. Longshore, S. Turner, and M. S. Ridgely. 2001. Drug courts—a bridge between criminal justice and health services. *Journal of Criminal Justice* 29: 241–53.

Werb, D., T. Kerr, W. Small, K. Li, J. Montaner, and E. Wood. 2008. HIV risks associated with incarceration among injection drug users: Implications for prison-based public health strategies. *Journal of Public Health* 30: 126–32.

Wermuth, L. 2000. Methamphetamine use: Hazards and social influences. *Journal of Drug Education* 30: 423–33.

West, Angela D. 2005. Horton the elephant is a criminal: Using Dr. Seuss to teach social process, conflict, and labeling theory. *Journal of Criminal Justice Education* 16: 340–58.

Wexler, D. B., and B. J. Winick. 2003. Putting therapeutic jurisprudence to work. *ABA Journal* 89: 54–57.

Wexler, H. K. 2003. The promise of prison-based treatment for dually diagnosed inmates. *Journal of Substance Abuse Treatment* 25: 223–31.

White, Helene R., Charles B. Fleming, Kim Min Jung, Richard F. Catalano, and Barbara J. McMorris. 2008. Identifying two potential mechanisms for changes in alcohol use among college-attending and non-college-attending emerging adults. *Developmental Psychology* 44: 1625–39.

White, T. 2002. Controlling and policing substance use(rs). *Substance Use & Misuse* 37: 973–83.

Whitzman, C. 2007. Stuck at the front door: Gender, fear of crime and the challenge of creating safer space. *Environment and Planning A* 39: 2715–32.

Wilcox, P., D. C. May, and S. D. Roberts. 2006. Student weapon possession and the fear and victimization hypothesis: Unraveling the temporal order. *Justice Quarterly* 23: 502–29.

Wild, T. C. 2006. Social control and coercion in addiction treatment: Towards evidence-based policy and practice. *Addiction* 101: 40–49.

Wiles, P., J. Simmons, and K. Pease. 2003. Crime victimization: Its extent and communication. *Journal of the Royal Statistical Society Series A: Statistics in Society* 166: 247–52.

Wilhite, A., and W. D. Allen. 2008. Crime, protection, and incarceration. *Journal of Economic Behavior & Organization* 67: 481–94.

Wilson, A. B., and J. Draine. 2006. Collaborations between criminal justice and mental health systems for prisoner reentry. *Psychiatric Services* 57: 875–78.

Wilson, D. B., D. C. Gottfredson, and S. S. Najaka. 2001. School-based prevention of problem behaviors: A meta-analysis. *Journal of Quantitative Criminology* 17: 247–72.

Winick, B. J. 1999. Redefining the role of the criminal defense lawyer at plea bargaining and sentencing—a therapeutic jurisprudence/preventive law model. *Psychology, Public Policy, and Law* 5: 1034–83.

———. 2003. Outpatient commitment—a therapeutic jurisprudence analysis. *Psychology, Public Policy, and Law* 9: 107–44.

———. 2008. A therapeutic jurisprudence approach to dealing with coercion in the mental health system. *Psychiatry, Psychology and Law* 15: 25–39.

Wolf, E., and C. Colyer. 2001. Everyday hassles: Barriers to recovery in drug court. *Journal of Drug Issues* 31: 233–58.

Wolf, Robert V. 2008. Breaking with tradition: Introducing problem solving in conventional courts. *International Review of Law, Computers & Technology* 22: 77–93.

Wolfe, E. L., J. Guydish, W. Woods, and B. Tajima. 2004. Perspectives on the drug court model across systems: A process evaluation. *Journal of Psychoactive Drugs* 36: 379–86.

Wolff, N., C. L. Blitz, and J. Shi. 2007. Rates of sexual victimization in prison for inmates with and without mental disorders. *Psychiatric Services* 58: 1087–94.

Wooldredge, J., and A. Thistlethwaite. 2002. Reconsidering domestic violence recidivism: Conditioned effects of legal controls by individual and aggregate levels of stake in conformity. *Journal of Quantitative Criminology* 18: 45–70.

Wright, U. T. 2003. Institutional ethnography: A tool for merging research and practice. Paper presented at the Midwest Research-to-Practice Conference in Adult, Continuing, and Community Education, Ohio State University, Columbus, Ohio, 243–49.

Yates, J. 1997. Racial incarceration disparity among states. *Social Science Quarterly* 78: 1001–10.

Yates, J., and R. Fording. 2005. Politics and state punitiveness in black and white. *Journal of Politics* 67: 1099–121.

Yu, J. 2000. Punishment and alcohol problems—recidivism among drinking-driving offenders. *Journal of Criminal Justice* 28: 261–70.

Zaller, N. D., L. Holmes, A. C. Dyl, J. A. Mitty, C. G. Beckwith, T. P. Flanigan, and J. D. Rich. 2008. Linkage to treatment and supportive services among HIV-positive ex-offenders in Project Bridge. *Journal of Health Care for the Poor and Underserved* 19: 522–31.

Zasu, Y. 2007. Sanctions by social norms and the law: Substitutes or complements? *Journal of Legal Studies* 36: 379–96.

Ziegler, R., and D. B. Mitchell. 2003. Aging and fear of crime: An experimental approach to an apparent paradox. *Experimental Aging Research* 29: 173–87.

Index

About the Authors

JoAnn Miller is associate dean for the College of Liberal Arts and professor of sociology at Purdue University. She is the author of several books, most recently *Family Abuse and Violence*, and journal articles on partner violence and appropriate punishments. She is past president of the Society for the Study of Social Problems and has been the cocreator, with Donald C. Johnson, of problem solving courts.

Donald C. Johnson has implemented and run three problem solving courts in Indiana—one for offenders with mental illness and addiction problems, another for incarcerated felons who are preparing to reenter society, and a program for sex offenders. He was three times elected as a superior court judge in Indiana, following a fifteen-year legal practice. He was a special agent for the FBI and served as deputy prosecutor.

Breinigsville, PA USA
15 December 2010
251519BV00001B/2/P